River of Mountains

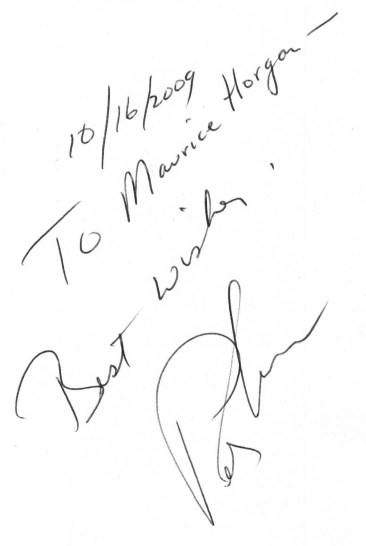

10/16/2009

To Maurice Horgan—

Best Wishes

River of Mountains

A Canoe Journey down the Hudson

PETER LOURIE

 Syracuse University Press

First Edition 1995
96 97 98 99 00   6 5 4 3 2

Except when noted, all photographs courtesy of the author.

This book is published with the assistance
of the John Ben Snow Foundation.

The paper used in this publication meets the minimum requirements of American National Standard for Information Sciences—Permanence of Paper for Printed Library Materials, ANSI Z39.48-1984. ∞™

Library of Congress Cataloging-in-Publication Data
Lourie, Peter.
    River of mountains : a canoe journey down the Hudson / Peter
Lourie.
        p.   cm.
    ISBN 0-8156-0315-0 (cloth : alk. paper)
    1. Hudson River Valley (N.Y. and N.J.)—Description and travel.
    2. Lourie, Peter—Journeys—Hudson River Valley (N.Y. and N.J.)
    3. Canoes and canoeing—Hudson River Valley (N.Y. and N.J.)
    I. Title.
F127.H8L94   1995
917.47'30443—dc20   94-48997

Manufactured in the United States of America

For my daughter Suzanna
and for my good pal Ernie LaPrairie

Peter Lourie has written books about his journeys on many rivers, from the Amazon and the Everglades to the Yukon and the Missouri. His most recent book is *Erie Canal: Canoeing America's Great Waterway*, describing a 500-mile paddle from Lake Erie to his home in Middlebury, Vermont. He has taught creative writing at Columbia University, the University of Vermont, and Middlebury College, and he is now working on two books, one about the Rio Grande and the other about Incan treasure.

Anyone who plans to canoe a river start to finish has to set his sights both broad and narrow, to combine the wide sweep with the deep detailed scrutiny.

John Rugge and Jim Davidson
The Complete Wilderness Paddler

Whatever else travel is, it is also an occasion to dream and remember.

Paul Theroux

Contents

PART THREE

The Tide

PART FOUR

River of Mountains to the Sea

Illustrations

MAPS

Acknowledgments

I wish to thank the following people for their encouragement and advice: Brian Kunz, Pam Painter, Larry Rosler, Mike Chandler, Jean Craighead George, Eric Ashworth, Susan Ramer, Lynn O'Malley, Robert Boyle, Betsy Folwell, Jeanne Mullin, and Mel Huff.

I also cannot forget the many good people who helped me along the way: Herb Helms, Gary Roberts, John Chambers, Peter Barton, Helen Donohue, Milda Burns, Robbie Frenette, John Cronin and his staff at the Riverkeeper, Mike Cichanowski and Dick Weber and their fabulous Wenonah canoes, Carol Sondheimer, Laura Haight, Pete Seeger, Jamie and Randy Frasier, Evelyn Thompson, Jim Pine, Hallie Bond, Jim Swedberg, Pat Shafer, Jim Britt, John Berry, Joan Patton, Peter Bishop and his whole family, Don Lourie, Selma Rayfiel, Alexis Nadeau, Bob Smith, Fred Godfrey, Jim Nichols, Jim Shaughnessy, Maggie and Forrest Hartley, Lee Butler, John Bennett, the Hadley-Luzerne Historical Society, Nelson Jessup, Ann Brewer, Don Winchell, Scott Overdorf, Patty McCool, John Paradis, Finch, Pruyn & Company, Ann Bannerman Bowes, Ellie Osborn, Alana Rosenberg, Tim DeGroat, John and Linda Cutten, Carol and Partick Poliseno, Frank Parslow, Joe Hyde, Daniel deNoyelles, and all the people restoring the Saugerties Lighthouse.

Also a big thanks goes to Bob and Nancy Stout, Kim LaPrairie, and most of all to Melissa who let her husband wander off while she held the fort.

In expressing my gratitude to all these people, it is possible that I unwittingly have omitted some names from these paragraphs, and for this I apologize. Any omissions or errors found in this book are entirely my own.

PART ONE

Adirondack Hudson

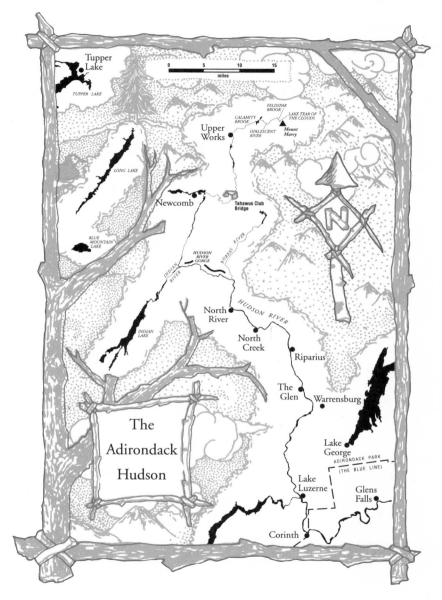

1. From Lake Tear of the Clouds to Lake Luzerne.

1

Preparation

Three feet below the surface of the headwaters of the Hudson River, the brown rocks give a clear indication of the speed of our canoe. They appear to be moving at twice the speed of the water itself, which means that two strong paddlers can easily reach six miles an hour on this three-mile-an-hour current. We are entering our first set of rapids. The roar crescendoes as we are swept into the windy, white torrent.

Ernie LaPrairie and I should have paddled together before today, but as busy fathers of infants, we delayed this whitewater practice until two days before our attempt to run the entire Hudson River, source to mouth, 315 miles in a canoe—a journey that has never been tried before.

This is only my second time in whitewater. My first attempt two months ago was a disaster, and today I seem to be fighting my partner on our first run through Perry Ehlers, a short set of rapids in front of the North River General Store on Route 28 near Warrensburg in the Adirondack Park. The more nervous I become, the more unsteady our canoe. I need to relax. The few times I actually let my body loose, the instability of our canoe disappears as if by magic.

Part of the problem is that I've been thrown off guard. We had agreed I would be in the bow, but just before we put the canoe in the water a few minutes ago, Ernie decided I should sit behind him. I am taller and heavier, and the canoe needs to ride higher in front in order to ship less water in the waves. So I feel terribly unsure of myself in the stern of this skittish, forty-seven-pound, eighteen-foot, six-inch Kevlar canoe. Being able to see the long, thin hull in front of me with Ernie deftly working his paddle as he judges what invisible path to take in the fierce river inspires little security. I've always believed the guy in the stern has final control of the canoe, but if this were the case now, we would be in big trouble.

In whitewater, Ernie says, teamwork is everything. But we have only these few hours to become a team because next week we will begin our trip by canoeing the forty-five miles of Class II (medium difficult), III (difficult), and IV (very difficult) rapids of the wild Adirondack section of the Hudson. Before studying the river, I never knew there were so many rapids on the Hudson or that they were this severe. An international whitewater rating system describes Class IV rivers as having long extended stretches of rapids, high irregular waves with boulders directly in the current; boiling eddies, broken water, abrupt bends. It warns that scouting is mandatory and that powerful and precise maneuvering is required.

I also had no idea that the Hudson drops a thousand feet in these forty-five miles of whitewater and that the headwaters of the Hudson are considered one of the greatest whitewater challenges in the East, a notion that motorists stuck in a traffic jam on the West Side Highway of Manhattan might never contemplate as they gaze at the wide, grey slab of river below the George Washington Bridge.

On this bright June day, the wind rises off the rocky turbulence. My arm aches from the violent maneuvers of my paddle as I help Ernie dodge boulders and keep the canoe parallel to the river. We hit the loud foam, and some ancient fear explodes inside me at the sound of the white mass rushing over buried boulders—at the sheer power of the river funneling through stone. At any moment a submerged geology could rip the bottom out of our delicate craft.

When we finally pull out of the rapids to rest in the calm of an eddy, I feel raw elation. Joy bolts into my blood—an antidote to fear—and I realize I haven't felt so alive in years.

Originally, my plan was to canoe upriver from Manhattan to Lake Tear of the Clouds, the highest pond source of the Hudson (also the highest body of water in the state). This marshy little pool ringed with balsam rests just below the summit of New York's tallest mountain, which Native Americans called *Tahawus*, or "Cloud-Splitter." Twelve crow-flying miles south of Lake Placid, 4,300–foot Lake Tear sits on the shoulder of Mount Marcy in the High Peaks region of the Adirondack Mountains, a lost gem of water on the cloudy brink of the timber line.

I wanted to aim my canoe for the solitude of the North Country. I needed to revive something dormant or dying in me. After years of traveling in South America, I had finally married, bought a home, and recently become a father. I welcomed the changes and found satisfaction in my late thirties fixing up our Victorian home in the as-yet unyuppified, industrial river city of Beacon along the Hudson's wide Newburgh Bay south of Poughkeepsie. But the rooted feeling, the good-wallpapering, fix-it-yourself satisfaction of home ownership was offset by an hour-long commute in heavy traffic to a teaching job downriver in Dobbs Ferry. I began to long for bachelor days in the jungle, freedom from schedules, new discoveries, and the physical challenge of long treks in the Andes. A book of mine about Incan treasure had been accepted for publication. Everything I'd ever written had come directly out of my travels, but now I was stationary and not writing—cocooned in the new busyness of dog walking, work, baby bottles, house chores. I longed for the old adventuring spirit. To break loose.

Then Melissa asked me at breakfast one day, "How about taking a trip somewhere? It might be good for us . . . you know . . . for our marriage."

Is it that bad? I wondered.

"You just look like you need a new project," she said.

After the initial shock of her honesty, I rose to her suggestion like a hungry bass for an early-morning popper. I discovered I had married a woman who could let her husband leave home.

"Only one condition," she said at lunch. "Don't be gone more than a month, and I'll need a mother's helper." Every June and July, Melissa produced the Hudson Valley Shakespeare Festival in Garrison, New York. Without me as baby-sitter, she would need some assistance.

"But that's two conditions," I said.

"For a month of freedom? Not bad."

So now I had the green light: a trip. But where? Surely not South America. It would have to be a domestic adventure, close to telephones and frequent news about our baby Suzanna.

I threw this one out at bedtime: "How about a month canoeing up the Hudson River after school lets out? In fact, why not the whole river, mouth to source?"

The idea really frightened me. It was a big river.

For seven years I'd lived in the Hudson Highlands, fifty miles north of the city, but had been on the river only once, when I helped my best friend scatter his wife's ashes from a canoe in front of the chapel where he had been married. Three years ago Melissa and I took our vows in that same stark, miniature Greek Revival chapel high on a bank of the Hudson.

Seven miles north of the chapel, I could now see the Hudson from my bedroom but had never taken any interest in the dull, grey-brown, barge-plying slug of a river. Like many people who live near it, I pretended the Hudson wasn't there. It was nothing but a nuisance, really, spanned by expensive bridges. Years ago the river had been part of the rhythms of everyday commerce, but today it seemed so massively uninspired.

Then, suddenly, I wanted to paddle the river—not just a portion of it either, but the whole thing—to follow the water out of civilization's nadir up to nature's tea-tinted lake; to flee the metropolitan maw in search of pure Lake Tear, its apex, the river's source. Having ignored the Hudson, now I wanted to embrace this river as a kind of path to self-renewal. Although I planned to paddle the whole river, I knew what interested me most was the upper river, the unknown Hudson, the half of the river that lies above Albany, a large portion of which runs through the Adirondacks where I'd spent every summer of my life since 1956, when I was four years old.

Impetuosity must run in my family. After my twin brother and I were born in 1952, my restless father took up skydiving, infuriating my mother's father by risking his life just when he had become a family man. I too craved a flirtation with danger. Perhaps Suzanna's birth drove me to it. Deciding to make this trip instantly stirred the muck of boredom and routine with a dangerous and physical task.

I quickly discovered what a strange river the Hudson is. The northern half is a true river with a strong current, but the lower half is tidal, a leviathan's arm of the sea, an estuary, a sunken river from the days of the glaciers, not a normal river at all. In the first 165 miles from Lake Tear to Albany, the Hudson drops nearly 4,300 feet. But from Albany to Manhattan, for another 150 miles, the Hudson drops a mere 1 foot.

Years ago I spent a few months in the jungles of Ecuador, 3,000 miles from the Atlantic and only 800 feet above sea level. That 800-foot drop in 3,000 miles of the Amazon River meant flooding and seasonal saturation for a whole basin nearly the size of the continental United States. Such a slow-dropping river in the rain forest made sense. But here in my own backyard it seemed an anomaly. The Amazon's 800-foot, 3,000-mile drop is in fact very steep compared to the Hudson's 1-foot, 150-mile drop to the sea. If the lower Hudson were to drop the Amazonian equivalent of 800 feet, it would take 120,000 miles of river to reach the sea.

In the history of our nation, the Hudson has been an industrial workhorse, and maybe that is one reason I hadn't noticed it. I had never thought much about barges or tankers, bricks or lumber. But as I began to read books about the river, I learned that before I would reach the eighty-five miles of the wilderness section of the Adirondacks (which *did* interest me), I would confront huge power dams, mills, and locks built in the early nineteenth century. Powerboats would ply the old barge channels from Fort Edward to Troy along the Hudson's forty miles of the Champlain Canal system. Before the excitement of the rapids, there would be a lot to learn about this river's tides and the old river industries of mining, logging, ice cutting, and fishing.

But I wondered whether I was strong enough to paddle the entire distance. I had no idea if it could be done or what the obstacles might be. Perhaps I would capsize in the wake of a freighter bound for the port of Albany. Or get mugged and be left bleeding in my tent on the shores of Yonkers.

Native Americans called the Hudson, "Water That Flows Both Ways." Experts agreed I could easily canoe on the flood tide 154 miles from Manhattan to Troy. But then to paddle any farther north against the current, or carry around the miles and miles of rapids only to reach the famous fifteen-mile Hudson River Gorge (which I had never heard of before) with its boulder fields and Class IV whitewater would be the journey of a Sisyphus looking for extra rocks to roll uphill. Against the current, my trip could take months.

So I changed my heading in the face of strong inductive logic and the prevailing flow of water and decided to canoe the reasonable route—from the mountains to the sea. Instead of aiming for a North Country Eden, I would start up high, drop more than 4,000 feet to sea level, and direct my canoe home, where, just two days ago, my little girl uttered the sweetest word in the English language—"Dadada." Finally it was not just the gibberish of an infant. In her singsong, silvery voice, she repeated the syllable that stood for me and no one else, which made it painfully difficult to leave home.

There is so much to learn today. Ernie is trying to teach me the cardinal rules of whitewater paddling: how never to let go of my paddle even if we capsize, how to lean downstream if we get stuck on a rock (a strategy that runs counter to the natural tendency to save oneself), how to help bring this long canoe (much too long for whitewater where we have to maneuver quickly and precisely) around behind a rock into the quiet safety of an eddy, a little pool of bubbling water paradoxically flowing upstream, and—perhaps most important— how to use a brace, the whitewater canoeist's steadying arm of safety. A brace, Ernie says, is simply an extended paddle, the blade either flat out on the surface or just below the surface, a slight feathering movement in the water to ease the boat's skittishness and to keep it from turning over.

Ernie yells at me our first time through Perry Ehlers, his voice faint in the roar. Then his voice grows sharp.

"Stead . . . steady. STEADY. Settle down. Settle DOWN."

We take on water. Because of my constant attempt to correct the canoe, the canoe is acting like a tightrope walker without a steadying pole.

My arm is killing me. Years ago Ernie damaged his left shoulder while racing. From the outset I paddle on the left while he takes the right side. What this means is that after a week of whitewater, my left arm will either be strong enough to lift an automobile or will simply fall off.

I found it remarkable that in this day of wild expeditions, of rounding the Horn in kayaks, parachuting on the North Pole, and riding bicycles around the equator, no one had thought of canoeing the whole length of this major American river. Or if someone had dreamed of such a canoe journey from the river's source to its mouth, no one as far as I could tell from my research had actually made it entirely by canoe.

I did discover one outdoorsman who had taken a combination of rafts, kayaks, and canoes, not from Lake Tear but from the first navigable part of the Hudson all the way down to Manhattan. Listening to what he had faced, I came to understand why no one had taken just a canoe down the river. It is a complicated river with wildly diverse challenges for a canoeist. The first nine miles are simply not canoeable. If I really wanted to paddle the source at Lake Tear, I would have to portage. There is no road to Lake Tear, and few people would be dumb enough to lug a canoe nine miles up steep trails of roots and rocks and low-hanging pines merely to paddle for a few minutes on a glacial lake, then lug that same canoe back down the trail to where the Hudson first becomes vaguely navigable.

The rapids then make canoeing the upper Hudson extremely difficult, especially one segment of those rapids called the Gorge. Only whitewater enthusiasts take open canoes through the notorious and treacherous Class IV rapids of the Hudson River Gorge, famous as a rafting location, especially in the powerful spring runoff. Perhaps no one has ever taken a traditional, flat-water, eighteen-foot canoe (which I needed for the flat-water bulk of my journey) through the Gorge—or at least no one who knew the Gorge existed and who then planned to trek on down to the city for a deli sandwich.

Having survived the Hudson's northern rapids in a low-tech craft, few would be masochistic enough to paddle the remaining 230 miles, portaging around power dams and dodging tugboats with barges in tow, all the way down to the highest tech city in the world, a place most canoeists avoid at all costs.

But I wanted to make the trek up Mount Marcy in order to paddle a few perfect moments on the river's source in the very same canoe I would then take to Battery Park. To many it seemed foolish, but I found the idea symmetrically important.

In my enthusiasm I said to Melissa, "I'll hunt off the land." She countered, "You'll hunt hot dogs and canned peaches, you mean." She was right. I did not have to camp out every night. I'd bring a tent and sleeping bag, but if I had the chance I'd also sleep in people's homes, motels, hotels, camp areas. I'd cook on a portable stove but I would also eat in restaurants, diners, marinas, backyard barbecue pits. Unlike what I had encountered along the Amazon, here on the Hudson there would be Coke machines in yacht clubs, potable water from friendly natives' faucets, ice for my seltzer. The inhabitants along the banks would speak English. I would learn about the river not from books, but from the river people themselves. I'd be a kind of foreign traveler in a familiar land. To see the river for myself was the goal—not through the eyes of the Hudson River school of painters, nor from the tourist boats to West Point, not even through the polemics of the environmentalists. Mine would be a paddler's view, a muscling to someone's dock, an unexpected conversation, and then a long paddle of leave taking.

I had heard about the river's incredible *diversity*, that it is hard to reconcile the upper wilderness Hudson with the ocean-shipping, tidal Hudson, so I wanted my journey to glue the river's pieces together, my canoe to become a sort of river yoke.

The water looks the most dangerous just before the bottom of the rapids. Each curl of foam appears booby trapped. In fact, the water here is deep and safe. The main danger is taking on too much water over the gunwales from the standing waves, huge lips of water that form above buried rocks. The more the canoe fills up, the harder it is to control.

Ernie advises to look for dark, fast water.

At the end of the rapid, Ernie tells me how my stroke speeded up as panic set in. I am like an animal struggling against suffocation. It's true: I hardly notice my body stiffening. Fear makes me a sort of fanatic tin paddler.

Two grey-haired fishermen at the bottom of the rapids wade into deep, black pools, watching placidly as they cast their fly rods into the river where it comes to rest. Nearly swamped now, grateful to reach shore, we put our feet over the sides onto the rocks and begin to bail the forty-degree June runoff from the High Peaks. I can tell Ernie is a bit embarrassed, maybe even ashamed. He's too good a paddler to seem so bad in a small rapid like this one.

He says, "I think you're afraid of swimming, Pete," then adds, "I've swum every part of this river. Nothing wrong with a swim." It's a gentle remonstrance. Ernie is modest and patient. Translated into a more demanding instructor's mouth, his words would be: "God damn, Pete, don't be so chicken shit."

When I was searching for help through the rapids, knowing that I wouldn't have time to carry my canoe around them, everyone in the vicinity of the Hudson's source, from the staff at the Adirondack Museum in Blue Mountain Lake, to canoeists and outfitters in North Creek, Tupper Lake, and Minerva, agreed that Ernest LaPrairie would be the best man to keep a whitewater novice alive in the famous Hudson River Gorge. I badly needed advice on what kind of canoe to use and on how to get past the big rapids.

So in February I drove up to Tupper Lake to see if LaPrairie would be for hire the following June. LaPrairie, I'd been told, had been through those rapids more than anyone alive. He was head guide for the Hudson River Rafting Company in North Creek, which runs five-hour trips through the Gorge, March through May. Ernie was also a licensed Adirondack guide with five generations of guides on both sides of his family, perhaps the last true guide in the north woods. The forest rangers at regional headquarters of the Department of Environmental Conservation (the DEC) in Warrensburg had placed his name at the top of a list of qualified volunteers for whitewater rescue. In the navy in Vietnam, he ran Recon missions on patrol boats in the Mekong Delta—the kind of junket Martin Sheen makes in the movie *Apocalypse Now*.

Like many in the north, Ernie makes his living doing this and that. When spring rafting season ends, LaPrairie sells canoes and camping gear from his outfitter store on Blue Mountain Lake. He is caretaker for four camps, and he rents canoes at a state campground just out of town. Until the new-housing market went bust in 1980, he used to "go into the woods" to cut timber as an independent contractor. With the onset of the long, bleak Adirondack winter, he was now working as assistant manager of a small ski area in Tupper Lake.

The day I arrived the snow was thick on the mountain, and huge flakes were falling in slow motion from a lead sky. Even so, I could tell from the desolate parking lot and the absence of lines at the chairlift that Big Tupper was hurting for skiers.

Brightly colored parkas moved about the ski lodge, and the astronaut boots of the skiers pounded the rude wooden floors. The smell of hot chocolate and hot dogs rose from the cafeteria. We had spoken twice on the phone. I'd told LaPrairie briefly about my trip, but he was skeptical, and I wanted to go over the details in person. I got a cup of coffee and found Ernie renting skis behind the ski-shop counter downstairs. He took me into a wood-paneled office that smelled of new ski gloves.

Right away he asked, "So how do you propose to get the canoe up to Marcy and back to where you can put into the river?"

His tone seemed challenging, calling me to account for such a ridiculous idea for a journey.

LaPrairie was clearly not a company man. A rough-and-tumble, reliable-looking fellow, Ernie is a short, compact man of forty-two with a sandy-grey beard and a thick head of hair. He seems scraggly around the edges, the type of person you might see in a bar in the back country of any northern place on the fringes of culture. He looks a lot like those wonderful portraits of bearded men from the Civil War, their eyes shining out of war-hardened faces.

There is something heroic yet humble about him, too. Perhaps it's the combination of tattoo on his left arm and his kind, soft voice, his forgiving blue eyes. Or maybe it's the fact that Ernie's family settled in the Adirondacks with the first white men. Until the 1830s, these mountains remained uninhabited, a landscape so harsh that even the Algonquins and Iroquois came here only to hunt, but never to live. When Ernie's relatives settled in Blue Mountain Lake in the mid-1800s, many desolate winters were spent listening to the wind rake the pines. The moment I met him, I could tell that Ernie still had the blood of a pioneer racing through him, and that he also had the patience and endurance of a first settler.

1. The author and Ernie LaPrairie before the carry
to Lake Tear of the Clouds.
Photograph by Herb Helms.

"That's the problem, you know," he said, his voice softening.
"And how many canoes will you use for your trip?" This last question seemed more like curiosity than challenge.

"Well," I said, feeling pretty stupid, "I was hoping you and I could take just one canoe."

The axe came hurtling down on my proposal.

"Can't be done," he said curtly. My heart took a dip. "You'll need at least three canoes for your trip." Ernie described the boats: first, I would need a Peter Hornbeck "Lost Pond," a fourteen-pound pack canoe for the long carry to Tear; then I'd need a John Berry ME Mad River whitewater design for the rapids above Warrensburg; and finally I would have to get a good-tracking, longer Wenonah Odyssey for the open stretch of the long trip home.

I told him I didn't have a lot of money and liked the idea of taking only one canoe. I asked again if he was sure the trip could not be done in a single craft.

Ernie shook his head. "If you're crazy enough, I suppose. It would have to be the Wenonah Odyssey, which has no keel so you can maneuver in the rapids. But I don't think *you* can do it."

When I told him I had a fourteen-foot Grumman, he laughed. He said what everyone else had said: I might as well paddle a barge downriver. With that clunky old aluminum canoe I'd have to work three times as hard and go about three times slower than with a Kevlar Odyssey. Also, whenever my aluminum boat ran up against a rock, it would stick to that rock and not just flow off it as Kevlar does. Aluminum canoes, he said, are much more dangerous in rapids. When they get stuck on a rock, they tip easily.

"How much are the Odysseys?" I asked.

Ernie said he had a secondhand Odyssey in his shop. By trading in my Grumman, I could buy it for a thousand dollars.

One thousand dollars would surpass my projected budget for the entire journey by $300, and I wouldn't even have bought any food or camping gear yet.

"I'll buy it," I said.

From the moment I met him, I knew Ernie LaPrairie would make the perfect companion for my journey. I'd traveled alone for several years in Ecuador, and now I wanted to go with a friend. But here was the expert of the upper Hudson telling me my trip was nearly impossible. His air of competence made his decision seem final.

Then Ernie repeated something he had said, and the repetition made me hopeful. A man who repeats himself is perhaps toying with an idea.

"The big problem is getting that canoe up Marcy and back down."

"What's the trail to Lake Tear look like?" I asked helplessly.

"It's pretty well cleared. But you're talking about taking an eighteen-foot canoe for eighteen miles by foot. Do you know how steep it is?"

Limply I said, "It'll be a first."

I did not admit to Ernie that I knew exactly what the trail to Marcy was like. Last August I'd scouted it. The hike to Lake Tear took me five hours from the parking lot at Upper Works in Tahawus, the ghost cottages of the abandoned MacIntyre iron mine near the town of Newcomb. The last two miles up, I had to stop every ten steps to rub my legs that cramped on what seemed like the foggy edge of the world. The valley below filled with mist, and the mountains rose out of the fog on all sides. I followed the trail, which became a knife's edge. I knew exactly how hard it would be to drag a canoe up there and to face this hardship even before the source-to-mouth journey began! Toward the top, the hemlocks and balsam would scrape the hull, and the roots and mud and rocks would make it a nightmare of a portage. When I had thought of doing this alone, I'd planned to take my time: a week if necessary to drag my canoe up there, my old sixty-nine-pound, fourteen-foot Grumman barge.

A man from Saranac Lake had just written in *Adirondack Life* about his trip with a partner up to Lake Tear with one of Peter Hornbeck's fourteen-pound pack canoes. As far as he knew, this was the first time anyone had ever taken any kind of canoe up to the lake. "The bow of the midget canoe kept hitting tree limbs as I carried it upside-down over my head," Charles Brumley wrote. "Every few hundred feet of elevation gain, my partner . . . spelled me. . . . The idea of carrying a canoe to Lake Tear, the highest body of water in New York, on Mount Marcy's shoulder, was Turner's. It must have been, or I wouldn't have felt so . . . well, so conscripted."

At Big Tupper on that dark, snowy February afternoon I wondered just how I could conscript a hesitating LaPrairie to make this trek not with some light pack canoe, but with a traditional eighteen-footer.

Ernie asked, "What does your wife say about this trip?"

"She's all for it."

Ernie gazed at the floor. The clomping skiers pounded on the wood above. Ernie looked a little tired, as if making a living in the Adirondacks had drained him. Later he told me that every night at two or three in the morning he gets up to read for an hour, a habit he developed long ago.

"It's great your wife'll let you go. I'm sure Kimball would let me go, too." Ernie's voice wasn't all that convincing. "I just can't afford to be away a whole month." This I believed. Ernie's daughter was only eight months old, and Kimball had just quit her job as program coordinator at the Adirondack Lakes Center for the Arts.

I felt a bond of new fatherhood, and now I wanted even more to paddle with him. For the next ten minutes the fixed smiles of a proud father played about his lips as we talked about the little critters who kept us up all night, straining our marriages and wallets, taking us to new limits of endurance. All the while, I could tell Ernie was revolving the idea of my trip in his mind as if it were a slab of meat roasting on a spit over a slow fire. He started to doodle on a pad, then took a few notes about the equipment I'd need. His guide's instinct for organization was obvious: sleeping bag, tent, mess kit, stove. "And you'll need a Bills bag to keep all your gear dry if you capsize." A Bills bag is a special waterproof duffle bag that canoeists use for river trips, Ernie said, and he could sell me one from his store at cost.

Suddenly he looked hard at me and said quietly, "Okay, I'll go. But only for three days—and only if you come up next spring for a trial run. I have to depend on my partner."

"Don't worry. I know the J-stroke," I said. But it had been a long time since canoe camp in Ontario, 1965, where, at thirteen, I'd taken seven- and ten-day canoe treks through virgin lakes and wilderness streams and come back feeling like a Canadian voyageur, confident about canoes and canoeing ever since . . . until these rapids, that is.

The last thing Ernie said at the ski lodge before I left was, "People will think I'm crazy to go on this trip."

I was happy to see he was grinning.

Ernie and I ready ourselves for another run through Perry Ehlers. He says, "Time in a canoe together, that's all we need." This is kind, I think. But will it really help? Is there any *time* left?

"Ernie, if I get nervous in the Gorge, just tell me to relax, okay? I can feel the canoe settle down when you tell me to relax."

"I'll be nervous, too," he says.

I wish he hadn't said that.

"If we have a problem, you know, it's always the fault of the guy in the stern." Is Ernie joking? I can't tell. "I have no problem being in the bow," he continues. His declaration of confidence gives me the feeling he is in fact a little nervous about my being in the stern. When he used to race tandem whitewater canoes, he was always in the bow, but that was with a partner he had known and trusted for years.

I suppose I'm clutching at some control over Providence while my heart scrapes at the very bottom of a fear I haven't felt in years. I wonder what childishness makes me say, "I hope you can keep me alive in the Gorge."

"No." Ernie, annoyed, shakes his head. "That's not *my* job. You have to keep *yourself* alive. I'm not taking *that* responsibility." Ernie's creed is a Yukon creed: individuals survive on their own strength; if you don't make it alive, it is neither the fault of the government, nor of society, nor of any other fellow human.

Our second time through Perry Ehlers is a much better run, calmer, less raw fear welling up inside me. My paddling strokes are smoother. The canoe, steadier, takes on practically no water at all as I brace through the standing waves, hoping the fishermen can observe our progress. But I see they've already left the river.

By March, Ernie had grown fond of the idea of such an unusual trip. On the phone he said he would take me for a whole week, first to Lake Tear, and from there to Lake Luzerne, the last town in the Adirondack Park. He wouldn't even charge me for two days out of those seven. I asked why not. He said, "The two days getting to Lake Tear will be just plain fun." He said his wife had been urging him to ask for more than his guiding fee of a hundred a day, but he loved being in the woods and just couldn't charge too much for something he loved.

He especially loved the Hudson River Gorge. Gary Roberts of the DEC who has performed a decade of river rescues in the Gorge told me, "I don't like whitewater. All I see are white faces." He explained that before the rafting companies started up ten years ago around 1980, there would be at least a few drownings in the Gorge every year. Two men from the city had gone through the Gorge a few years back in an open canoe, without life vests, with little food, and no preparation. When the doctor examined their dead bodies after an all-night rescue operation, he had never seen two more perfect specimens of human strength. Like so many who have died in the Hudson River Gorge, these men had probably measured the inch or two on their road atlas and had figured they could get their canoe down that river in a few hours, no problem. An afternoon float, that was all. Perhaps they took sandwiches and beer.

The thing about the Gorge, said Roberts, is that the only rescue after a certain point is by river. It's complete wilderness on either side with only a few old logging roads in and out. He said, "If you ever have an accident in there, whatever you do, don't, under any circumstances, leave the river. Follow it down."

After organized rafting trips began, those who might otherwise have taken their own canoes through the wilderness river now tended to join the rafters. Ernie agreed the Gorge had gotten safer, and cleaner, too, because the rafting business depended on customers in search of a pristine river experience. Rafting had been good for the river even though on a Saturday morning in May you might find as many as 2,000 people in this once untouched wilderness.

Perhaps if I had known exactly what was in the Gorge, I would not have opted for only one boat on my 315-mile journey. I would have used a whitewater canoe for those rapids, or I might have canceled the trip altogether. But I preferred the simplicity of using Ernie's Odyssey as the best all-around canoe for my multi-water journey. At eighteen feet, six inches, this tandem expedition canoe moved through the water like one of those very fast water spiders that skim the surface on a calm day. Its lines were long, its waist narrow.

Kevlar is a petroleum weave made by Dupont and best known for its use in the construction of bulletproof vests. Six inches of Kevlar have the same resistance as ten inches of steel. Ernie told me the U.S. Army was designing tanks made out of Kevlar because it is so light and indestructible. But when Kevlar is used in light canoes like the Odyssey, its skin is thin and flexes like canvas. My unpainted Odyssey was a thatch color, a kind of wicker tan, almost translucent and very "natural" looking for a high-tech product of the oil industry. From a distance on a sunny day, through the Kevlar skin, you could see the shadow of the canoe's contents (including my legs).

This particular canoe of Ernie's already had scratches on its hull, and the extra flotation panels had been stripped to make it lighter. The gunwales were straps of mahogany and the seats Kevlar buckets that moved forward and backward on light aluminum piping. The main thing was the canoe was light enough for the climb to Tear. Of course it would be perfect for the open water of the Hudson below the rapids all the way down to the Battery, about 230 miles of sun-beating, flat river.

In April, Ernie dropped a solo seat just aft of center for the hundreds of miles I'd be alone after he left me in Luzerne. I tried not to think what it would be like to say good-bye to my companion after a hard week's trekking together.

Ernie did most of the planning. Food, whitewater gear, car shuttles. We needed an air bag for the Gorge so the canoe would ride high when we capsized, which Ernie was sure we'd do. As extra precaution, Ernie planned for us to wear wet suits, helmets, and life vests.

That April was a particularly high-water rafting season. A woman fell out, smashed her head on a rock in Cedar Ledges in the Gorge, and drowned. Ernie was one of the first on the scene. Knowing first aid and CPR, various people tried their best to revive the dying woman. A few doctors happened along on other rafts, and the woman was revived many times while valiantly being hiked out on the Northwoods Club trail. She died finally in the middle of the night in the Saranac Lake hospital.

April and May were scary months for me, thinking about that dead woman. No wonder I was so jumpy in Perry Ehlers with Ernie two days before we set out for Lake Tear on June 11.

There was another reason rapids terrified me. Just this past April, on my first time ever in whitewater, I'd turned turtle and nearly become a white face in whitewater. I had taken my old Grumman to Connecticut with some kayaking friends from school. The spring runoff had swollen the Ten Mile River a little more than my expert and champion whitewater buddy, Scott Overdorf, would have preferred for my first time out. The water swirled and shot high over the banks. I wore one of his old wet suits and put my aluminum canoe into the swift water. I practiced ferrying across and turning with the current and dodging a few boulders. I loved it. There seemed little difficulty to this whitewater business—just paddling and occasionally steering to one side of a rock.

Simple, I thought.

Then we got out of our boats to scout what seemed like a small set of rapids. We walked fifty feet downriver. Scott said, "Until now you've done pretty well. You're aggressive. That's good. So I'm going to let you try this one if you want. You've got a fifty-fifty chance of making it to the bottom. But you must stay to the right. Go left into that standing wave there, and you're history. Stay right of the eddy and then (his hand drew an ideal itinerary for me in the air) pass down around that log and around that rock there, see it? And then into that eddy below."

Scott's hand pointed right, left, right, at eddies and buried rocks and specific waves I couldn't even see. I had nothing to compare these things to. The rapids looked easy enough, even though Scott had told me about the "Three-Fold Factor," which in whitewater lingo refers to actual waves in a rapid being three times as big as they appear from shore.

"Now, remember, Pete, stay right of that hydraulic there and pass around that log and into the eddy below." *Hydraulic?* The first time I ever heard the word, I couldn't help seeing the river as a machine, part shredder, part compactor. What for God's sake is a hydraulic? I wondered. Scott explained it was where the river flows over a rock and tumbles back on itself with such force that it actually flows up-river. If you get caught in a hydraulic, you have to dive into it to reach the tongue of water that flows downstream right along the riverbed. In a perfect hydraulic, the water doubles back along the bottom, and there's no way out.

When I got back into my canoe, I paddled so hard for the right bank of the wild little rapid that I could not stop my bullet of aluminum. The canoe hit the log with such force, the log broke in half. I bounced back toward the center of the very wave I was supposed to avoid. The canoe went broadside, and I saw Scott yelling something at me. I thought he was screaming, "Hold On! Hold On!"

I grabbed the gunwales, fearing a 180-degree turn in whitewater, and looked helplessly up at the huge wave about to topple me over in apparent slow motion into that stop-breathing ice water awash in rocks and foam. After it was all over, I discovered he had actually been yelling, "Paddle hard! Paddle hard!" Apparently with forward thrust you gain stability. My fear of going stern first was ill founded because a canoe can take a rapid either stern or bow forward so long as the canoe remains parallel to the general flow. Sideways was the very worst approach to the waves and rocks.

What scares me now through Perry Ehlers is the very swimming Ernie says I can't be afraid of. In that April rapid in Connecticut, what I had always thought of as a graceful canoe, my companion in flat water for twenty years, suddenly became a submerged metal enemy—a hulky, pounding mass of aluminum swamped up to the gunwales. (Underwater it actually moved more slowly than I did, which is dangerous because a swimmer must remain upstream from a canoe to prevent himself from being pinned against a rock.)

I learned how powerful whitewater can be when I was tossed and dunked every which way, the river doing everything possible to position me ahead of my old Grumman friend, now turned diabolical metal assassin. My hypothalamus must have been in a deep freeze in the cold spring water. I couldn't even kick my feet. I was a victim of thrust and bounce.

First, the traitorous canoe hit a rock and, WHAM, I heard the sound inside my brain. Then my tailbone hit the same rock, and I kicked the canoe away from me. I tried vainly to work my way to shore, still not believing I'd gone into the river. But I did remember that Scott said I should always go through rapids feetfirst. This saved me.

Feetfirst, I am thinking with Ernie. I must remember I will be okay if I put my feet up in front of me. To ward off rocks.

On our last run, with the wind and roar and foam, I feel great. In the afternoon driving home, I think how Ernie complimented me at the end of the day. With his paddle resting on the gunwale in front of him and with a warm grin from beneath the Civil War beard, he shouted, "All right, Pete!"

He looked surprised at how fast I'd picked up some of his pointers. I liked the way he knew how to encourage me, the way a good teacher knows how to embolden a student. His instruction was often stern, but when I did something right, he was all smiles.

The next time we do this, it'll be for real. We'll have at least two full days of Hudson rapids, one after another with a night's rest in between, and then back at it until the arms are ready to fall off. But for now, driving home, I feel tipsy, the way my father must have felt after his first skydive, thrilled to have actually jumped from the plane and planning to make thousands of future jumps. What I cannot seem to forget, though, is Ernie's response when I asked what class Perry Ehlers rapid was. I was thinking he'd say Class III (large regular waves covering boat, numerous rapids; passages clear though narrow, requiring expertise in maneuver . . .) or maybe even a short IV. But he said, "Class II. *Maybe.*"

Later I looked at a book on canoeing and found a description of a Class II river: regular waves, easy eddies, easy bends, course generally easy to recognize.

I could see I had a lot to learn.

2

The Great Portage

June 10. It's early, and Suzanna is waving at me as I pull out of the driveway, leaving home again only the day after I got back from our practice run in North River. My canoe sits on top of the car, life vest, tent, and gear packed away in the trunk. Suzanna smiles from Melissa's arms, unaware that I'll probably be gone for one twelfth of her life.

A mile from my house, on Interstate 84, I cross the Hudson at Newburgh, a wide, solemn, brown, still expanse of river. A certain gloom fills the car while the sky above is a mocking perfection of blue backdrop to puffy clouds. With every easy mile north on the road, I reckon it will be a hard multitude of strokes and hot river paddling to regain what my car fritters away. To drive the entire length of the navigable Hudson, 304 miles of it anyway, takes only six hours. I wonder what it will take to canoe my way home. If I can possibly make it in three weeks (and this is a big *if*), it might take me 504 hours, most of which will be spent dipping a paddle into water.

The miles zip by. I pass two cars with canoes on top, one Mad River and one Old Town. Whenever I see canoes on cars, some hardness in me melts. I think, "There are special people in that car." Even on the highway, canoes muffle the machines they rest on. With their round hulls and mellow curves, they look like soft shields against a heartless sky.

Canoeists are good people, I've always believed—they have a special love of quiet. After many years away from this fraternity, I'm glad to be a part of a growing sport in an age of back-to-basics. Let the bloated, stock-on-margin '80s be buried in junk bonds. Give me rivers and lakes and the soft roll of a canoe belly.

Four hours later at Ernie's house across from the Adirondack Museum in Blue Mountain Lake, the sky has clouded over with a good chance of rain for our climb to Lake Tear tomorrow.

June 11. Monday, 4 A.M. Rain all night and worry about what the trail must look like up to Tear. Ernie knocks on the door to wake me, but I'm already awake. His baby cried all night with the rain.

Ernie says at the coffee machine downstairs, "I heard the rain. I didn't want to get up today." We both complain, but Ernie, I know, is as excited as I am. Our shared moaning is the beginning of our friendship. I feel the way I used to feel when suiting up for a hockey game, the cold from the ice rink seeping into the dressing room, too nervous to speak seriously, too much gut-goings-on to tell my teammates how much I like them all. This is the early morning camaraderie of sport.

I follow him out to his garage. He calls out, "Baaaabbiess. Baaabbbieesss," at which there arises a holler of geese, goats, and chickens, such a racket of barnyard pets racing down to his little shed at the side of the old garage where he feeds his animals, talking to them, loving them, his two old dogs, one blind, right behind.

When Ernie is out packing the truck, Kimball tells me about his passion for rafting in the Hudson River Gorge. A friend of theirs went with him last spring when the river was at its peak and the friend had come back terrified. "He asked me, 'Does your husband have life insurance?'" The question scared her, for Ernie indeed did not. Apparently, in the height of the river's vengeance, Ernie had sat in the stern of that rubber tube with eight people on board all paddling for their lives—he had steered them through the waves and the rocks and the 17,000-cubic-inches-per-second rush, and smiled the whole way. Everyone else in the raft, even the veteran guides, were fossilized with fear. No one had seen the river quite this high. Shooting the river at lower levels just doesn't prepare you for that.

Kimball, a little grumpy from her baby's sleeplessness, but tolerant too of her husband's love of danger, says in a tone of loving dismay, "Ernie was actually smiling!" And she laughs.

5:12 A.M. Coffee'd, banana'd, packed, we set off in the grey wet day from Blue Mountain Lake for the hour drive to Upper Works parking lot above the town of Newcomb. That old adventure and dawn-coffee feeling percolates in the gut.

We ride with Ernie's brother-in-law, who will drive Ernie's pickup back to Blue Mountain after we reach the trail and get started. In a few days he and his wife will bring it back so it'll be waiting for us when we come down from Lake Tear. Ernie's brother-in-law, a gentle, quiet man, says, "The bear's back. Last night he tore the sign down again."

For the past month the hamlet of Blue Mountain Lake has been hosting a bear, reluctantly supplying it with garbage. The bear has broken into a number of homes to rampage through garbage cans. Last night, sharpening its claws, it tore down the town beach sign.

On the mostly quiet drive I tape my weak knee twice with Ace bandages. Two months ago I could hardly walk. My doctor told me I'd torn a meniscus cartilage and would probably have to have arthroscopic surgery. I've been worried about our long hike at the beginning of this journey. I hope the Ace bandages help.

Over a heavy sock I also tape, on the same leg, an old, bad ankle, sprained too many times in the past, twice skiing, once hiking in these High Peaks.

"Ernie," I say into the morning silence, "if this left leg goes bad on me on this trip, just cut it off or shoot me." He gives a short chuckle, but truly I'm worried: maybe I'm getting too old for this kind of thing.

From Newcomb we take the long drive up the mining road. At a stop sign beside the road in the mud, Ernie spots coyote tracks. He says, "In the last fifteen years, the fur market has been so bad, the population of coyote in the Park has gone way up. There's not much trapping anymore, and the coyote has few natural enemies."

6:30 A.M. Ernie's brother-in-law cracks a few jokes about our trek, then drives off. Ernie balances the canoe on his shoulders like a throwing dagger on a forefinger. The two paddles are lashed along the inner sides of the hull. We walk ten yards and immediately face our first obstacle. We've come to a gate erected by the state to prevent off-road vehicles from going up the trail. Ernie manages to negotiate the canoe around the metal posts by ramming the canoe into some pines.

I carry the sixty-pound pack with a strap around my stomach, feeling its burden already. To save four pounds, we've decided not to take my tent. Instead, we'll use a lean-to near Lake Tear. We'll try to make the Hudson's source today, then hike back a mile or so to the sleeping place, which will eliminate some of the weight of carrying gear for two people for two nights.

The plan is to switch off whenever we get tired carrying the loads we have chosen first. I am glad we'll change off. I'm anxious to try the canoe on my shoulders.

In the old days of Ernie's ancestors, Adirondack guides often carried their guide boats as well as the provisions for their clients, whom they called "sports." Many sports carried nothing too heavy. The fact that Ernie has chosen to begin the trip carrying the canoe is fine by me, but I do feel a little strange for hiring a guide in the first place. I've never hired a guide before.

We start out at a leisurely pace. First I lead, then Ernie leads. I keep looking back when I'm in front of him, to see if he's okay. Every time I turn and do not pay attention to the trail, I stumble.

A cool light rain falls on a muddy, wide trail. The roots and rocks are completely exposed from the feet of so many High Peak travelers. This is only one of the overused trails leading to Marcy. Twenty years ago when my family came here from our camp on a lake only an hour away, these trails were still wild. Thank God the public schools aren't out for two more weeks. After July Fourth, in the heart of summer, there's no solitude in the High Peaks at all.

But this morning the woods feel fresh as spring after a harsh winter: grey sky, clouds low, wind picking up. Ernie is good at carrying this awkward canoe through the woods. He misses the higher branches, and he is graceful at judging the trees. When he takes a corner, the tail end of the canoe just misses trunks and rocks. It's as if he has an instinctive sense of proportion.

In *Adirondack Canoe Waters: North Flow*, Paul Jamieson suggests that any carry of more than five miles is a thing of the past and "not recommended for revival." Humbug, I say. Give me an old-fashioned carry if the trip is worth it. Yet I'm glad it's Ernie who begins with the canoe, for the nine-mile trail to Marcy is not a traditional carry. Just how absurd this portage is will become increasingly clear as we approach the summit.

In the summer of 1859, the artist Benson J. Lossing and his wife hiked—without a canoe—this same route up Mount Marcy on their way down the length of the river. On their way to the river's mouth, they bypassed the most beautiful section of all, from Tahawus to Warrensburg, because Lossing did not think it worth the effort, but they did cover most of the Hudson's distance. Lossing made sketches en route, which he later incorporated in his book *The Hudson: From the Wilderness to the Sea.* Of course Lossing and his wife didn't travel today's manicured trails. Yet he wrote in such a gentlemanly tone, the hardships they must have faced on such a journey nearly 140 years ago can only be guessed at. Accompanied by Adirondack guides, they left Upper Works for Marcy's peak, having been warned that a tourist should never enter this wilderness before the middle of August, for by then the "flies and mosquitoes, the intolerable pests of the forests, are rapidly disappearing, and fine weather may be expected." On a hot sunny day during blackfly season in the deep woods, the insects can drive deer, bears, and men insane.

If the day heats up, I'll wish I hadn't come in blackfly season. So far it's too cool for the intolerable pests. Blackfly season is the only time a canoe can safely run the Hudson rapids. The water level in the Gorge has to be just right for us to get through. April and May with the wild, high water would be too early. Later in the summer, certainly by August, the river will dry up and my journey would surely fail. So I'll take the bugs if it means the chance for success.

Our first day on the trail we're grateful for the very weather that had me worried last night. Early June before the summer hikers come to the High Peaks is a wonderful time to be in the woods, except for the black flies.

Before blackfly season I'd gone to Ernie's mom's house in Blue Mountain Lake. I wanted to meet Ernie's mom, whose great-grandfather, grandfather, father, and late husband had all been guides, and whose son now was a guide. I wondered what kind of traits an Adirondack guide had to have.

Evelyn was eating pork chops at the kitchen table with her daughter and son-in-law when Ernie and I reached the house. She seemed much younger than her sixty-one years and as modest as her son.

I sat down at the kitchen counter. Ernie stood while his mom kept eating. When she finished, she turned and answered me: "To be a guide you have to know the woods. I think it's something you have to grow up with. Very few guides now have any real background."

Ernie agreed: "There are probably more licensed New York State guides than ever before, but they're not real guides. They don't have years of experience in the outdoors that the older folks had. They don't *depend* on guiding as a living. There are a lot of casual guides. Maybe that's the biggest difference."

"How old were you when you trapped your first muskrat?" Evelyn looked at her son. "You were always in the woods with your father from the time you could wander, from when you were five or six."

"I sold my first furs to old Galusha when I was six," Ernie said. "I had twelve muskrats and he got me for seventy-five cents apiece." We all laughed.

Adirondack guides have always been a special breed. In each hamlet—Tupper Lake, Minerva, North Creek, Blue Mountain—there were only a few guides. Revered in town, they seldom guided outside their areas, and certain guides had reputations for either fishing or hunting, but not necessarily both.

Ernie said, "My dad guided hunters, not fishermen. I'm the same way. I won't guide people for fishing. And I enjoy my own hunting too much to take anyone else out. I guide mostly for canoe camping on rivers and lakes. Mom's dad guided mostly for fishing. He raised nine kids guiding. He didn't work at any other job until he was sixty-eight when he finally worked for someone else. He'd go off guiding weeks at a time."

We follow the trail along Calamity Brook to Calamity Pond. Suddenly, through a cloud, comes the backdrop of a huge spruce-covered mountain. It is spectacular, almost a Rocky Mountain drama, more so because the scene is unexpected. In front of the mountain lie a large marsh and tiny pool of dark water. In the 1800s it was called Duck Hole.

At the edge of the marsh I expect to see moose, but discover instead an eight-foot sandstone monument erected after a Scotsman named David Henderson accidentally shot himself and gave this pond its present name. The monument bears the following inscription: "This monument was erected by filial affection to the memory of David Henderson, who lost his life on this spot, 3rd September, 1845."

Henderson, who was fifty-two years old and one of the founders of the great MacIntyre iron mine, was heading a party in search of an additional source of water to power the blast furnace at Upper Works, not far from where we began this morning at the parking lot. (A redirected stream of water would power a wheel that would provide compressed air for the "blast.")

Henderson was accompanied by his ten-year-old son and a famous Adirondack guide by the name of John Cheney, who claimed to have killed 600 deer, 400 sable, 19 moose, 28 bears, and 6 wolves. When the group arrived at the duck hole, Henderson handed his pistol to Cheney so Cheney could shoot some ducks. Cheney moved forward, but the ducks flew out of range, and Cheney handed the pistol back to Henderson, who put it in its holster. A little while later a shot rang out. A man named Dornburgh who was in the party wrote:

> Mr. Cheaney [*sic*] knew Mr. Henderson was shot by the movement he made, and he ran to him as fast as possible. Upon arriving at Mr. Henderson's side the fallen man turned his eyes to him and said: "John, you must have left the pistol cocked." Mr. Cheaney could make no reply, not knowing but that might have been the case. Mr. Henderson looked around and said: "This is a horrible place for a man to die," and then, calling his son to him he gently said, "Archy, be a good boy and give my love to your mother." This was all he said, although his lips kept moving for a few minutes as if in prayer.

Henderson had probably taken off his knapsack, put it on a rock, unbuckled his belt, and taken hold of the gun's muzzle. When he laid it down on the rock, the hammer struck, and the gun went off with the muzzle pointed at his abdomen just below the naval. The duck hole was renamed Calamity Pond.

Early the next morning the party brought Henderson's body down to the mining village at Tahawus, then called Adirondac. A year later a historian named Headley ascended Marcy with the same John Cheney. Headley wrote of his visit to Calamity Pond:

> The first few miles there is a rough path, which was cut last summer in order to bring out the body of Mr. Henderson. It is a great help, but filled with sad associations. At length we came to the spot where 25 workmen watched with the body in the forest all night. It was too late to get through, and here they kindled their camp fire and stayed. The rough poles are still there on which the corpse rested. "Here," says Cheney, "On this log I sat all night and held in my arms Mr. Henderson's little son. . . . Oh! how he cried to be taken to his mother, but it was impossible to find our way through the woods; and he at length cried himself to sleep in my arms. Oh! it was a dreadful night."

I step carefully as we cross two suspension bridges over a rushing torrent. Such a long way to go yet. Those bridges sway with the weight of our loads as if they will snap.

Wind slapping the canoe from side to side upsets the balance that might allow Ernie to rest his arms. The weight of the canoe itself is not as painful as having to keep his arms up to correct the tipping.

As we walk through light rain, I tell Ernie about the book that will be published, tell him about the old treasure hunter I met, my German friend Eugene Brunner, who considered himself the Heinrich Schliemann of Ecuador, who had made a forty-five-year quest for an Incan treasure of 750 tons of gold and silver. I tell him how Brunner searched for gold every year of his life since 1937, when he had fled Nazi Germany and had found refuge in Quito, and about the old man's missions taking dead bodies out of the cloud forest for the Ecuadorian Air Force when their own planes crashed in unmapped terrain. I tell him about Brunner's death a few years ago, which had made me sad because I'd learned so much from the old treasure hunter. As I speak, I wonder if by telling Ernie about Brunner, I am trying to replace the old friend with a new one.

"What memories," Ernie says from underneath his Kevlar helmet. Talking to a man carrying a canoe up a mountain is like speaking to a man without a head.

I'd like to draw a picture of Ernie beneath that long canoe, but at this point, it's impossible for me to take any kind of notes. The rain and wind grow stronger the higher we climb. From Calamity Pond we follow the trail to something called Flowed Lands, an area that was flooded by the mining company in order to direct the water away from the Opalescent River and into Calamity Brook to work the blast furnace below. After Henderson's "calamity," the company thrived for a time, then stopped operations and reopened again later. In 1990 the area continues to be mined under the management of National Lead Industries, not for iron anymore but for titanium, an impurity in iron ore used as a pigment in paint.

8:35 A.M. Ernie still has the canoe two hours after we started. Every time I stop to say, "Ernie, do you want me to carry the canoe now?" He replies, "Well," sounding a little hesitant, "if you want to. Sure." I realize, of course, I cannot take the canoe away from him, not yet anyway. He's enjoying this, and I won't insist.

Suddenly, as in a dream, we pass two hikers. We say "Hi," but they don't return our greeting. Hardly looking at us as we pass, their eyes are fixed to the ground. Then from behind we hear their delayed reactions: "Hi." But they pass on, stunned by their own hard walking. I wonder where they imagine we're taking this leviathan.

Ernie points to a lovely pink flower in the pine needles, "Lady-slipper," he says. "The Orchid of the Adirondacks." Then he adds, "Right under that spruce there, see it?"

"No." I always get the trees mixed up. "Which one's a spruce?"

But Ernie interjects, "Trilliums! Gosh, the trilliums are still blooming here. I love the woods."

I, too, love the names of the brooks and rivers and mountains up here. Our route is taking us from Calamity Brook to Calamity Pond to Flowed Lands to Lake Colden to Opalescent River to Feldspar Brook to Lake Tear of the Clouds. These are the names of the wilderness, of preindustrial America, names from a time when we all lived closer to roots and rocks and mud, unlike those names of the lower river, which are thoroughly Dutch-settled names (Peekskill, Fishkill, Rensselaer) or machine-factory-fort names (Mechanicville, Beacon, Fort

Montgomery, Fort Lee)—man-made names for the Industrial Age. I have come to explore the upper, unknown Hudson perhaps simply to hear the names as we pass the wild places. This forest is enchanted with its nineteenth-century history of logging, mining, and Indian hunting parties, filled with the raw names of survival. The upper part of the river is the beginning of America; it reminds us of what we used to endure, through the bleakness of winters and want.

I long for Ernie's life in the mountains. Eons apart from him, Melissa and I live so far from here yet along this same river. We live in a poor factory town that is like so many former industrial river towns on the lower Hudson, among the abandoned buildings of brick, with the weeds in the cracks of the weathered stone. We live in a graceless, suburban wasteland without the dignity of this Adirondack Hudson.

Finally we reach Flowed Lands where we drop the canoe on a wide beach, take a photograph, rest in one of the lean-tos, and eat gorp—that high-energy mix of peanuts, raisins and M & M's—in a wet, cold British drizzle. Behind the lake at Flowed Lands is Lake Colden. While exploring the region in 1836, Henderson and Cheney gave the lake its name. They found fresh panther tracks, and along the shore they came across "the warm and mangled remains of a deer that two wolves were disposing of when frightened away by the approach of the party." The twin lakes, Colden and Flowed Lands, are lovely, and still wild.

When we load the canoe and begin to paddle across the lake (saving us a mile of trail that scoots along Flowed Land's northwestern shore), Ernie says, "Excellent. Sure beats hiking."

Ernie is strong from rafting all spring. His upper body is powerful. During the hike, however, he has worried about how his legs would manage in the woods on a long walk ten years after he stopped logging. But now that we are paddling, it seems that all of his sinews are dedicated to water.

We're both glad to be off the trail. The sky is free of branches; the world is visible again, flooded with grey light. But Flowed Lands is hardly deep, and we have a hard time finding the channel that leads across to the continuation of the trail. Sometimes we get stuck, but since the canoe's "draw" is shallow (it needs only a few inches of water to float in), we manage to pass over many shoals that are only three or four inches deep. Here the pebbles are clearly visible, and if I wanted, I could reach out and grab a handful of stones from the icy water.

Ernie has warned me that the Adirondacks are famous for capricious weather changes. As if to illustrate the point, the wind suddenly picks up and we're paddling furiously, making many false starts into the marsh looking for the channel, then turning back and trying again. We fight the wind, then also the current. We scrape pebbles with the tips of our paddles. We pole our canoe over the sandy shoals, even get out a few times to drag the canoe across the marsh.

There's no one around for miles in the cold gloom of the day, and the lovely Mount Marcy and Mount Colden loom like monstrous porcupines rolled into balls.

Canoeing, which at first seemed a nice break from hiking, is no longer so nice. The wind picks up to a near gale, and whitecaps beat our hull. Then it seems we're about to turn turtle in the few inches of water in this diminutive lake. Ernie and I are paddling so hard, we tip and sway. My arms feel numb from paddling, yet we're making little headway. My hands are frozen; it's September in the Yukon.

I remember how, as the weeks got closer to my leaving, Melissa would ask over and over: "Aren't you going to exercise for this trip?" Each day she'd ask again, "So when are you going to start training?" I told her I'd never done any preparation before, not when I climbed into the cloud forest of Ecuador or on any other trip. "My arms will build up by canoeing each day," I said.

She said, "But you're older now. One of these days, it'll be the end of you. You'll have a heart attack. It's *not normal!*"

Paddling on Flowed Lands, still miles from Lake Tear, I know she was right. I should have used the NordicTrack while I had the chance.

Finally, we find the channel in the marsh and drag the canoe across sand. Then we're on the trail again, the wildest hike of all.

The next four miles of trail—from Colden to Lake Tear—run along the edge of cliffs above the dreamlike Opalescent River and Feldspar Brook. There is hardly a moment when we cannot hear or see the torrents of green water plowing over huge boulders or the white rush dropping in great flumes. On this leg of the portage we can hardly speak to one another; the river is so loud, and we're struggling too much for words.

In 1859, Lossing and his wife saw a similar but less dramatic Opalescent. They walked more than four miles in the bed of the dried-up river. "We crossed it a hundred times or more," Lossing wrote, "picking our way, and sometimes compelled to go into the woods in passing a cascade. The stream is broken into falls and swift rapids the whole distance." Describing the scintillating geology of the Opalescent with an artist's eye, Lossing says:

> The stones in this river vary in size, from tiny pebbles to boulders of a thousand tons. . . . They are composed chiefly of the beautiful labradorite, or opalescent feldspar, which form the great mass of the . . . Black Mountain range, as the Indians called this Adirondack group, because of the dark aspect with their somber cedars, and spruce, and cliffs present at a distance. The bed of the stream is full of that exquisitely beautiful mineral. We saw it glittering in splendour, in pebbles and large boulders, when the sunlight fell full upon the shallow water. A rich blue is the predominant colour, sometimes mingled with a brilliant green. Gold and bronze-coloured specimens have been discovered, and, occasionally, a completely iridescent piece may be found. It is to the abundance of these stones that the river is indebted for its beautiful name. It is one of the main sources of the Hudson.

The soil that used to cover the labyrinthine root systems of the trees has been worn away by summer hikers. The mud sucks our boots. Ernie negotiates the long canoe ever so gracefully, then hits a tree or two, after which I can hear a Kevlar-muffled expletive.

There's a lot of time for thinking on a long hike. I remember the day I told my stepfather about this trip. Pop's grandfather had once owned much of the Adirondack Mountains during the decades in which he was president of the Santa Clara Lumber Company of Tupper Lake. Pop had spent sixty-five summers in the Adirondacks, had hiked the High Peaks, and he thought I was certifiably crazy when I told him about my plan to canoe the whole Hudson River, which meant carrying my canoe eighteen miles to Lake Tear and back. He said, "You've got to be kidding. That's nuts! That's not a portage—It's just plain stupid."

It is to Pop I owe my love of wilderness. Ever since I've known him, he's had a topographic map of some wilderness river in Alaska on his desk, and it was he who showed me the quotation from John Rugge's and Jim Davidson's *The Complete Wilderness Paddler:* "Few of us ever take the leap and actually get into genuine honest-to-God wilderness to see it for ourselves. . . . Most people . . . just aren't sufficiently aware of the need to think big: they let the books convince them that the wilderness is somehow a quality of the heart, some- thing INSIDE them. Nonsense. The wilderness is plain open space, the sheer physical presence of the earth unwinding without us people."

Ernie and I stop to rest on the lip of a deep gorge of emerald green water. I'm breathing now like a panther after a chase. For someone as out of shape as I am, toting a sixty-pound pack is not a lot of fun.

Ernie says, "Getting to the lake is becoming an obsession with me now." I won't ask again if he wants help with the canoe. Ernie, if he can manage, will be the first ever to lug an eighteen-foot canoe to the source of the Hudson. So I'll let him. I have a long enough journey after that. Ernie can be the hero of the north woods.

He keeps asking about my knee. "It's okay," I tell him, glad for his solicitude. He says, "You'd better not carry the canoe. You could slip on these rocks and ruin that knee so bad your trip would stop before it started."

Ten minutes later, at yet another rest stop, I say, "Your depth per- ception is fantastic, the way you clear those rocks and trees on the trail."

"Just luck," he says.

We are hanging over a ledge; the balsam fir smells sharp. We're looking out over the valley in this cool, bug-less day, and I feel happy.

The wind in gusts is like the fist of God knocking the canoe into the stunted trees of these upper elevations. I hear a little more swear- ing now from under the Kevlar helmet as I stumble behind Ernie, and there are longer and longer pauses before finding footholds in boul- ders the size of large pigs.

We reach the juncture of the Opalescent and Feldspar and the last lean-to, where we planned to spend the night after dropping the canoe up at Tear. But we find three young forlorn campers tucked deeply into their sleeping bags in the middle of the day. Unwilling to move, they're waiting for the long rain to stop.

2. The steep trail up Mount Marcy.

Maybe the rain will never stop. We drop the canoe and the paddles in the woods right on the trail and hike the pack down to the previous lean-to, two miles back. Inside the little open-ended hut, written in a scrawl, a message is posted on a nail: "A Big Bear got our food. Be careful. May 22, 1990."

"We'll leave everything here and take the chance. These bears aren't grizzlies," Ern says. I have started calling him Ern. Hard labor and the long day make the nickname seem right. "Ern."

Perhaps the worst section of this hike is the next. The trail marker says it is 1.2 miles from the Feldspar/Opalescent junction to Lake Tear. But it seems more like three. Very, very steep. This also is one of the most marvelous hikes in the High Peaks. You walk along a trail that follows a knife's edge, with brooks crashing below on either side of you. The roar of Feldspar is on your left. The mist and the great peaks of the MacIntyre range are behind you. Here is cool freedom and peace.

1 P.M. We are making great time. Ernie lifts the canoe. Arctic mist blows up the side of the valley on our backs.

We follow Feldspar now. What a wonderful name: "Feldspar." It rolls in the mouth like rock candy and reminds me of my first love affair with geology when I kept a rock collection in the fourth grade.

Thoughts ramble at high altitudes. I mumble to Ernie, "I wish I knew what was for dinner."

"Nope. Not telling."

I'm glad he's not telling: the food will taste better if it's a surprise.

Now I am carrying just the two paddles and a small day pack.

"I wouldn't take that canoe from you—not for all the money in the world, not when we're this close." We are like members of a football team heading into the last quarter knowing we'll probably win the ball game.

"And I wouldn't let you, either," Ernie says, the difficulty of the hike and the wind, the fist of God, making him bold in his desire to get his guide's job done. I wonder if he's thinking of his father and his father's father and his mother's father and all the Adirondack guides before him. Probably he's not thinking at all—there's too much pain in his neck. He probably just wonders where to place his foot next so he won't stumble. A lot of pride rests on not stumbling. He hasn't fallen once.

Perfect climbing temperature, too: perhaps fifty-four degrees. Rain cutting off a little.

I say, "You're doing great. We're almost there."

Mostly, silence is best.

Up here every other tree is a Christmas tree. The air is so sweetly balsam and rain. The thump of our boots echoes off the sky like the pumping of startled pheasants.

We rest every ten minutes. I take a photo of Ernie. The word *Wenonah* blazes along the side of the canoe. Ernie hears the click and says, "Wenonah, on the trail to Marcy." I repeat the motto of the Wenonah Company—"For the people who know and love canoeing."

I feel like shouting with joy. This wilderness part of the river is a great secret to the people who live in the southern half of the state, the majority of the 20 million residents of New York. When I decided to canoe the whole river, I asked around if anyone had done it before. People on the tidal river from Albany south to Manhattan, including environmentalists and fishermen, knew almost nothing about the

Hudson this far north. In fact, for most people the Hudson seemed to begin somewhere near the state capital of Albany and was only about 150 miles long. (After all, Hudson himself went only as far as Albany and Troy.) The unknown river, the 160 miles above Troy, to them was like another river. Never mind that it shared the name.

Lower and upper river people are often unaware of each other. Ernie hadn't ever heard of John Cronin, the Riverkeeper, an important environmentalist from the Hudson Highlands. By the same token, Cronin knew nothing of LaPrairie's Adirondack fame.

In some ways I feel like a river diplomat, hoping to introduce the various people along the river to one another.

Finally, I got the name of someone who claimed he had made the trip not once, but three times. At Raquette River Outfitters in Tupper Lake, Robbie Frenette said there had been a fellow in last year by the name of Brian Kunz, the director of the outdoor program at Dartmouth College, who might be an expert on the Hudson.

In February I drove to Hanover to meet Brian. I don't know why, but I expected to find a charlatan. That no one else I could find had ever made this trip except this one fellow—who said he'd done it "often"—did not seem exactly plausible.

I began to believe his story, however, after he told me on the phone, yes, he had done it with a group from Boston University, three years in a row in June and July in the early '70s, but he said the river might have changed since then. The group had hiked without any boats from Marcy to Upper Works. From the old MacIntyre furnace they'd launched kayaks, then switched to rafts (and occasionally inner tubes) through the serious rapids. At the Glen, above Warrensburg, they got back into kayaks and canoes for the rest of the trip.

I went to see Brian to get a better idea about how to break up my own trip, about where to sleep, what to expect, what the river looked like as a whole, and of course to see if this guy was for real.

On a sunny New Hampshire day I found his cape perched on a high field of snow. He, his girlfriend, and some friends had just come back from a morning's ten-mile cross-country ski. We stepped inside, and he launched right into a discussion about the Hudson. I could see that Brian, who was now about forty and whose face was friendly, handsome, almost boyish, was still enchanted with those trips he had made nearly twenty years ago. Even now he could recall in wonderful detail the actual campsites and the river's rhythms.

Like a lot of outdoors people, Brian seemed much younger than his years. His passion for rivers had preserved his youth, and there was something wonderfully innocent about him, too. In this age of cynicism and irony, he was a positive fellow. In the face of the world's environmental despair, Brian and his outdoor friends imparted love and joy for the wild places that remain. He got me fired up about the trip. He spoke with all the enthusiasm of Huck Finn.

"That's the great thing about rivers," he said as the steam from his coffee curled into the sunlight slanting through a picture window. "You can just drag your canoe up into the bushes, stake out your little area, and sleep. You're invisible. Then you launch in the morning, and you're off. Big boats don't see you. People on shore might be able to point you out, but they can't get to you. Fact is, there are very few parts of the Hudson that have roads right up along the river. Imagine a world without roads and cars. You'd be surprised. The river is surrounded by a *no man's land.*"

No man's land—I liked the sound of the river's edge—as if the river had its own inviolable idea of space and time. While humanity races along the river and over it in so many frenetic cars, the great river keeps its steady course.

Their trips had started from the Adirondak Loj, Brian said. They hiked to Marcy from the opposite side of the Opalescent and Calamity Brook. At the summit he would compare their upcoming Hudson journey to an expedition down the Amazon. He would say, "You'll be dealing with problems, barriers, as they come up on your trek. You'll start at the source and continue all the way to Manhattan, past rapids, paper mills, power dams. The river is barricaded in places. Sometimes you'll have to hike through towns with your boats. It'll be up to you to solve the river's challenges. At the dams, maybe you can negotiate with the big companies to let you through their compounds; maybe they won't let you. Your decisions will determine the outcome of your journey. Good luck. This is *real adventure.*"

After the rapids, the character of the river changes, Brian told me. "Did you know that there are nine huge dams on the river? And locks on the forty miles from Glens Falls to Troy?"

"Locks? Like on the Erie Canal?"

"The same. But as soon as you get to the locks, there's no more portaging. The lock tenders can lock you through." On the words "lock you through," Brian had begun to smile serenely. He kept smiling for the rest of the interview.

"You must speak to those guys. They're fantastic people. They've been tending the locks on the Hudson for generations. You just paddle into those big chambers. Then they'll lower the water level so you can paddle out the other end. Most people don't know this section of the Hudson is part of the Champlain Canal."

The idea of locks on the Hudson so delighted Brian that his delight delighted me, and I too was in a good mood for the rest of the day.

He said that around Troy I'd come to the worst pollution on the river, worse than Manhattan. Suddenly there would be big ships from overseas. Yet it was magic here too, to be on a new river: a *tidal* river of barges and ocean freighters and container boats.

"Big water," he said, his delight unfazed by the mention of pollution. "But the same river, too. Very strange, and wonderful. You can paddle with the tides every six hours. A few times we paddled at night. That was exciting. You get into the rhythm of the river. When the tide goes, you go. And you sleep when you aren't battling the wind that can really whip up out there. Plenty of places to pull over and rest. At dusk and again at dawn you have calm water. Sometimes the tide may be going with you but the wind'll be against you. This makes for big chop. It's better to sit it out sometimes. Pull out a good book. No hurry. Go with the flow. The river's always changing."

That is what Brian said about the upper Hudson, too. One year it would be high water; the next, low. Everything depended on rain and beaver dams. If the beaver made a lot of dams that year, the level of the upper Hudson could drop way below normal. Or a few days of heavy rains could turn the rapids into really dangerous whitewater. Drought could also make it impossible to get through. Some years the water was so low, Brian's boats got scratched badly on the rocks and were ruined.

It was Brian Kunz and his delight in speaking about his trips from twenty years ago that fired my imagination about the river as a whole. At one point in the conversation, his friend, Earl, also an outdoor program director at a New England college, said, "You know,

I've heard these stories ever since I met Brian. Over and over I keep hearing them, yet the river seems more mysterious every time I hear them."

Brian kept smiling, remembering.

1:23 P.M. Stunted trees scrape the hull. Wind. Wham. "Shit" from the belly of the canoe. "SHIT! SHIT!" Ernie, who loves boats as much as he loves canoeing, gets upset whenever he inflicts a scratch on a good canoe.

The bow has rammed a trunk. The path twists into much tighter turns now.

There was a phone call just before I left home. A friend wanted me to represent an environmentalist. John Cronin is the Hudson Riverkeeper. He patrols the lower Hudson in a boat also called the *Riverkeeper*. Cronin's job is to look for polluters of the river and to bring them to court. Cronin himself asked if I wanted to be sponsored and have some of my expenses covered. I hesitated because I didn't want helicopters dogging my 315-mile trek, and I didn't want the public pressure of having to be in certain towns for press conferences. But my friend Scott Overdorf, who grew up on the river in Pough-keepsie, convinced me to work with the group. He said I'd be "giving the river something in return." He explained that river runners, kay-akers and rafters alike, should make a sacrifice to a river before a trip. "This appeases the river gods," he said, "and believe me, every river does have a god!" It would be dangerous, indeed, if I ever bad-mouthed a river or took it for granted and did not acknowledge its power.

So I joined in the Riverkeeper's cause, but with the proviso that all environmental press should be focused on the lower river. I was worried that if I were perceived in the North Country as an "environ-mentalist," some people might not talk to me. The paper and power companies are really touchy these days about anyone who might give them bad press, and in June there had been massive demonstrations by park residents against the recommendations made in the Commis-sion on the Adirondacks in the Twenty-first Century, which, among other things, suggested a moratorium on future building in the park.

Focusing her efforts on the Big Apple, Cronin's publicist would try to arrange a "historic landing" at the Battery. Mayor Dinkins might even come to the press conference at Battery Park to meet me and make a speech on environmental policy.

The idea would be to help the Riverkeeper make his point that the upper river and the lower river were still accessible to a canoeist and that it was all part of the same larger river system that people around Manhattan should learn to respect. Most of the lawsuits that Cronin had filed through his attorney, Robert F. Kennedy Jr., were against the city of New York anyway, and my press coverage could help bring needed public pressure on the city, by far the worst polluter on the lower Hudson.

I agreed to help. But all of this made me nervous, for I'd planned the trip for no one but me.

3

Lake Tear of the Clouds

The wind grows worse. Then the trail suddenly flattens out, and the trees are dwarfed by altitude and the bitter caprice of Adirondack weather. The last few hundred yards are like walking on top of the world.

Then, finally, a misty Lake Tear appears, and somewhere above, Cloud-Splitter's summit is lost in fog. Miniature whitecaps blow up against Feldspar outlet where the trail meets the lake, this trickling brook, the beginning of the Hudson River.

In Theodore Roosevelt's day at the turn of the century, Lake Tear was 500 feet long and 5 feet deep, but since then it has been filling in through the natural process of eutrophication. Today the lake is only 200 feet long and no more than 2 feet deep. The side of the lake up against Mount Marcy is all bog. In another hundred years or so, some lower body of water could well become the highest pond source of the Hudson because Lake Tear will cease to exist.

The marsh is surrounded by stands of hemlock and balsam severely bent from the constant winds that lash down off Marcy's summit. Mist in those ragged trees lends the little lake a primordial look. This scene could be from the beginning of the world.

Lake Tear of the Clouds itself was not discovered as the source of the Hudson until Verplanck Colvin, an Adirondack enthusiast and official New York State surveyor for the Adirondacks, described it in

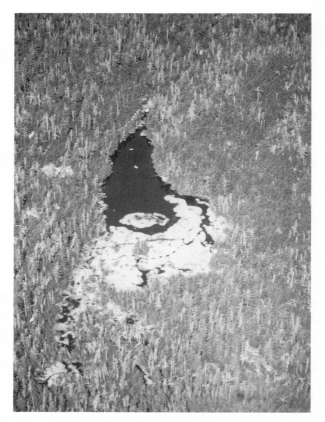

3. Aerial shot of Lake Tear of the Clouds.

1872 as "a minute, unpretending tear of the clouds, as it were, a lonely pool, shivering in the breezes of the mountains, and sending its limpid surplus through Feldspar Brook and to the Opalescent River, the wellspring of the Hudson."

At an elevation of 4,293 feet, the trail runs right into the lake at the very spot Theodore Roosevelt was sitting with his lunch when an Adirondack guide by the name of Harrison came up the trail with a note telling him that President McKinley's condition had worsened and that the president would probably die soon.

McKinley had been shot on September 6, 1901, by an anarchist terrorist while the president was attending the Pan-American Exposition in Buffalo. Vice-President Roosevelt, who had been vacationing in Vermont, quickly left Lake Champlain at the news of the attempted assassination and arrived in Buffalo the next day, where he was assured by the doctor that the president was out of danger. So Roosevelt then left Buffalo to join his family at the Tahawus Club in the Adirondacks.

On September 13 Roosevelt engaged an Adirondack Guide named Noah LaCasse for a trip up Marcy. The vice-president and his guide proceeded up the route Ernie and I had just climbed. The trail was slippery. The visibility on Marcy was terrible. They stopped for lunch at Lake Tear and sat in the grass a few feet from the source of the Hudson.

Roosevelt opened a can of ox tongue and served his guide saying, "Noah's the one to be waited on first. He's been doing all the work." Then suddenly Roosevelt spotted a man coming up the trail. Another Adirondack guide had hiked up to Lake Tear to hand the vice-president a note that said the president was dying and that Roosevelt should come back to Buffalo right away.

Miniature whitecaps drive into the shore off the pond. Ernie puts down the canoe with a grunt, breathing hard, and says: "When you first spoke to me about this trip, I said to myself, 'No way, I'll never do that. Never.' But here we are!" Like Noah LaCasse, Ernie has been doing all the work. But I don't have a can of ox tongue to offer him. Instead we have candy bars, and I give him one I've been saving.

After little rest, Ernie says, "If we're going to leave the canoe here for the night, I better hide these paddles so no one will take the canoe for a ride. Everything we've done today would be for nothing."

We've chosen to paddle the lake tomorrow and pray for better weather. We just can't muster the energy today; we're too tired.

Ernie dives into the thick tangle of brush and spends a good ten minutes hiding the paddles. Before I discovered the park rule that you cannot camp anywhere above 4,000 feet, I had envisioned setting up our tent here by Tear of the Clouds and paddling around quietly before dinner. But the rule is a good one; the high-altitude vegetation has an Arctic-tundra delicacy. And since we must go below 4,000 feet, and since it's raining, we might as well go down to the lean-to with the bear.

We leave the canoe on the trail, pulled partially into the trees. A plane buzzes behind the clouds. Perhaps it's some journalist who has heard about our trip, out looking for us in vain through a thick cover of grey. Today in both the *New York Post* and the Glens Falls *Post-Star*, articles will have appeared about Ernie and me, about our trip bringing attention to a neglected river.

Before we head down the trail, I can half-imagine Mr. R. with his guide LaCasse eating ox tongue. Nothing has changed. The source of the Hudson, except for being a bit more bog and a little less pond, is the way it was. But I wonder what the river becomes as it grows, what I will find below the trail to the Upper Works, the ghost town of the MacIntyre Mine at Tahawus, the unrunnable rapids from the Tahawus Club bridge to Newcomb, the great Gorge, North Creek and Warrensburg, and finally below Glens Falls and the power dams and the locks of the Champlain Canal system; then below Saratoga, Troy and Albany, and into the one-foot drop and the 154-mile tide. Perhaps my trip is a journey backward in time, then forward into the present, and maybe into the future too, from the nineteenth century to the twenty-first century. I had not expected time travel, only spatial trekking, only a move from A to Z, from source to mouth. But the nature of a simple idea is that it grows more complex.

Already my journey isn't exactly what I expected it to be.

The summit of Marcy almost blows clear. The rock baldness above the tree line climbs as the mist climbs.

"Think anyone'll steal our canoe?" I worry.

Laughter.

Ernie says, "If they do, we'll catch them below."

"Not if they decide to go over Marcy."

Ernie says, "That'd be pretty stupid. It's a mile straight up from here to Marcy, then another eight or so out the other side."

"Yeah, but what if . . . " My worry is no match for the fatigue and the elation.

We fill our water bottles from Feldspar Brook as it tumbles out of Tear. The whitecaps drive at us from behind, whipping up the purest water of the ancient Hudson. We drink a toast to each other and to the timeless lake. We did it.

To show how daring we feel, we cast aside our water purifying tablets, although they are recommended everywhere in the High Peaks these days because of all the camping. Giardia protozoa have invaded the clear streams. Not using the tablets is a small but bold moment at the trickling source of a mighty river. A statement for the way we want things to be.

5 P.M. Like children returning home at dusk after a long day at play, we scamper down the mountain. We race to the lean-to with its hard-packed dirt floor and aluminum sheet that covers big holes in the leaky roof.

In mud and rain, we scatter for wood. Legs and arms don't work so well. The camp smoke puffs into mist. Wet socks and shoes hang on the limbs of pines. Now I see what's for dinner. The indefatigable Adirondack guide proudly cooks steak, Lipton's freeze-dried stroganoff, and cowboy coffee, the best coffee this side of the Mississippi, the grounds boiling in a pot of Feldspar water. I feel no guilt for not cooking. I'm too tired, wrapped in a sleeping bag, unable to move. "Ernie," I say, "I expected macaroni for lunch, macaroni for breakfast, and macaroni for dinner."

"You think guides like macaroni?" he says. "Well, I prefer steak."

"So do I, so do I. Do you always eat this well when you guide?"

"I sure try to." Laughter.

After dinner, with dark descending fast, I ask Ernie, "So how does it feel to be the first and only person to carry an eighteen-foot, six-inch canoe all the way to Lake Tear?"

Ernie stokes the fire, then sits on a big log. Sipping his coffee from a tin cup, he stares into the embers.

"Great. But I'll never do it again." We laugh happily. Ernie takes two Advil with coffee for his sore muscles.

"You can tell your great-great grandchildren about it."

With mirth and pride in his eyes, he says, "Well, I'm glad I came. Makes me feel good." He slaps a mosquito on his face and throws the last two dead branches on the fire before hunkering down in his sleeping bag.

"So why did you finally decide to come with me?" This is a question for my mini-cassette recorder, which I have pulled from a small dry-pack strapped around my neck. Before we left Blue Mountain Lake yesterday, Ernie opened his outfitter's store, ducked in, and came out with this wonderful little waterproof case. Made by the Mad River Canoe company of Vermont for kayakers who want to keep vital things dry, this little zip-lock plastic folder is just large enough for a tape recorder, a few mini-cassettes, a pen, some money, and a driver's license, though God knows why I need my license on a river. I suppose it's for identification in case of an accident.

"So why did you decide to do such a crazy thing?"

Ernie has pulled out his flashlight to read before he goes to sleep. Billows of smoke rise into our faces; chunks of steak roll in our bellies like warm stones.

"I thought it'd be a great idea to float on the headwaters of the Hudson. Nobody has ever done it before."

"So why won't you go with me the whole way?"

"The boat traffic on the lower Hudson worries me more than anything up here. My job is just to get you started." Ernie says he's content to go no farther south than the park boundary, around Luzerne. Ernie actually says, "I don't want to go any farther south than the 'Blue Line.'" This is a common way of talking about the park's perimeter. The border of the park was for many years drawn in blue on state maps.

Ernie has been interviewed for a number of films on the Adirondacks. Journalists contact him when they need information because there are so few real Adirondack guides and because he's more articulate than most. But often he chooses silence.

He tells me about a man who once came to him looking for a talkative guide. "He said, 'I need an Adirondack guide who'll talk to me. Guides never talk. They're so quiet in the woods. Will you talk to me in the woods?' I told him, 'Nope, you've got the wrong person.'"

Mosquitoes are bad tonight, and reading in my sleeping bag by the light of a miniature K-Mart flashlight isn't easy. While waiting for that bear to show up, I look at a slim Adirondack Museum publication called *The MacIntyre Mine—From Failure to Fortune* by Harold Hochschild and read aloud a piece of it to Ernie, some history of Lake Tear he doesn't know. I also read from *The Story of Adirondac* by Arthur H. Masten.

One hundred and sixty-four years before us, white men camped here, lusting for the rich veins of iron ore that run through these mountains.

Ernie listens quietly as I read. A young Scottish friend of the McIntyre family, David Henderson went into these woods in October, 1826, prospecting for silver. An Abenaki Indian named Lewis Elijah Benedict claimed that he could lead him to a place where there was much iron ore.

For three days the prospectors traveled deep into the woods. Near the headwaters of the Hudson in a narrow pass (Henderson later wrote in a letter), Lewis Elijah "took us to a ledge five feet high running into the River, which was nothing but *pure ore.*"

"Henderson sounds like a treasure hunter," I comment on the reading, then continue.

"On the top of the vein are large chunks which at first we thought stone, but lifting one up . . . and letting it fall it crumbled into a thousand pieces of pure ore. In short, the thing was past all our conceptions."

Then the race was on to make the claim. The prospectors traveled as fast as they could to Albany. They kept Lewis Elijah with them "where, under McIntyre's watchfulness, he would be safe from temptations that might be offered him to show others the way to the ore body." The Abenaki grew sick in the city until McIntyre had secured title to his mine.

Next morning early. Adirondack High Peak weather is indeed a caprice. Today is ocean-photographer blue and all sunsplash. The cold, cloudy anger of the peaks has vanished as if bad weather might never return. The morning is perfect, a gift from the Cloud-Splitter. The rain on Marcy has stopped. But Feldspar is swollen and fierce with falling water. The sound of tumbling is so loud it pounds on the back of my skull as I climb in the bright sunlight.

I hike alone up to the lake, hoping to catch a secret from the glass-blue sky. Ernie has volunteered to take the pack down to Flowed Lands and wait there for the photographer, and then to come back with Jim Swedberg and meet me up at Tear for our historic paddle.

When planning this section of the trip, we allowed for two nights and three days, but it looks as if we'll try to hike back out to the Upper Works parking lot today, leaving me an extra day to dawdle somewhere along the river if I get into a dawdling spirit, or if I need extra time to make up for unforeseen delays downriver.

Hiking alone to Tear is the essence of joy; legs are good and sore. The strong sunlight brings out a perfume of evergreen, yesterday's rain, the intoxicating smell of Christmas trees. But even in sunlight, the climb is tough and long.

From Ernie's house, the night before last, I arranged with the Riverkeeper's publicist to arrive at the Battery on July 2. "July third is too close to the fourth," she said. "We don't want fireworks to steal your thunder. Christ, if you came in on the fourth, you wouldn't even get on the news."

In order to plan the gala arrival of a solo canoeist paddling for a cleaner river, she needed a firm date, so we fixed on the second of July.

It'll be a push to make that deadline, but I have to admit I'm addicted to the feeling of moving on, of leaving one place for another. This has made me less than a good traveler. Once in the great Rift Valley of Kenya, I refused to linger on the magnificent savannah as my primatologist fellow traveler wanted to do. It was getting dark, and we had already had two flat tires. The next puncture might have meant spending the night isolated on an untraveled dusty track, the hyenas not far off. When the primatologist spotted a dead baboon carcass, I knew he wanted to get out and study the bones. He was about to say something, but I blurted, "Absolutely not!" I was at the wheel, and we drove on to Nairobi in steel-silent darkness. I was anxious to reach our hotel.

Tonight we might sleep in a real bed, too, if we get down the mountain in time, perhaps at Ernie's house. Certainly tomorrow we'll be able to launch the canoe at the furnace of the old McIntyre mine, where the river first becomes navigable. Then there will be only 306 miles to paddle before I reach Battery Park!

When I reach the lake, it is absolutely still with Marcy's rock summit and the surrounding trees mirrored in the glassy water. How can this be the same lake as yesterday? Even the canoe looks different, so long, its hull cramped into the brambles on this insignificant trail. I easily lift the bow onto the dark tea of the water, leaving the stern pulled up a few feet onto the low bank.

Lake Tear is an anomaly. A glacial tarn left over from the retreating ice, it has an Alpine feel. A gem of clear, cold mountain water in rarefied air. To add to its dreaminess, there is not one living fish in Lake Tear, nor, for that matter, are there any fish in the lovely roaring Feldspar Brook. This is not because of acid rain, however, but rather because insects cannot live in the cascade; it is too steep, and the spring thaw scours the rocks of all life.

After a candy bar and some Tang from a canteen, knowing Ernie won't be here for some time, I dive into the wiry woods in search of paddles. Branches scrape my hands. My feet buckle on the roots, the vegetation unbelievably tangled at this altitude. I search for nearly twenty minutes. Then, where I never would have found them if I hadn't been looking, I spot a sliver of the unnaturally white epoxy blades from beneath the pine-needle brown.

I plow out of the brush, paddles in hand, then glide the canoe out onto the lake. Kneeling in the center, I am free of the trail; free of the long hike. Last night before he fell asleep, Ernie said, "I hate hiking. It's like walking through a tunnel."

Now I know exactly what he means because this lake is the antithesis of tunnel. The sky widens into a blue wash. Marcy stares down at me. On the rocky summit, a camper, only a dot, is waving as if from some other dimension, surely not from this planet. He waves, but there's no sound.

I'm certain I will not tell Ernie I've paddled alone on Tear of the Clouds. Forgive me, Ern. You have done the work getting the canoe up here, and I steal the show, although there's no one around to know it, except the camper. Who cares, really? Maybe you've chosen to hike back to Flowed Lands with the pack because you were sure I could find the paddles. Or maybe you thought I would not even look for them. Or maybe it doesn't really matter to you one way or the other. One of your guide's duties is complete, and perhaps you have turned your attention to the next job, which will be to get us safely through the Gorge.

It's a dream anyway: to paddle alone on top of the world.

When I first told some friends about my trip, they, who know only the lower, tidal Hudson, said, "Are you kidding me? You'll die out there. A canoe on the Hudson River? That's crazy!" They were thinking of tug boats, freighters, tides, and the wind off the three-mile-wide Haverstraw Bay, of the flimsy buoyancy of a canoe on all that expanse of industrial sludge. Imagine my friends seeing this—it takes me literally nine strokes to cross Lake Tear of the Clouds in my sleek canoe.

Before I left home, more than one person said to me, "I can't believe you're going to do what has been a lifelong dream of mine. I have always wanted to canoe the whole Hudson myself!"

But where, for Christ's sake, is Ernie? Enough speculation and reflection. I'm itching to hike out of here, to keep moving, to launch the canoe below and get on with the river.

6 P.M. Upper Works parking lot. I never thought we'd reach the pickup truck ever again, but after two days in the woods, here we are. Already, I feel removed from the world of newspapers, suburbia, and even my family. I almost wish to turn around, give it all up, and live back there on that mountain.

The photographer and Ernie finally arrived at the lake. It was late-ish morning and the sun was getting high. Ern and I enjoyed the attention of the lens.

Swedberg is a mutton-chopped man about Ernie's age, dark hair and grizzled beard; tall, lanky, and a bit awkward. He grew up in Long Lake, twelve miles from Ernie, and has taken pictures for *Adirondack Life* and *Outside,* among other journals. He's the official photographer for one of the rafting companies. He even has certain encampments in the Gorge from which he takes color photos of the rafts as they pass over the rocks into the spume. Then he races back to his lab, develops the film, and projects wonderful action shots on a large screen at his rafting base in North River. Only hours after defying Class IV rapids, the eager rafters order prints of themselves in the fray. It's a good business.

After today's shoot he'll send photographs of Ernie and me ahead to the Riverkeeper for publicity in the New York area, and some of his pictures may be used in the children's book I've contracted to write.

4. Paddling Lake Tear of the Clouds. *Courtesy Jim Swedberg.*

I brought a camera, too; but I'm a novice photographer, so we've chosen Jim, an expert kayaker who can go with us into the Gorge and accomplish what most photographers could not.

Another reason for having Swedberg along with us in the Gorge, I suppose, is simply for safety. Ernie says one should never attempt serious whitewater without an extra boat along.

But today I have wondered just how professional he is. Jim dropped one of his new lenses and broke it near Theodore Roosevelt's picnic spot. Then Ern and I dragged the canoe over some logs and pretended to be paddling down the first few feet of the trickling Feldspar.

Wasting no time after the light went blank just before midday, we began the long march down to Upper Works. Ernie said, "So now the real journey to New York City begins!" I thought of Pop and how, in the name of the purity of taking one canoe from here all the way to the Battery, I was finally completing what he'd called "a fool's carry."

Indeed, my 315-mile odyssey was *about to begin*.

The next six hours were as difficult as the climb, maybe worse. I carried the canoe down the mountain a long way myself. On the steepest, rocky sections, Ernie and I carried it together, the ends of the hulls on our shoulders, Indian-style, the upright canoe filling with sunlight. We had to keep changing shoulders when the path grew narrow over the big boulders.

The last few miles I put the canoe over my head and ran down the trail. It was light, and I found a good balance. I left Ernie with that bitching heavy pack in the mud behind me. I passed a pretty woman hiking alone and said in a voice that didn't sound like my own, "If you see a guy named LaPrairie straggling back there, tell him to the get the lead out." Her beautiful eyes stayed with me under my long Kevlar hat.

Lucky I had that canoe over me, too. For the day was hot and the blackflies were everywhere, but they couldn't find me inside a canoe.

When I took the canoe off my shoulders a hundred yards or so from the parking lot, the flies attacked my face. I made two switches of pine branches and kept them whirling around me to keep the intolerable pests from landing. Then I saw Ernie come up the trail. Even he was getting bitten today. He looked ragged and tired and angry, so I said nothing.

The pickup was waiting for us. We lashed the canoe onto the truck, threw our gear in the back, and wound the long miles down the old mining road to the town of Newcomb. We would be back tomorrow morning early to launch the canoe at the furnace here, but for now we would go home and have dinner with Ernie's family. He wanted to see his baby, and I needed to call home.

Of course I debated whether I should stay in my tent somewhere in the woods beside the river, in order to keep this trip "pure." But there was no stopping Ernie. He was going back to his house no matter what I did, and he said, "You're certainly welcome to come home with me." I could tell from the slight shake of his head that he thought I was a little nuts for wondering if I should stay here by the river when I had an open invitation to take a shower and eat a home-cooked meal.

Thinking of a soft bed in Blue Mountain Lake, and wondering why I had to be so purely rugged about this river trip, which would be continuous anyway, I said, "Okay, let's go home." It was one of the best decisions of the journey. I needed to build strength for the rapids that lay just ahead.

4

The Adirondack River

In the early-morning light, we've brought Ernie's pickup and my car. We have also brought, not one, but two canoes. Months ago Ernie and I asked Wenonah to donate a canoe for the whitewater section of the Hudson. A few weeks ago the president of Wenonah surprised us when he agreed to loan us an Odyssey for the rapids. This canoe is exactly the same as mine except it has an extra layer of Kevlar on its hull to withstand the pounding of the rocks.

In the grey light of dawn, my canoe looks worn with bright scratches in the yellowish-tan Kevlar. The new canoe sits gleaming on top of Ernie's truck, not a blemish or discoloration in it. We will first use my boat from the McIntyre furnace to the Tahawus Club bridge, a distance of nine miles. Then we'll switch to the Wenonah-donated Odyssey with its reinforced Kevlar hull, because the rapids from the bridge down to Newcomb are so bad that even Brian Kunz's group was unable to run this section either in rafts or inner tubes. They also couldn't swim it, Kunz told me; there were simply too many rocks. On each of Kunz's three trips, his party had had to hike out to the road, which runs parallel to the river here, and carry around the rapids to Lake Harris and the village of Newcomb.

This section of the Hudson is perhaps the least known on the whole river. Even Ernie has no idea what to expect, but he's fairly confident we'll need to line the canoe through a few miles of uncanoeable water. Lining is the technique of letting the canoe work itself through the rocks while the canoeist walks along shore. He holds long lines from the bow and stern, and coaxes and manipulates the craft marionette-style.

In the half-light we lift my canoe off my car and leave it at Upper Works, exactly where we put the canoe on his pickup yesterday. We don't cheat by an inch. At school last year, another teacher, one of the cynics, joked, "But how do we know you won't *cheat?*" "You're right," I said, "No one will know the truth except me."

Ernie and I shuttle his truck and the other canoe down to the Tahawus Club bridge, then drive back in my car to Upper Works. All this shuttling is laborious but necessary. Without an extra person, we have to go through many convolutions of transit in order to be self-sufficient.

At Upper Works the light grows stronger. Crows squawk loudly from a maple tree as we silently lift the Odyssey upright onto our shoulders and hike it down the road about a mile past the old mining houses. It's too early and too cool for bugs. Or talk.

Anticipation of beginning the rapids today is strong, and I feel the imminent danger of Class IV whitewater. But I try to think with my legs. I let them do the work as I peer at the old mining houses in this tiny ghost village. These wonderfully preserved, abandoned wood buildings are all that remain on the site of what was one of the busiest, most populated parts of the Adirondacks 150 years ago.

I've always loved mining and miners. Some evenings when my father came home from his office at St. Joe Lead Company in New York City, he would bring with him chunks of graphite, garnet, zinc, or lead. Mining makes me happy, the way archaeology—digging in the earth, embracing the past—makes me happy, too.

The beginning of the McIntyre mine was a primitive endeavor. In the early 1800s the mine consisted simply of a forge and a log building for the workmen. The charcoal for smelting the ore ate up an acre of hardwoods a day. A village sprang up around the mine and its furnace. First called McIntyre, then renamed Adirondac, the town became the most active place in the entire region.

Archibald McIntyre and his associates bought large tracts of land that would total 105,000 acres. In 1837 David Henderson married McIntyre's daughter and took charge of the business. He built a dam,

5. Ernie LaPrairie and the Odyssey in front
of the abandoned buildings at Upper Works.

a dock, a sawmill, and workmens' houses on the quiet Hudson in a
place later named Tahawus, referred to also as Lower Works. Here
the sawmill would later become the clubhouse of the prestigious Tahawus Club where Roosevelt and his family stayed as guests the
summer McKinley died.

At Upper Works, Henderson built a new blast furnace before Upper Works too became a village. But Henderson died just before the
mine reached its peak production in the years 1848 to 1853. The new
railroad spur that was to be built from the Delaware & Hudson's
North Creek station seemed not to materialize quickly enough (it was
not completed until 1876), and the company's original owners sold
the business in a deal negotiated by a Lake Luzerne lumberman
named Ben Butler. I mention his name only because I've been corre-
sponding with another Butler in Lake Luzerne, president of the

local historical society, who has planned a party in honor of my "historic canoe journey through our village." Luzerne will be the last town I'll visit inside the "Blue Line."

In 1856 floods on the upper Hudson destroyed the dam at Adirondac and both the dam and sawmill at Tahawus. When McIntyre died in 1858, operations halted. Benson Lossing visited the Upper Works in 1859 and declared it "the little deserted village." "The last cast from the furnace was still in the sand and the tools were left leaning against the wall of the cast house." The two mining villages were ghost towns. Visiting the sites in 1863, the Hudson Valley naturalist John Burroughs spoke of a man named Hunter who was paid a dollar a day as caretaker, "to live here and see that things were not wantonly destroyed but allowed to decay properly and decently."

One hundred and thirty years after Burroughs' observation, it seems the mine buildings still stand mostly because the Adirondack Mountains have been a great underpopulated secret. Huge tracts have been held in private hands. The history of the mine's hundred thousand acres passes from mining company to private club, part of it then to Finch, Pruyn paper company, and some most recently to the state through eminent domain. For this reason land demarcations are all jumbled, making it very difficult for canoeists to know what sections belong to whom. Even the trail to Tear, which is state land itself, passes through either Finch, Pruyn, or the old McIntyre property (now National Lead) just a few yards either side of the path. The Tahawus Club is the largest of perhaps forty-five other hunting and game clubs that lease land from Finch, Pruyn & Company, but even John Chambers, the forest ranger in this district, has to check his big, detailed map to recall which parts are leased and which are not.

In 1887 James MacNaughton, host to Roosevelt during his famous Adirondack stay, became the trustee of the heirs of the original owners. In *The MacIntyre Mine*, Harold Hochschild writes, "While anglers waded the streams and hunters roamed at will through the forests surrounding the deserted mine and furnaces, MacNaughton never lost his faith that the mine would some day again produce iron." MacNaughton researched the idea of changing over to mining titanium, and titanium was finally mined here beginning in 1916.

In 1921 the National Lead Company, a large paint manufacturer, bought the company. During World War II, after foreign sources of titanium dried up, McIntyre became the nation's largest titanium re-serve. In 1941, more than a century after the Abenaki had taken the prospectors to the ore, the National Lead Company began to mine titanium in earnest. Nine miles away, the town of Newcomb grew prosperous again with the resurgence of open-pit mining.

The big blast furnace, built in 1854 and capable of producing fourteen tons of iron a day, now sits abandoned in the ancient forest not far from the river. It was only "in blast" once, which is why it's so well preserved. Overgrown by weeds and obscured from the road by trees, it is a hidden monument of the past, its stonework cold, its technology defunct. The furnace inspires an eerie feeling as we pass the four-story stone structure. It's as if we've come upon an Adiron-dack version of a Mayan temple completely intact.

A hundred yards below the furnace, we launch the boat in a quiet, pristine, almost Northern Ontario river. This is the Hudson's first ca-noeable water. Here the spruce-laced banks are only about fifty feet across. The current is sluggish, the water almost black or black-green as it reflects the trees. Ernie's red life vest over his blue paddling shirt is the only bright color around.

"How come it's so still here?"

"Because it's flat," Ernie says. "There's no drop in elevation."

With not a rapid in sight, no sound of whitewater, we paddle, pause, paddle, and pause again, as if in disbelief. The canoe trip proper begins in perfect silence. Then we paddle faster, and Ernie's bare arms are two arcs flashing in the dim forest.

Ernie, in the bow, is the pacesetter. His paddle hits the water about every three seconds. He says, "If I get going too fast, if you want to slow down, just tell me. I used to race canoes, and I love to move." It is true that we have begun to dig at the river, our strokes much faster than the peaceful setting warrants, more like the strokes of voyageurs traversing Canada.

"You set the pace, Ernie," I say, and want to kick myself for not asking him to slow down. There are times when I struggle to extricate my camera from its waterproof bag. By the time I have the camera out and ready, the distant mountains have vanished around a bend, and Ernie's continued paddling on one side of the canoe has begun to turn us toward the bank.

When we talk to one another as we paddle, Ernie can hear me fine because I'm behind him, but when he speaks he sometimes has to hold his paddle in the air a moment or raise his head slightly and speak upward into the sky. Often his words fade into the muffling immensity of the forest.

I love the fluid sound of our paddles in still water.

"Boy, this is the way to go," I call to Ernie. "We're making time."

"And you don't have to work your feet so hard," Ernie says.

The river meanders. Again the purple and sienna mountains come into view. A pileated woodpecker follows us apiece from tree to tree along the shore. Ernie spots an otter slide on the bank, then raccoon and deer tracks in the sand. We are Lewis and Clark, we're Samuel de Champlain and Mark Twain. Ernie sees another otter slide and says, "I want to be an otter in my next life. Even when they're adults, they're the only animals that play for the sheer joy of playing."

Ernie is a different person out here.

Then, suddenly, we hear bulldozers and backhoes and the drone of a huge mining operation. In the town of Newcomb, during my weeks of research, I had been told the titanium mines were closing down, that the open pits were being planted with trees, that hundreds of jobs had been lost, that foreign producers of titanium were undercutting profits (titanium comes very cheaply off the beaches in India), and that if the price of the metal went up, the mine might resume operations some day. I also heard that significant reserves of other minerals besides titanium, such as molybdenum and vanadium, reside here, and that perhaps when the world market makes it economical to mine these exotics sometime in the future, the mining company will do so.

One of the Department of Environmental Conservation officers in Warrensburg had said about canoeing this section of the river, "The law says you can float on any river, which is public domain, but if the land on both sides is private, you cannot get out to portage any obstacles along the way." I'd been afraid Ernie and I might get stopped somewhere along this mining section. Kunz himself had warned me we might have to skirt a series of huge culverts that channel the river underneath a mining road.

I say to Ernie, "Sure sounds like the mine is going great guns still."

Forty-foot mounds of black tailings appear on the eastern bank, eerie, unnaturally dark hills from decades of scraping the iron earth. The sound of machines grows loud, steam shovels and dump truck activity out of sight from the level of the river. Ernie says some of his relatives used to work in the mine, but didn't stay long; they didn't like it.

Now we spot those culverts Kunz warned me about. From 200 yards away, I pray there is enough water to float right through them. I dread having to take out and portage over the mine road for fear that security guards will capture us the way they surround Green Peace antinuclear activists on Nevada test sites.

The closer we get, the louder the noise of the machines. Then I can see there's definitely not enough water in the river to get through those culverts. We will have to trespass: we'll have to go over the road.

We hear a truck pass above us. A close call. Like novice commandos who have forgotten to wear black or to smudge our faces with charcoal, we try to get out of the canoe on the steep bank of stones. On the first try, our feet slide back into the water. Ernie scampers up the mound to scout. He comes back quickly. "Okay, *now!*" he says, and I drag the canoe up and pass him one end. He takes it from me, and we clamber to the other side in the dust. Lucky for us it's a light canoe. The stone embankment on the other side is steep too. Up and over we dash, between dump truck runs. Now we're back in the water and paddling hard around the bend before anyone can see us.

The drone grows faint; my heart beats fast as we reenter the unadulterated Adirondacks. The great tailing mounds are behind us now, but you can see the red of the natural iron in the banks. From a distance those mounds look almost natural with the Sawtooth range behind them.

There is an ongoing movement in the Adirondacks to reclaim the rivers for the public. Too often canoeists are thwarted when they head down some wilderness river that passes through private land. I heard the story of one caretaker's vigilance. On one of the large estates in the park, a notorious caretaker waits for hapless paddlers to portage a certain natural dam. He creeps low in the bushes, and just when the paddlers get out of their canoes to traverse the dam, he pops up with his shotgun and drives them back the way they came.

Legally he's in the right. I'm confident the water in the river cannot be owned by National Lead, but the land on each bank and the riverbed itself are theirs, by law. As Paul Jamieson, a professor in Canton, New York, and a long-time canoeist and advocate for reclaiming the lost Adirondack canoe routes for the public, has written in a 1988 *Adirondack Life* article, "DEC officials, legal consultants, judges, landowners and members of the public interpret navigational rights in often contradictory ways. . . . Once legally upon a stream, can the boater proceed in either direction as long as he remains afloat even if both shores and the river bed are in private ownership?" Jamieson says the laws are unclear. What holds true in some districts is not so in others. He asks, "Can the boater walk on the privately owned bed of a stream where necessary for passage? Counsel for the Adirondack Park Agency (APA) says that he can pursuant to the right of navigation. . . . [But] When is a stream navigable? Is the test its capability of being used in commerce or recreation or both?" Jamieson believes the laws must be rewritten to clarify and to open up the rivers that pass through private land, especially now that there's another land rush in the park.

In the 1880s and 1890s people flocked to the Adirondacks, especially the wealthy. By 1892 clubs, associations, and individual owners had claimed as much as a quarter of the region.

Today the Adirondacks are being rediscovered, and the great trend to develop has begun again. Even as environmentalists try to preserve the forests and reclaim the rivers, the force of condominium construction is strong, and developers are often aided by park residents who want jobs and money for a traditionally impoverished region.

As an example of how in recent years the great secret of the Adirondack wilderness is being told again, as it was told perhaps a hundred years ago in the heyday of North Country retreats, I had heard that the new owner of the National Lead property, a Texan, on a helicopter tour of his land, was so taken by the wilderness he decided to keep *all* the National Lead land for his own estate and to refurbish

one of the old Tahawus Club camps into a magnificently modern retreat in the woods.

Here perhaps is a common Adirondack paradox. What has saved
this section of the river from destruction is not only the forethought of
individual landowners, but industry itself, big business, mining, and
logging. On the lower sections of the river, the railroad has cornered
much of the riverbank real estate, which has kept humans from ruining the Hudson. McIntyre got going before settlers came to the mountains, and Finch, Pruyn & Company has owned large Adirondack
tracts on the upper Hudson for more than a hundred years. If these
companies had not held onto their land over the decades, God knows
what building of cabins and condos would have spoiled the river
above Newcomb. As it is, above this little town there's not one dwelling—no tossing of domestic trash into the Hudson's headwaters. This
is true for the first thirty miles of the trek from Lake Tear. So I'm
indeed thankful for the mining and the logging operations on the
upper Hudson.

But when I look down into this limpid brown water, I can see
bottom and some pike grass, and I wonder just how the river has
been affected by the mining operation. It does not look dirty. I'm not
sure I'll drink it, though. It looks so beautiful, I wonder if I really *want*
to find pollution here.

Some people find pollution wherever they look, but my journey
should be a quest for the beauty of the Hudson, too. I will not simply
point my finger at the old tires beneath the water, the flotsam of rafting parties, the barges' oil leaks and kerosene spills.

Ernie has taken off his life vest. I've noticed that when he moves,
he has a kind of deliberate motion. It's not that he's awkward, yet
there is a stiff quality in his movement.

"So, Ernie," compelled to speak about the upcoming whitewater,
I ask, "what do you think the river's running on the North Creek
gauge?"

"Oh, maybe 3.9 or so."

In 1971 the U.S. Geological Survey placed a gauge in the Hudson
near the town of North Creek to measure its changing volume and to
help whitewater enthusiasts know the dangers of the Gorge. Local
stores and the town newspaper publish the readings daily, and the
gauge has been automated on a special telephone line that can give

the level of the river from any phone anywhere in the world. In the fall and spring when the water is high, Scott Overdorf calls the number maybe even hourly, just to see what the river is doing. On a moment's notice, Scott will drive up on Friday night after work to run the Gorge with his wife, Patty.

The upper Hudson is so protean, those who know how dramatically and suddenly the level of water can change check this number regularly. Those who have an up-to-date number hoard it like a gold artifact. Around the time of the spring whitewater derby in North Creek, you can try for days and never get anything but a busy signal.

In the *White Water Guide to the Upper Hudson River*, the great whitewater paddler John Berry says: "In general, levels between 2.6–3.2 are low and barely runnable with much scraping. The practicable minimum for all sections of whitewater on the river is 3.2. . . . The practicable maximum recommended for safety for any craft is 7.0. Above 7.0, wave patterns approach 5' to 6' high in long, continuous stretches. . . . Due to both river width and current speed, rescue is difficult under these conditions."

"What about that rain yesterday, Ernie? Won't that raise the level of water?" I wonder if Ernie can tell I'm getting scared.

"No. It has to rain for days before the level is affected."

He says 3.9 is a good level for us to take an open canoe into the Gorge. Not too high, but high enough so we can make it. If the level goes below 3, however, the river will not be runnable and we'll have to wait for rain. I don't mind waiting if I have to. I like the idea that my trip depends on rain. Then I ask Ernie about that time last spring when the river was at 9.2 and his friend Tom had gotten so scared.

"Kimball told me Tom asked her if you had any life insurance." Ernie laughs but does not refute the story. He says, "Yup."

Let me translate the river's caprice into fluctuations of volume in order to give some idea of the force of the Hudson when it runs at 9.2 on the North Creek gauge. When the river is running at 3.2, there is a volume of water flowing at about 718 cubic feet per second. When the river is running at 4.0, the volume increases to 1,530 c.f.s. At 8.0 the river is an exponentially larger 10,200 cubic feet per second, and at 9.2, which is about as high as the river can get short of a major flood, the volume is a walloping 17,000 c.f.s.

I've noticed there are times when asking too many questions of Ernie seems to bother him. Like people on a city street, questions seem to crowd him. But this morning, he answers each of my nervous questions without any irritation in his voice. To explain some answers, he will even stop paddling, turn, and speak directly at me while the canoe continues to glide on the water like a twig headed for a waterfall.

"Did you ever swim the river at 9 and above?"

"I did that day," he says.

"How long were you in the river?"

"Not too long," he laughs.

"What if you don't get back in the raft or canoe quickly?"

"You go for a long, cold swim."

"Hit any rocks?"

"A few. You don't have any choice. You're just washed down. If you're in the water and you have the presence of mind to get your feet right up on the surface, then you might hit a few rocks with your butt."

"You can't control yourself on a river so strong, can you?"

Our canoe arcs toward shore with no one at the helm. Ernie has taken this opportunity to lean back and and stretch his muscles. He's rubbing one shoulder. His bad arm seems to bother him. But it's hard to know for sure. He never complains.

"In a big river like this," Ernie says, "you're okay if you're over on your back and floating. But if you're being washed down and away from the raft, you watch and see what you're being pushed towards. Then you can use your body the way you use a canoe. You roll over on your belly and swim like crazy against the current. You can actually swim upstream and maneuver from one side of the river to the other the same way you ferry a canoe."

"Really?" I'll accept this if Ernie says it's true, but it sure does not sound possible to me. Our talk of rapids in so calm a scene seems a surreal dislocation.

Ernie resumes his steady stroke and says over his shoulder, "I love this kind of paddling, narrow, quiet. Such an old *old* river."

Why can't I enjoy this meandering water? Even in the solitude, I hear the roar of the white fever that lies ahead.

"Do you ever worry about anything?" I ask Ernie.

"No," comes an honest reply. "There's no use in it."

"I worry all the time. I'm a born worrier. My grandfather's a worrier, my mother's a worrier, my brother and sister, all of us worriers."

Face it, Pete, I tell myself, it's certain: we're going to tip over at least once in the canoe, and I'll be swimming again. So enjoy this silence while it lasts.

I understand why the Texan president of National Lead wants to adopt the land. Silence is something we all crave. We live in an age of movement, noise, activity, empty business, fierce gesticulation. There is never any time to get together with friends. When we do meet, finally, there's so little time to talk, and practically no time to share ideas of the heart. We live too much for the future, for the upcoming accomplishment of all the unaccomplished things.

So this day before the rapids begin, *this* is the future. I crave the stillness of these mountains and would like to go back to smother the bulldozers and dump trucks at the mine.

After the long, quiet meander, the river opens out into a bay of ducks and mosquitoes, then narrows again, the current only a knot or so. Certain stretches are blackfly territory; others are all mosquitoes. We paddle along with clouds of blackflies storming our heads. We put on Avon Skin So Soft, which works only a little. It was like this in the Amazon, long segments of river with no bugs, then a section with so many mosquitoes symphonically whining all night long on the outside of our mosquito nets, they kept us from sleeping. The air heating up feels like Amazon air.

"How long were you on the Amazon, Pete?"

"Three months. We rented beat-up old boats and followed rivers into little cowboy towns. It's a wild west down there."

Ernie points the blade of his paddle into the sky, spotting our first osprey wheeling over a marshy section of the river, about to dive for fish.

"Gosh," says Ernie, his paddle now resting on the gunwale, "Just look at that!"

The huge bird, brown with snowy head, stalls a hundred feet above the water, hovers, then plummets feetfirst. So majestic in flight, the bird becomes a terrorist in its claw-plunge to the water, diving with such desperate force it disappears into the river. A second later it rises, a fish splashing in its talons.

"So, Ernie, what was Vietnam like?" Ernie continues paddling. I have noticed he doesn't ever speak about the war unless I ask.

He saw a fair amount of fighting on river patrol boats often at night. "Snipers, fire fights, a few operations with the Seals," he says.

Today in his navy-blue paddling shirt, Ernie looks as if he might be on a mission. Ernie was in Vietnam only one year, 1968–69, back in what he calls "the good years." He volunteered for a second year, but they were turning his operations over to the Vietnamese.

"I always thought it funny," he says with perhaps a bit of irritation in his voice. "When everyone was protesting and trying to get out of the draft, I had to go and get letters from three different doctors *just to get in* because I have a screw in my ankle. I volunteered for Vietnam, but once I got in, they wouldn't give me my second year. And I was the only one from my town who went to war."

"When you came back, was it weird?"

"Not around here." The stroke of Ernie's paddle has speeded up.

"Any good memories of Vietnam?"

Ernie rests his paddle across the canoe, stretches his arms to the sky, and says, "In the Delta of the Mekong, it's so lush and green. We ran operations along the Cambodia border where the mountains meet the Delta. That was a nice contrast."

"What was it like up those little rivers?"

"Scary. You never knew when you'd be hit. Rifles, grenades, mortars. They blew up the first base we built. We were mortared at least once a week."

The river narrows to twenty-five feet. Ernie points to a muskrat home and to a large cedar tree on shore with a huge gash from the busy teeth of a beaver.

Ernie says with affection for the animal he used to trap, "Ah! Mr. Beaver."

Ahead, we have a choice of channels. They look the same, so we follow the strongest current along 180-degree bends.

Nine miles on a river takes a long time. Around every bend I expect the Tahawus Club bridge, but it will not appear for a few more hours. The only consolation is that every paddle takes me closer to Manhattan and my family.

"Why, for Christ's sake, Ernie, would I want to go all the way to Manhattan when I've got this?"

Ernie says, "I don't really know, Pete." We both laugh.

It is so hard to imagine this river ever changing. From where we sit, the implacable water seems as if it will never turn dangerous with rapids, or ugly with industry. But when we least expect it, here comes the clear sound of beginning rapids ahead. If silver were a sound, this murmuring Hudson moving into rocks would be the sound of silver. Silver, action, drama, youth, terror.

We pull over to where a green rowboat sits half-full of water, and take the canoe out on a path cut by the Tahawus Club. Railroad tracks, forlorn in the beginning stages of nature's reclamation, run through a meadow. These are the tracks built to get the titanium out from above. A few months ago the train ran for the last time, and already the tracks have that weedy look of abandonment. Deer graze on the railroad bed. The road to the mine is empty. A few feet beyond, we finally spot the Tahawus Club bridge. The clubhouse is only a short walk away.

Founded in 1877, the Tahawus Club (first called Adirondack Club and based not at Lower Works but in the old mining houses at Upper Works) is one of the oldest hunting clubs in the Adirondacks, one of the most prestigious, and perhaps the most threatened. Its history is the story of increasing restrictions, of changes still to come, of leasing land and, perhaps, of a death knell in the wind.

A few weeks ago I was invited to the club for dinner with the father of a schoolmate of mine. Nelson Jessup's distant ancestor, Ebenezer Jessup, had owned more than a million acres in the Adirondacks. In fact, the town of Corinth was once called Jessup's Landing. Jessup himself had been coming to the club for sixty-two years.

Jessup was up alone for Memorial Day to fish, to attend a club meeting, and to search for peace of mind. He offered me a drink.

At sixty-six, Jessup had thick sideburns and a curving white mustache. He had a kind of outpost, British Empire, turn-of-the-century ruggedness. He said he loved hunting and fishing. He was perhaps the last serious bird hunter in the club who still hunts woodcock. Jessup's father's old camp on Lake Sanford had been flooded out by National Lead in 1947, and only the stone chimney stands above the much wider, new Lake Sanford. Jessup had been renting camps at the club ever since. As Jessup told me about the ongoing tenuous state of the club, I detected a kind of bitterness and yet a codependent's congeniality toward both National Lead and Finch, Pruyn, from whom the club now leases 7,800 acres, which it is trying desperately to buy in order to gain control over its own destiny.

"We're only a pittance of what we used to be. We have fourteen family memberships. Our land has never been so threatened as it is today." He shook his head. When he was a kid, and the club was in full swing, his father said they used to lease 137,000 acres. "That's a big piece of property. One reason I never built after we lost our camp on Lake Sanford, however, is that the club has been running at a deficit every year. The Northwoods Club, downriver, survives because they *own* their own land. Every few years they sell off some of their timber. If we could buy this land, then we too could survive by selling timber."

For dinner we went to the clubhouse, which had been an old sawmill from the mining days. The building looked understated with its yellow clapboards and brown trim, its scattering of yellow wicker furniture on a wide wraparound porch. I got the feeling of going back to a more decent time as I stood looking out over green, freshly cut meadows and a valley below the tips of distant pine trees.

We waited outside for a moment for another old-time club member to arrive. Jessup had invited a woman named Ann Brewer, who had been coming to the club since the 1920s. Waves of blackflies danced over the dirt road in a steady wind at 5 P.M. The breeze kept them off the porch. I could hear the faint sound of the nearby Hudson mixing with that desolate Adirondack wind through pine needles.

Brewer hadn't arrived yet, so I sat down with Jessup at one of the few wooden tables. Jessup said, "The mine is closing, and I hear that the Texan entrepreneur who acquired National Lead is going to use the land up here as his own private preserve." There was a hint of irritation in Jessup's voice. "They say he's security conscious. Perhaps we're not going to be able to drive around as we used to."

Never having owned much land, the club had continued to survive through the handshakes of insiders. But now the two companies that would decide the club's fate had new owners. Outsiders had become insiders, and the gentlemen's handshakes had vanished.

Ann Brewer was very late, so Jessup and I served ourselves. Politely of course, we dove into the food, pork chops, baked potatoes, and broccoli that the caretaker's wife had prepared for us.

We gazed outside at the dwindling light. Jessup pointed to the controversial tennis court, which "had shocked everyone when it went in (this is, after all a hunting and fishing club!)" but which had subsequently been accepted as inevitable and which many members now felt they could not live without.

Ann Brewer, like Jessup, was up for the Memorial Day meeting. She arrived finally, a little unsteady on her feet, but ruddy and marvelously Victorian in her speech. Almost as soon as she sat down she asked, "I hear you are writing a book about the river. Will your book be about the environment?"

"No," I said, "not exactly."

"Good, I find that subject, the environment, I mean, so boring."

I said, "I'm here to find out about the Hudson River that runs through your club."

"I grew up in Hastings, not far from the city, but you'll find that the Hudson up here is quite a bit smaller, ha ha." When she spoke, her jaw jutted forward slightly. She was a person who, when told the coffee was "not Sanka," replied, "Thank God, Sanka keeps me up at night." This was of course accompanied by her own hearty laughter.

Both of Jessup's daughters had gone to Miss Porter's School, one of the few remaining all-girls' prep schools in America. Ann Brewer's mother apparently had been at Miss Masters School in the late 1800s when it was still a finishing school. Now, like Porter's, Masters is an all-girls' prep school. Last year I'd taken a job teaching at Masters, which somewhere along the line had dropped the *Miss*.

"My mother learned two things at Miss Masters school—how to wrap a perfect package and how to make a fluffy omelette. But nobody in the family would *eat* a fluffy omelette." Ann Brewer's face went red with laughter.

In spite of our differences about the environmental movement, I liked her and her Katherine Hepburn voice. "Any memories about the Hudson when you were children?" I asked.

Jessup's big mustache drooped only a little as the evening wore on. He said, "In my youth I remember Lake Sanford filled with logs. Big booms were used to hold the logs in the Lake. In the spring they'd let them go, and the lumberjacks would follow the logs down the Hudson through the Gorge. Finch, Pruyn would send their lumbering crews up here, back into the deep woods, and they'd live in those camps for a whole year. You can still find remains of the old loggers' cabins. But I was always in school during spring ice-out when the logs began to move in late April or May. Not many club members came up in springtime. I doubt if there's anyone alive today who saw the great logs move in the spring." The last real lumbering for Finch, Pruyn on this upper section of the Hudson came in the late '30s, he said.

Mrs. Brewer came to the club first on her wedding trip in 1923. Her husband had come up as a baby in '99: "And I don't mean 1999." Jessup's father came up as a ten-year-old in 1900. Brewer and Jessup were two of the three oldest survivors of the club.

Huge moths slammed into the window. Mrs. Brewer told the story about how the Roosevelts first came to the Tahawus Club. "My father-in-law operated on Alice Roosevelt's jaw, and he advised her family to go somewhere quiet where she wouldn't have to do much talking. So she came here. Doctor Brewer first came here as a guest because in those days, the club always needed a doctor for the summer season. . . . Will you be going to the Northwoods Club, too?" she asked. "Did you know that Winslow Homer painted most of his Adirondack pictures at Northwoods? You know, *that* club was founded as a sort of offshoot of *this* club. But you must go there."

Northwoods was adjacent to the Gorge. Ernie had cut logs there years ago, and two days after canoeing past the Tahawus Club bridge, we would follow the river along Northwoods Club land.

"Well," said Mrs. Brewer, "I wish I could tell you more about the river." She was thinking hard when suddenly she smiled, "Oh, I do know *one* thing. Do you know what Albany is the capital of, Mr. Lourie?"

"New York?"

"No. It's the East Coast capital *of bananas!* [pronounced "bahh-nahhnahhs"]. Bananas from South America are brought up the Hudson and then are shipped everywhere from Albany, of all places!"

Later I discovered that Chiquita had recently stopped bringing its bananas up the Hudson, and now shipped them on container boats to Newark instead. This is why I hadn't seen any Chiquita freighters on the river near my house in Beacon in the past year or so. The banana boats had been one of those odd lower-Hudson sights, huge Chiquita boats steaming through the Hudson Highlands, coming all the way from Honduras and now heading into the heart of the state.

Jessup's final words were, "God, how I love this place. I am lucky, I know it. This kind of privacy will be the most precious commodity of the future. The Adirondacks haven't really changed in hundreds of years. When the wind drops at night, I love that roar the silence makes. If we let Tahawus go, we'll never find such a place again."

I said good-bye, leaving Jessup and Brewer inside, and stepped out onto the historic porch, feeling strongly the very mystique about the Adirondacks Jessup was talking about, which I have always felt and hope to feel forever, this perfection of silence and wind, this desolate beauty of North Country dusk in the immediate, sound-conducting air, and this tinge of sadness that comes from the lonely wind in the pine needles that makes me think of change. How we're all changing, and dying bit by bit.

Before dinner, Jessup had driven me to the Tahawus Club bridge. He let his jeep idle in the middle of the empty road so we could view a piece of the river below. We saw the rocks begin, the white of the water where the Hudson makes a sudden drop into the silvery rapids.

We could see the river bow out of sight.

"Nope," he said. "You'll have to take your canoe out here. Too many rocks below. Can't run it."

5

The Gorge

Ernie and I are suiting up. We've carried the canoe to Ernie's truck parked by the little bridge, and after driving to Upper Works to shuttle my car down to Newcomb, we've switched canoes. We will need the reinforced Kevlar canoe for the whitewater stretch from here to Lake Luzerne, the edge of the Adirondack Park and the so-called Blue Line.

We pour bug dope all over our life vests, safety helmets, and wet suits. We dowse ourselves as if the pesticide were a liquid gold, a treasure we cannot get enough of. Something in the excess of our actions describes the anticipation I feel.

Because of its difficulty, the next section will have to be lined. So Ernie is attaching long nylon ropes to the stern and bow of the Odyssey. When lining a canoe there's not a lot of pressure on the craft, but we're not taking any chances: this thin, high-tech line has the tensile strength of 2,000 pounds. Ernie works in a cloud of blackflies. He says, "Lining is not a chicken way out. It's just plain smart. It's pointless to do too much. Especially this early in your trip." Ernie wants my trip to be a success, and I appreciate this.

Walter Burmeister, in *Appalachian Waters 2: The Hudson River and its Tributaries* (which I studied carefully because it is a detailed record for anyone seriously thinking of canoeing the Hudson), points out that this next section holds one of the worst danger spots on the whole Hudson River. Up ahead there are two drops of eighty feet within one mile.

I knew that after dropping more than 4,000 feet on the first half of the river, the Hudson fell a mere foot in the 150 miles from Albany to the Atlantic Ocean. But I wondered why these eighty-feet-per-mile drops should be so treacherous. I needed a comparison, so I asked my school buddy, Scott Overdorf. In parts of the Grand Canyon, he said, the Colorado River is Class V whitewater but drops only twenty to thirty feet per mile. In fact, he said, most of the big whitewater rivers in the West drop much less than equivalent rivers here in the East, but get their heavy rapids from the sheer volume of water passing between the banks.

I learned, too, that these drops of eighty feet per mile below the Tahawus Club bridge were much greater than the average drop, even in the Gorge below. In the Gorge's ten miles from the Indian River to the Boreas River, the average drop is thirty feet per mile. The maximum drop in the Gorge is perhaps seventy feet per mile, but this figure applies to only one set of rapids just below Blue Ledge Pool, called the "Narrows."

Rugge and Davidson, in *The Complete Wilderness Paddler*, say, "Give a stream of water—any stream—a vertical drop of two inches and it will bubble and slurp. Give it 100 feet in a mile and it will crash and roar and spell catastrophe for open boats. Even 50 feet in a mile bodes an impossible drop for open boats in most rivers. Between 10 and 50 feet, you and the river have to negotiate."

There is one consolation: after these two big drops today, we will have a nice paddle because the river then meanders softly for almost eight miles to the bridge at Newcomb where we plan to take out for the night. From Newcomb to the Glen, forty-five miles or so of intermittent rapids, we'll be in territory Ernie knows well. We will also be with Swedberg, who will follow us in his kayak from the Newcomb bridge, taking pictures and adding an element of safety to our trip.

But today is different. We're alone in completely unknown territory. When I told the manager of National Lead operations in Newcomb that I planned to run the river here, he said, "That's crazy. You can't canoe from Tahawus to Newcomb."

Around two in the afternoon, Ernie and I slide the shiny new canoe down a steep bank into the river and glide into our first white-water since that day last week when we practiced in Perry Ehlers. Swiftly we paddle into channels between boulders. Ernie's face is set like steel, without expression, with neither fear nor joy.

Rocks sprout on the surface. Rocks clutter the stream. Our paddles work fast. The increasing wind and roar of mounting turbulence are a sound that simultaneously makes me drunk with enthusiasm and sober with terror. Our paddles work even faster, our brains like computer chips making decisions without the cumbersomeness of thought.

I feel tipsy from this sudden action after months of anticipation. I yell, "Okay, Ernie, let's run 'em!" My heart is a hawk in a cage beating for escape. I attack the river. Ernie shouts, "Steady. We'll take our time."

But, damn it, I'm ready to run the whole thing, tip over, I don't care. Just get us through. My paddle is churning back and forth and to the sides, bracing constantly to steady the canoe. But Ernie's caution, his long-standing knowledge of the real dangers out here, and his calling out commands to back-paddle, then go forward, then sweep or pry and go left, or right—all this has a sobering effect.

With Ernie in the bow drawing from the left, I can tell he wants to go left so I pry the paddle against the gunwale. Or I sweep my paddle in a wide arc out from the canoe if he draws from the right, knowing he wants the canoe to go around to the right of a rock. Ernie decides. He decides how we will pick our way through these boulders, and I simply help execute his decision.

He takes the bow of the canoe around another rock, and after I help him get the bow in position, I then concentrate on bringing the stern around, too. This pattern is repeated over and over: one minute I'm helping the canoe go left, then I quickly make it go right; and vice versa. It's a two-pronged operation. There is no right without a countering left. We use the flow of water around a rock to propel us to the next rock. We ride its watery side like a surfboard on a good wave. The water forms a kind of shoulder that helps our canoe along.

The eddies that gurgle behind the rocks are amazing, too. The water actually runs upstream here. When the river gets too crazy and we're going too fast, when we need a breather, we head for an eddy. We enter it perpendicularly, then quickly swing the boat around to face upstream, Ernie drawing, say, from the left, and me drawing also from the left, then quickly sweeping on the right to steady the canoe into place. Then, here we are, pointing upstream in an absolute stasis with the whole river crashing furiously all around. But it's only a temporary truce with no need for paddles; we are held in place by river dynamics. The texture of these eddies is soft and bubbly, even puffy, and the upstreaming water allows the canoe to nudge up against the protecting boulder as softly as kissing the head of a horse.

We rest before we enter the skirmish again. It seems we *do* have control.

This is what Ernie has been saying all along, and which I find awesome. When you think of rushing water through rocks, over rocks, around rocks, in spite of rocks, you don't think you can just take your time in the flood. You don't imagine you *own* your own destiny. You think you're at the mercy of water fever. You are convinced you must run it at full speed like shushing a mountain. But in fact what Ernie is showing me is that we can indeed take our time. We *have* the final say. In whitewater, reason must prevail. We can back-paddle. Or we can actually stop midstream, set ourselves up accurately for the approach, move right, move left, turn our boat around, go upstream, or ferry across by angling the canoe, bow against the current, almost parallel to the river bank, but a little off to one side, letting the water rush around us, even allowing the canoe to move across the river in the middle of large standing waves.

This tandem feeling is wonderful, too. Ernie can read the river the way a classicist reads Greek inflections. To be his partner makes for a kind of human closeness not easy to describe.

Suddenly Ernie yells out, "Pull over," and we paddle crazily for shore. "Too many rocks. I don't want to ruin this canoe." Ernie, who has never run this section of the Hudson before, is being cautious. But I can't help thinking, if we stay in the water, we will quickly reach the end of the rapids.

"Aw, come on Ernie. Let's run it." I feel like a kid with a bad fever. I have a whitewater infection. But I love it. "I don't want to stop, we're doing so well. I'm just getting the swing of it."

"No."

"Okay."

The river's loud roar numbs the nerves. When we pull up to

shore and get out, I see the scrapes. Already this canoe has taken some heavy blows on its hull. It will be a long, scraping day on rocks, and then the same for the next three days, until we get to Luzerne.

After we pull the canoe onto the boulders and tip it over to get some water out, Ernie prepares to line the canoe. He takes the stern and bow lines in his hand and sends the empty canoe into the white froth. By jerking on one of the lines, he can work the canoe around the rocks through narrow channels. How elegant and graceful our light canoe seems as it is slowly shoved outward into a treachery of boulders, picking up speed, then coming to rest in the eddies of other boulders. When Ernie sends the craft out into the river, it seems a soul floating free of a body. At first it does not know what to do but looks like a suicide in a dangerous daze as it heads, unresisting, straight into the big waves. Then Ernie jerks on the bow line and the canoe jumps to face downriver. It picks up speed and floats gracefully between two large rocks. Ernie pulls the stern to keep it moving along the narrow channels.

I must have been crazy. There's no way in hell we could have canoed this section. Boulders and rocks bubble up so close to one another they might be all part of one huge submerged dinosaur's back.

From time to time, Ernie shoots the Odyssey back out into the rushing, deeper water. It obeys. Now the Odyssey reminds me of a doe or fawn. It is a beautiful thing to watch a canoe being lined through rugged water.

The few times I step into the river to help because the canoe has run up on the edge of a rock and is about to swamp, Ernie violently motions me away. He wants to control the canoe with ropes. There's no use taking a chance getting pinned against some rock or taken under in the swift current.

I jump from boulder to boulder along shore, the white rush in my ears, watching Ernie like a kid with a kite, playing those ropes ever so tenderly. As he did in the "big grunt" up to Lake Tear, Ernie is again doing all the work. I follow my guide, eyes fixed on that Odyssey as if it were my only hope for a river rescue. I'm dying to try this lining business but will wait until we get closer to the end of the rapids. On my topographic map I see we have come only a fraction of an inch.

6. Lining the canoe. *Courtesy Jim Swedberg.*

Lining is slow travel. If we ran this section, we would be through in a matter of minutes.

In fact, Ernie does all the lining today. I'll have to try it another day. I'm disappointed that he didn't give me the canoe, but we're paddling now, and succeed where Kunz failed. Kunz never used canoes here, so he was not able to line. We hear cars passing on the road where Kunz lifted his rafts and inner tubes out of the river and then hiked them into Newcomb. Now we're paddling the soft, slow, unknown river, and I am proud we haven't given up. I would like to find that foreman at National Lead and let him know of our success.

It is 6 P.M., and twelve hours have passed since we began nearly twenty miles ago at the old mine of the Upper Works parking lot. Five hours after lining through our last rapid, we finally reach the Newcomb bridge. As the bridge comes into sight, we pass a small hunting cabin, the first residence in thirty miles from the source of the Hudson. Seeing it here, empty and human, chairs propped on the bank for easy gazing on the river's sunset, I think, "What a shame. I like the Hudson better with no people." From here on, there will be scattered cabins and houses with a distinct pioneer look. The peopled Hudson begins even though it will not be until the edge of the park in Luzerne when, like a star exploding, the river will fill with speedboats.

Okay. June 13, 1990. 4 A.M. We spent the night again at Ernie's. This morning when Ernie and I meet together down by the coffee machine, he turns to me and says, "Short night." Ernie likes coffee as much as I do. When the machine has made a full pot, we drain it like desert walkers drinking from a canteen.

Our voices are hoarse from lack of sleep. Every tendon in my body aches. I pray I don't have girardia from drinking out of Feldspar Brook. Today will be a big day; tomorrow will be an even bigger day. Two monolithic days in the Gorge, and then after forty-five miles of rapids and another twenty of gentle paddling, I will be out of the park and alone.

We'll travel light in the Gorge. We plan to camp at Blue Ledge Pool in the middle of the heaviest rapids. A friend of Ernie's, Jamie Frasier, who is training to be an Adirondack guide, will hike our tents and food and sleeping gear into Blue Ledge on the Northwoods Club trail from Minerva, so if we go over, we'll be in less danger of losing everything. We will travel with two extra paddles tied beneath the gunwales and a big yellow airbag inflated under the thwarts.

Yesterday the sky grew grey with horsetail and high cirrus clouds. Today it's fish belly. Tomorrow it will probably rain. Ernie says that's the general pattern in the Adirondacks. Will the rain affect our safety in the Gorge? I wonder. "Probably not," says Ernie in a reassuring tone.

At Newcomb at 6 A.M., Jim Swedberg arrives from Long Lake slightly grey-eyed and sluggish. Jim takes his sleek, little kayak off his car, then places a few bags of gear inside the plastic hull.

Today Swedberg seems even more ponderous, almost too much to be a sportsman, but Ernie says he's an excellent kayaker and knows the Hudson as well as anyone. Ernie apparently never knew Jim when they were growing up, even though they have mutual friends and acquaintances and are almost the same age. They've run into each other mostly on the Hudson during rafting season these past few years while Jim is taking photos of the rafters and Ernie is leading rafts through the Gorge.

Jim's early morning stupor disappears in a volley of loud laughs. Ernie jokes with Jim in a warm way, and I'm glad to have the extra person along. Jim finishes packing his kayak with camera gear and tells me that, yes, his equipment is at some risk, but that he has done this sort of trip many times, and always manages to keep his cameras safe.

We take some preliminary pictures by the sign on the bridge above the river. I am the explorer leaning on the neatly printed, white-on-green "Source of the Hudson River" sign with not much swagger this early in the morning, not much conviction in my grin. A few blackflies and mosquitoes find me in the dawn mugginess. We cut the bottoms of two plastic Clorox bleach bottles to make bailers for the bow and stern and tie them with a piece of line to the thwarts. I take a picture of the river above the bridge, clouds reflecting in perfect glass—not at all a Hudson scene anyone below Troy would recognize.

Then we're off. The clouds are high, but some leftover mist from the night sits low in the hills. The gentle green slopes of the forest leading down to the water remind me of the Amazon.

As a kind of pregame pep talk, Ernie says, "From Newcomb it's nice to the mouth of the Indian. In high water it's maybe Class III +. Not canoed a whole lot. First, we'll come to Ord Falls, then after a three-mile run, it's Blackwell Stillwater to the mouth of the Cedar River, then two miles to the mouth of the Indian, then three miles from the Indian to Blue Ledges, where Jamie will have our food for us. We may decide to hike the canoe around Blue Ledges tonight—

7. Paddling below Newcomb in the still water between rapids.
Courtesy Jim Swedberg.

depending on the water level—then start at the top of 'Mile-long'
tomorrow."

"'Mile-long'? The rapid is a whole mile long?" I ask.

Yes, Ernie says, but he'll take a look at it and make a decision
when we get there. If he thinks we can run it, we'll go for it. But the
standing waves in the "Narrows" at the top of "Mile-long" even at
lower water are big enough to swamp an open boat. "It's pointless to
swim if we don't have to. That's not a very long section of river to
line the canoe," he says.

This game plan sounds scary.

I ask, "So what should I remember, Ernie, for today?" On the
verge of my biggest whitewater battle, I have forgotten what I learned
in boot camp yesterday.

"Just relax," he smiles. "That's the main thing."

This is a little like telling a man who's having a heart attack, "Whatever you do, *don't panic.*"

"If your body's relaxed, you have control of your boat. Just relax and watch the water. See what's happening ahead of you. Then go for the black water. That's where the channels are clean. Any place you see whitewater, you know there's a rock upstream. If it's white and flat, it's a big hydraulic. If it's white and standing waves, if you see a series of waves in a row, normally that indicates there's a channel, a shoot, and all your water's funneling and piling up on itself."

"Wish we had a spray skirt for the canoe."

Ernie says, "Then it wouldn't be an open canoe, would it?"

"Guess not."

An open canoe like ours without a spray skirt to cover it and keep the water out is a big problem in standing waves. Ernie says we have to avoid all the holes. We will pull to the side to bail if we ship water.

We set off in a grey, uncontrasting light. The buried boulders in the water are nearly impossible to see until we're right on top of them. This means Ernie will have to make split-timing decisions. If it were sunny, it would be a lot easier to see those rocks and to read the river.

Swedberg kayaks over to us, and Ernie asks, "Jim, would you take a squint at the boat and see what our trim is like."

Jim says we're a bit heavy toward the rear. So Ernie moves his sliding seat forward a notch until the line of the canoe gunwale is almost parallel to the water level, perhaps a little higher still in the bow.

Wearing these damn safety helmets, it seems we have to talk louder than normal in order to be heard. There's an echo when we speak. I can hardly hear Ernie who says, quite casually, "I haven't been through here in nine years. It was the day before Thanksgiving, and we hit a snowstorm in Blackwell Stillwater. No one else was around. *That* was beautiful."

Children's swimming ropes dangle over the edge of the banks. These are the first of many ropes to be draped by children over the Hudson's brink. The ropes are deserted. It is still too early in the season to swim.

Then all at once I'm busy working my paddle in the mesmerizing beauty of one rapid after another, endless whitewater punctuated by a few commas of peaceful paddling on black, black liquid. Our first two big sets of rapids are one at Ord Falls and one just after Blackwell Stillwater. We can judge the biggest rapids by looking at the treetops ahead. On both sides of the river the trees drop precipitously out of sight. The lower they seem from where we sit, the steeper the gradient.

The morning blends into the afternoon, and somewhere along the flat light of the merging hours just when I'm getting the hang of reading what is known as "technical" whitewater (technical because of all the maneuvering involved), just when I feel I can run all forty miles of rapids successfully because Ernie and I are bonding with this Odyssey, because we become teammates of the river, we suddenly stop for lunch.

Certain images of rapids will never leave me. First, there are the quiet Class II rapids, maybe a quarter mile long, like the ones leading into Ord Falls, then Class III whitewater where my arms become adept. My sense of when to pry and when to sweep grows keen. More than once, when a rapid is over and we sit gliding without using our paddles in the diminishing standing waves, in a small state of happy shock, Ernie says, "All right, Pete. You're doin' great." As in Perry Ehlers, he seems somewhat surprised, but always complimentary. It makes me feel good, too. After all, Ernie has jeopardized his life to accompany a stranger, who, lucky for him, just happens to be an okay partner.

There on the piled branches on shore, a large television set has washed up in the spring flow. Its screen faces us like an omen from another era. Swedberg takes photographs of Ernie and me leaning over the tubeless TV, grinning over this serendipity of river pollution. Through all of our laughter, I feel a sadness too. Other human junk lies in the water here and there, old tires, an occasional Styrofoam cup, bits of black plastic tarps.

We push onward into the next rapid, and again, the next. Arm stiffening, relaxing, stiffening again. We stop once to scamper up the banks of Blackwell Stillwater, a slow-moving, ink-dark portion of the river. Nearby are the few simple cabins of the Polaris Club, another hunting and fishing fraternity. We look for that big old pine tree that a friend of Ernie's from North River told me had a cross cut into its bark to commemorate the death of a logger here nearly a hundred years ago. We stumble around on the bank until Ernie spots the cross about thirty feet up now, the gouged lines turned faintly white with sap.

Ernie says, "Back then the companies used to take care of their men."

In the canoe I feel happy to have witnessed a souvenir of the logging days. We glide on perfect, spider-skimming water, passing the ruins now of a splash dam that was used to hold the spring water at a much higher level until it was needed to help the lumberjacks flood the logs downriver.

The river's volume grows all the while. Huge tributaries, like the Goodnow, Cedar, Indian, and Boreas, feed it from both sides. We paddle all the way to the mouth of the Indian River. This is where the rafting companies begin their twelve-mile run through the Hudson River Gorge proper. We climb out of our boat to look for the remains of one of Finch, Pruyn's main logging camps from the lumber days, but with little luck. Leaning his head back onto his folded hands, six feet from the river on a tiny beach of white sand, Ernie tells me that in 1865 his great-great-grandfather had a working farm right here on the banks of the Hudson.

Then, finally, we pack our gear and head into the heart of the Gorge. "You see some strange sights in the Gorge," Ernie says smiling. He remembers once when an osprey followed Ernie's raft for more than ten miles from tree to tree. "It was odd," he says. Another time he saw a woman run the Gorge in an open canoe. While he watched from shore, she did a handstand in her boat, "right in the biggest rapids!" Ernie clapped and cheered. He also once saw a guy in an aluminum canoe poling, not paddling, through Class IV. "That guy ran the gorge just as slick and clean as anyone could." Once, too, Ernie saw a girl break her paddle in the rapids only to grab a long pine branch floating alongside that she then used to guide her way through.

Nothing brings home this sense of a tumbling river and rocky channels more than following a few feet behind Swedberg's kayak as we engage in river battle. With that double-bladed paddle, Jim turns his craft easily as he weaves his path through stone. Going first, he signals which channels to avoid and which to take. He raises his paddle into the air at an angle to give us directions.

The sleek bullet disappears into the waves. He is only a few yards

8. Shooting whitewater. *Courtesy Jim Swedberg.*

away but we cannot see him anymore. Then there, there he is waving us on. So we paddle in a two-person frenzy to prevent the powerful sweep of the river from driving us from our course. We follow him down the hill of the river descending in the deafening white noise of the river's steady rush. Sometimes he leads us astray into an impossible channel, and suddenly we have to back-paddle hard, looking for that stasis in the river a moment, to give us a chance for Ernie to cross his paddle to the opposite gunwale to direct the canoe along a totally new route through the rocks. Then we paddle forward, dig like dying men at the water, constantly shifting this long canoe right, left, left left, right, left, right right.

We do this out of instinct now, too. Ernie has stopped calling out commands. I know what he wants. Even before he moves to direct the canoe one way, I've anticipated him and start the process in motion. Sometimes I see the rocks before he does and act quickly to avoid them. I have a great deal of control in the stern.

So busy are we that when we come barreling into what locals call the Ledges, the sudden quiet water of this deep Blue Ledge Pool is like some trick. Amazingly, we fly right into a crowd of people sitting on a spit of land in a ninety-degree turn in the river. They must have hiked here on the Northwoods Club Trail.

Blue Ledge Pool is one of the few places on the Hudson's 315-mile course to the sea where the river shifts due east. Leading right up to this bend and the great sluggish pool itself is long Blue Ledge rapids, which nearly toppled us, but didn't.

There has been a kind of fierce grace in our tandem paddling late in the day. Then quite magically, perhaps as a reward for so much work, there appears this perfect pond of serenity in a canyon of blue-grey rock. The scene would be serene, I should say, if it weren't for this crowd of hikers sitting on the rocks like languishing penguins. We make the wide arc of the turn going very fast and leaning into it as two people on a motorcycle might lean around a bend.

The boat shushes to a halt.

On one side of the pool is a sheer cliff with pines growing out of its 300-foot face. Ernie says there used to be eagles up there on those beautiful blue ledges, but now the ravens have usurped the old eagle nests.

We step out of our water chariot onto a beach of white sand. My legs wobble as I place my foot into a bevy of deer tracks. Today alone, from Newcomb to Blue Ledge, we've dropped 220 feet in fifteen miles of paddling. We made it this far without tipping over.

We'll make camp here, thank God, but tomorrow could be quite a different story. From Blue Ledge to the end of the rapids at the Glen, we will drop 610 feet and travel at least another thirty miles.

Ernie and I, feeling proud of our achievement, pause on the sand to talk about tomorrow. It is strange to stand up after canoeing rapids. The land seems to move all around us, as if we're still in the boat.

9. Relaxing at Blue Ledge Pool. *Courtesy Jim Swedberg.*

"What's up tomorrow, partner?"

Ernie unzips his tight-fitting wet suit. He wrestles his helmet off and says, "First thing at dawn we'll enter the 'Narrows.' It's a mile long. I've never taken it in an open boat without dumping."

I check to see if Ernie is kidding, but he's not even smiling.

"Then there is mile-long 'Big Nasty Rapids,' 'Wrap Rapids,' 'Giveny's Rift' [alias 'The Soup Strainer'], then mile-long 'Harris Rift.' Harris is a big one and is followed by 'Fox Den Rapids' and 'Bobcat

Den Rapids,' then the confluence of the Boreas River and finally 'Black Hole,' which some call 'Greyhound Bus Stop.'"

"All that?" I ask but try only to think about the beauty of Blue Ledges. It looks like good trout fishing here.

The hikers are drooped over the rocks not far from the beach. They are white-haired and older. From the crowd, looking rather exhausted as they recline on the big rocks below the cliffs, a silver-haired man with a soft voice saunters over leaning on his cane to say, "Hi, there. We're the Crooked Cane Club. We hike all over the northeast. This is my cane." He lifts a wooden antique with a lion's-head handle. He asks if we mean to camp here or move on today. We say yes, we'll camp.

He notices his group starting to move off along the three-mile trail back to the Northwoods Club road. "Good luck," he says. "I have to skedaddle. Bye." He doesn't ask who we are, or what our big plan could be. He hurries to reach the others already filing into the trees and up the trail. His cane slips on one of the boulders. He does not fall. He will never know about my journey or why I might be doing it.

In a few minutes, Jamie and his cousin Randy appear with backpacks. Randy wears a baseball hat that seems too big for his head. Randy never says a word. He's one of those blond, tough, probably very nice, but silent, north-woods kids. Jamie on the other hand is twenty-five and a nonstop talker. Ever good-natured, when he yaps, his sketchy blond mustache jumps around on his face like the fin of a frantic fish.

Jamie's passion is fishing. He wants desperately to make his living as a guide. Ernie hires Jamie as a raft guide in the spring. Ernie, who has the streak of a big brother, tells me, "It's tough to make a living as an Adirondack guide these days, but I give him work when I find it. We're thinking of starting a partnership. I'm too busy with the shop and the family. I can't afford to be away for long trips anymore." Apparently my trip is one of two that Ernie has planned for the summer.

Jamie and Ernie put up our tents. Randy collects firewood for tonight's feast. I would make myself useful if I had any energy left, but I don't. I flop down on a boulder. To rest after so much paddling is undiluted bliss. Stopping by a loud, moving river after a full day of rapids is like dreaming and never waking up. Even when I take off all my clothes and lay them on the boulder in the northern sun and take a bar of soap and splash in the freezing Hudson, I do not wake from this dream. I stand at the top of the Narrows, perhaps the Hudson's roughest water, splash-bathing. I can see Swedberg run the river, heading his kayak upstream in a kind of standoff. As if he hasn't had enough whitewater for the day, he dunks over, falls back, rolls himself upright, only to attack the river again and to move ever-so-slowly upstream like a wounded salmon fighting a spring current to spawn.

I stand alone at the head of the 315-mile river's major rapids, which we've saved for dawn, and without my wet suit and thermal long underwear, with no vest, no paddle, I feel as vulnerable in my pale skin to this temperate sun and to this river of mountains as I have ever felt in my life to anything. Not even when I am naked and a woman's hand reaches for a first touch, not even then am I as pliant as I am here.

An hour later Jamie has caught three rainbow trout, and he lends me his little spinning rod. I walk on boulders on the spit of land vacated by the Crooked Cane Club. I cast twice into the safety of eddies and catch two tiny rainbows like colorful Floridian shells in this brown-grey northern landscape. I toss them back, the smell of fresh fish on my hands, and return to camp.

Jamie will cook his trout. To my surprise he starts to unpack some slabs of meat wrapped in tinfoil. "I brought some meat," he says in his cheery way. In fact, he has brought bear meat. Yes, bear meat—as well as caribou meat, venison, moose meat, and steak from the Grand Union.

Now he's cooking this carnivore's delight, all of it. The fat hits the flame, and the sizzling meat explodes before us.

"I sure love to eat," says the warm-hearted, voluble Jamie in that clipped Adirondack, leftover French-Canadian accent. Ernie counters good-naturedly, "I never noticed." We all laugh.

With Jamie, a conversation can turn quickly from one topic to another. Somehow we move from meat to Jamie's wife's pregnancy. Jamie's wife, the doctor predicts, might have twins. "Lord, love a

10. Aerial view of Blue Ledges and the Narrows.

duck. Twins!" laughs Jamie. "Forget fishing for the next twenty years," says Ernie. Jamie looks much too young to be a father already.

The fire is wonderful: it discourages mosquitoes. Between the daytime blackflies, the dusk mosquitoes, and the all-night no-see-ums, insects have us ambushed twenty-four hours a day. The gnats take the graveyard shift, an irritating but comparatively insignificant artillery. Blackflies are the armored personnel carriers of the woods, leaving welts the size of pennies on my neck and ankles. If Saddam

Hussein had utilized blackfly warfare, he could have won in the Persian Gulf.

Jamie doesn't want to charge for any of the meat, partly because he's famous for eating whatever is to be eaten, and partly because he is a generous man. Before we leave tomorrow I'll give him fifty dollars, "for the twins." Chomping first on bear meat ("The bear is not as good solo," he says, "as it is wrapped in bacon. Sorry I didn't bring any bacon." "Okay this time, Jamie, but don't let it happen again."), then moving on to sweet caribou that Jamie's father shot in Newfoundland, then on to the venison Jamie himself shot last hunting season, I stand in the direct billow of the smoke to keep the mosquitoes away. I feel like Homo erectus by Lake Olduvai feeding on Pleistocene hyena. Nothing has tasted this good in weeks. Meat, a glory of meat. I consume more meat than anyone here, including Ernie who is, I think, showing a gentlemanly, woodsmanly restraint.

After dinner, dark descends, and Jim stokes the fire to get some shots of Ernie and me, trading lore. It's a timeless sound, this crackling flame with the rush of invisible rapids thirty feet behind us. In the prehistoric sparks of the campfire, holding his coffee in a tin cup, Ernie talks of the old days, of how his grandfather's family used to own these woods but gave up the land at some point, land that now would be worth a fortune. Ernie is a rich man, his wallet not filled with money, but with banknotes of history and long settlement in these parts. His family tree is as old as white men in these mountains. Uninterrupted lineage is wealth; connection to land is wealth; knowledge of place is wealth; love of place is riches beyond the largest treasure ever buried by the Incas against the conquistador lust. Many of us Americans are poor, our family histories atomized by the automobile. We live in condominiums with treeless front yards. Ernie's yard is the Adirondacks themselves. My twin brother lives on the opposite side of the continent, my sister is moving to Colorado, my mother is retiring to Florida, and Melissa and I are thinking about a move to Vermont. But Ernie will stay in this pine-smelling land of his great-great-grandfather. He thinks the Adirondacks are getting crowded, and occasionally he talks of moving to the Yukon Territory, but he will never leave here.

Ernie, who had planned to sleep in my tent, discovers it's just too small for two grown men. So he sleeps in Jim's four-man tent, and I am glad to be alone.

I'm so tired, I cannot even worry about tomorrow.

Boom. Asleep.

All night the dark water runs wild beside our tents and through our dreams.

Before anyone stirs in the early dawn, I can hear the river's sound unchanged. When I peek out of the tent, I see the sky is one big grey smudge. My stomach grows weaker. Today we face chutes and boulders and ledges and talus slopes—some of the most furious rapids on the East Coast, these final two miles of the Gorge.

Outside, Jim Swedberg looks up from rekindling the fire, and says with a big, teasing smile on his dark face, "So are you ready for today, Pete?" I would like to punch him one because he's playing that male game of making light of fear, and today I don't have any spare emotional room for games.

"As ready as I'll ever be," I say politely, but my legs are extra weak.

"You'll do fine," he says.

I understand Jim's levity. It's the same reassurance that Ernie gives me under the strain of whitewater. My grandfather once said, "Pete, you can get through life if you have a sense of humor, but without it you're lost." Even so, finding humor where fear has eclipsed laughter is not easy this morning. Swedberg's assurances do not exactly work.

Looking at Ernie's competent if serious face, however, does help somewhat.

Then Jamie is out of his tent and already breaking camp, whistling loudly. Ernie is cooking Quaker Oats instant oatmeal and cowboy coffee.

Our bellies are warm while we suit up before we've spoken even a paragraph to each other. Useless to speak now. Better just get going. Get it over with. This isn't exactly fun.

"Let's do a little scouting first," says Ernie. "We'll paddle to the other side and walk through the woods."

"I'll set up below," says Swedberg as he casts his feather-light kayak into the white foam, paddling easily down the slope of the Narrows and quickly out of sight around the bend. Ernie and I hike through the woods around the now southward-arcing river to scout the mile-long Narrows. Before running a Class IV river, one should always "scout" it by walking along the rapids and studying them carefully.

Wearing helmet and wet suit, I feel as armored and anxious as I used to before a big hockey game. It's a long walk, and we keep peeking at the river, then diving back into the woods. "Yup," says Ernie, "we want to stay right; then left."

Ernie and I scout nearly all of the Narrows, then hike back through the woods. We stand by our boat poised for action. We can hardly hear each other shout. The roar of the Narrows is deafening, as loud, it seems, as standing on an airport runway. This is the roar of doom, I think.

We don our life vests. He shouts close to my ear, "Okay, Pete, let's keep right. Then we want to go left of that big rock. It's going to be a little bit tight. Just do what you were doing yesterday and we'll be fine." He shows me with his hand where, more or less, he wants the boat to go.

"Stay in the black water over there. Just don't let the boat go over into that hole, okay?"

"Okay." My knees tremble. What hole is he talking about? I don't see it. Black water? It all looks feverish white to me.

I feel all mushy inside. I have lost that nerve I earned so slowly in the difficulties of yesterday. For the beginner in whitewater, the start of every day is a fresh look at terror. Recalling Scott Overdorf's *Three-Fold Factor*, I think to myself, if the Narrows are *three times bigger* than they look from shore, then this will be a day to remember.

Now we're in it. There's no going back. Heavy holes and waves like thunder, towering roar and the wild jerking of a massive Hudson pulling and pushing and twisting this long twig of a canoe, sucking it along. Waves above us, we are deep in the holes. Picking up speed. Bracing, bracing. My nerves are as bad as they were that first day in Perry Ehlers. We're terribly unstable because I'm about as bad and jittery as I have ever been in a canoe. But there's no time even for Ernie to admonish or to yell to steady up. He is working too hard,

11. Shooting more rapids. *Courtesy Jim Swedberg.*

and it just goes on and on. Sometimes Ernie disappears into the river's holes. My arm is about to explode off my shoulder. I follow him into the hole. On and on. Right side, then left side of the river, then cross again and again, seeking channels in the blasting roar. The Hudson River god nudges a huge wet palm against our Lilliputian boat.

Not once do we take refuge in an eddy. Not once do we back-paddle in the Narrows. It's too early in the morning to be anything but green and awkward yet unstoppable downriver.

Then we're near the end. We have come this far.

But suddenly—good Lord!—a rock in the Little Narrows catches our belly and swings us around broadside to the massive flow.

The canoe tilts dangerously. We're caught on a rock. Marooned. Ernie and I shove and poke the culprit stone with our paddles. But in vain. Until—in slow motion—*I forget one of the cardinal whitewater rules.*

Ernie shouts, "Don't lean upstream!" But I can't help leaning the way my body tells me to lean. The upstream gunwale catches the water. Thousands of all-at-once gallons flood the canoe. Before we can register what has happened, we're both swimming, the canoe alongside us bashing rocks as it somersaults downriver.

Stunned. At first the body does not respond: it balks in frozen disbelief. Then in slow motion the body acts like somebody else's body, slowly in the icy water, someone else's arms beginning to flail toward shore.

Stupid idiot, Pete. Not only have I forgotten cardinal rule 1, but in my shock I also forget *cardinal rule 2.* My paddle disappears into the rapids.

Ernie, holding the canoe now by the stern, swims it to shore, and manages to keep it parallel to the river. Swedberg has found my paddle below, thank God, and I'm clinging to a rock, my wet suit so heavy with water I can hardly stand. Ernie's face strains from the heavy work of directing a waterlogged Odyssey toward shore. But what a pro. Slowly he lands it the way my stepfather lands a great northern pike on a fly rod.

Ernie's wet face is as unemotional as stone. He does not speak to me, so I won't speak to him. He might be angry, or he might simply be recovering from the exertion of rescue. Now he's tipping the canoe to get the water out in the big eddy below the Narrows, called Square Eddy.

He says, "Get in." Then he smiles. "Now you're not afraid to swim, eh?"

"You bet." I do feel less fear now, it's true.

Then we're back in the paddling business, and I feel like a vet. Always get back on the horse that throws you. Come on, river. Come on. Try that again. I dare you. My paddling grows confident, and now finally we're the same team that we were yesterday as we banked into Blue Ledge Pool.

We take a break at Carter's Landing, a big beach that used to be the site of a logging camp with a forty-foot shanty. We find no lumberjack remains.

Ernie is worried about the next rapid, "Mile Long," alias "Carter Landing Rapids," or to some, "Big Nasty." He says there will be a lot of maneuvering, big rocks, standing waves. "We'll play it by ear," he says. "If there's a spot where we can get out and dump the water, we will. At the bottom of Big Nasty is Wrap Rapids."

"Rap rapids, as in rap music?"

"No. Wrap, as in Wrap Around a Rock."

"Oh, that's encouraging," I say.

Big Nasty takes us fifteen minutes of solid technical maneuvering. Watching Ernie in the bow leaning way out downstream with his paddle deep into the river, pulling us to one side—it is so beautiful. There's such graceful, poetic power in that stroke. Then he will shoot his paddle through the water with his blade parallel to the flow, and quickly turn the paddle to a perpendicular position and pull it back again as hard as he can. Once, we have to redirect the canoe by ferrying across the river back-paddling. We actually move upriver, then race forward into the fray.

When we make it through, I have never felt this feeling of teamwork and grace in motion before. I know now why some paddlers won't paddle solo in whitewater. Ernie is really excited. He says, "Fantastic."

In the peaceful aftermath of Big Nasty, Swedberg says, "I liked that little ferry you guys pulled to get back into position. That was nice."

Ernie pays me the best tribute. He says, "We've got plenty of power. When I want to put the bow somewhere, Pete knows what I'm thinking. You're working well with me, Pete." There is spunk in his voice, and gratitude.

We stop at OK Slip Brook, where a little waterfall is set back into the woods. After a ten-minute break, we hit another nasty rapid called, variously, "Kettle Mountain Rapid," "Giveny's Rift," or "Soup Strainer." From these towering cliffs of rock on each side of the river, the ledges have tumbled down over the centuries and made such a messy field of boulders, we have to get out and line the Odyssey now. Ernie says, "At five feet on the North Creek gauge, we might run this. There'd be enough water to give us channels that wouldn't be so restricted. But not now. Too many rocks."

Ernie lets me do some lining, and it feels great. The canoe is like a delicate fish. I play the fish for what seems like hours, and the fish grows weary and malleable. I shoot the craft into the current, quickly feeding it line, and the bow comes around nicely just short of the big whitewater. Then I snap the bow downriver. The canoe glides smoothly through the rocks. All the time, the roar, the numbing roar continues.

In the middle of the river, we spot the Soup Strainer, a rock normally buried, but the river is too low now to cover it, and it looks just like a hippo out of water. Leaping the boulders, we find the remains of an ABS plastic Old Town canoe, torn in half by the rocks. I wonder if the canoeist is alive.

The beginning of the next rapid (mile-long Harris Rift) is like softening jazz. The river abruptly widens, the hills on either side diminish, and we enter a kind of endless rock garden. The channels, more open, are easier to run.

Admiration for the beauty of this rapid doesn't last long. We work for fifteen minutes before the river hears my dare and tries to knock us over again. Caught on another invisible rock, neither of us makes a wrong move, but we tip over anyway. Later Ernie will say, "There was no mistake that time. Just sheer water power took us over. Couldn't be helped, Pete."

And for our second time today we swim a long way, but I hold my paddle in a tight grip. Something else is wrong. Ernie is standing on a rock in the middle of the river, holding the canoe with one hand. He's leaning upstream with the water turning white around his legs, and he's cursing into the roar of the river. Apparently I have tied the nylon line too tightly around the back thwart, and he needs to get the line free in order to be able to work the canoe to shore.

Ernie keeps cursing while I find the rocky bank. Then he gets the line free and he's walking the boat to shore, his legs turning the water white where he steps. I wish Swedberg were taking pictures of this, but he's out there as he should be, following Ernie in case he should stumble.

I worry that Ernie might really be angry this time when he comes ashore. But he's calm now that the canoe is safe. Without words we tip the Odyssey; the water drains out, and we get on our way again. I have a little blood on my face and hands, from scratches only.

Silence reigns in our canoe unless I say something, so now I break that silence once again: "Ernie, if we did the Narrows again right now, we wouldn't tip over would we?"

"Yes we would," he laughs.

"Let's go back and do it again," I say.

"You can go back, Pete."

"I just don't think I'd make the same mistake again, that's all."

"It takes hours in a boat, Pete. You've got to pay your dues first. I've paid mine plenty of times."

I ask Ernie how the loggers ever got the logs down through the Gorge. He says it was amazing what they could drive logs through.

There are a few more sets of rapids until we pass under the railway bridge of the Delaware & Hudson at the entrance of the Boreas River. Here the Hudson takes a sharp bend to the right. After the Gorge's predominantly eastern flow, the river turns due south again toward Battery Park, my distant destination.

We spot four Canada geese swimming along shore. Ernie and Jim are surprised. They've never seen geese on this part of the river.

"I'll be darned," says Ernie. "Maybe they're going to nest here."

Now the whitewater river holds one last surprise. Just below the Boreas, Swedberg sets up cameras on a rock directly adjacent to the infamous Greyhound Bus Stop. We pull ashore to pee, then head for the North River Black Hole, as the residents of nearby North River call it, a huge flat ledge of rock extending underwater from the right-hand shore, forming a solid wall, like a dam. The danger of dams is that they can be perfect hydraulics, where the water tumbles over the ledge and down to the riverbed before it curls back toward itself along the bottom of the river, leaving no room below the curl for a person to dive down and out. For this reason, some of the worst swimming accidents on rivers can occur in the smallest, man-made dams—dams that are only two feet high.

Greyhound Bus Stop has such a huge single hydraulic that Ernie says we will have to build a lot of speed to get through. I can feel the adrenaline come into my body like a rush of jealousy. After this, there is nothing much until Perry Ehlers, he assures me. The Black Hole is an isolated danger. "If we have a problem, we'll be in slow, flat water just below," Ernie says.

Swedberg raises his arm for the okay. Ernie and I build up speed. We are confident. We've been tested. This run feels like the final touchdown in a game we cannot help but win.

When we plow into Greyhound Bus Stop, the bow of our Odyssey dives like a kingfisher into the rim of the Black Hole, water spraying, and, wham, we're out of it in one piece and with only a fraction of an inch of water at our boots.

Ernie and I cheer. Jim is waving and pointing to his camera because he got the photograph.

6

~~~

Adirondack Miners, Loggers, and Good-bye

At the confluence of the Boreas, the Hudson River undergoes a metamorphosis. The great vertical drop ceases, the hills flatten out, and everything opens up. The river calms into a wider, gentler creature. Along shore, boulders disappear. Black and brown pebbles line the streambed. The river is much shallower, and we can watch our speed in the stones within paddle reach. The sound, too, is a soft aftermath of fury, like tender lovers lying abed following sexual fever.

Already I miss the stark canyons that have vanished. An osprey follows us partway downriver as if to say farewell. We're too tired to speak. We paddle steadily but not hard, our arms firm, our strokes like the churning of well-oiled machines.

It is a long, beautiful, peopleless paddle out of the Gorge into the hamlet of North River, where we find the Hudson's first serious cluster of homes. On Route 28, cars zip alongside the river.

North River is not exactly a crowded area, but a string of homes, a store, and a post office along the road that follows the Hudson. Jim says, "It'll get much worse from here on, Pete." He means numbers of people.

Just above Perry Ehlers, we pass the headquarters of the Barton Garnet Mine, an odd four-story, boxlike hanger on the right bank. In the hills away from the river, the open-pit mine, the second oldest—and only other—mining operation on the upper Hudson, produces 90 percent of the world's commercial garnet and has been in the Barton family since 1878. It was Peter Barton's great-grandfather, Henry Hudson Barton, who discovered the rich deposits of garnet on Gore Mountain. Now Peter, in his late thirties, runs the company from his office on the banks of the Hudson.

I visited Peter last spring when I was preparing for this journey. I climbed the four flights of stairs to his office overlooking the river and found him extremely receptive to my canoe trip. Peter went to school in Bozeman, Montana, and never imagined he would end up in the family business. But he came home for a summer and stayed working at the mine for fifteen years, taking over the family company in part "because no one else wanted it."

Peter is a gentle man, soft-voiced, tall, and lean. He is also a whitewater enthusiast. When I met him, he was about to be engaged. He had bought a Wenonah Odyssey from Ernie years ago, which now hung in his garage. Once or twice a year he takes it down for a river trip. "It's a beautiful canoe," he said reverently.

"How's the social life up here?" I asked.

"You have to love the outdoors," Peter smiled. "When the family gathers for our annual meeting, my cousins say, 'How do you live up here all year long? It's so *desolate.*' I tell them I keep very busy in the woods."

I liked Peter. Where else in the world could a stranger stride into the office of an unknown company and just sit down with the company's vice-president and talk casually about the noble river flowing outside his office window? When I asked him what it was like to live and work beside the Hudson, he said he sometimes gazes at the water for hours. "I love the river," he said. "And it's always changing with the seasons. I never tire of the Hudson."

I told Peter that my father had worked for a mining company, too, and I had a special fascination with miners. Peter said his garnet was superior to garnet the world over. "The best women's nail files use our garnet. You can always tell it's North Creek garnet by looking closely at the file," he said. "If the garnet is dark it's ours. If there are little red flecks in the file, it's inferior Japanese garnet. Those nail files won't last nearly as long as ones made with our stone."

The story of the Barton mine is wedded to the story of commercial abrasives and sandpaper. In 1846 Henry Hudson Barton, the son of Daniel Barton of Castle Dunbarton in Scotland, came to Boston from England as a young man in his teens. Apprenticed to a Boston jeweler, Henry Hudson Barton one day saw a man dump a heap of stones on his jeweler's counter. They were garnets from the Adirondacks, the visitor explained, but Henry's boss was not interested in the brown-red stones. Years later Henry would remember them.

In 1858 he married Josephine Baeder, whose father was a pioneer in the manufacture of sandpaper in the United States. In 1869 Henry Hudson Barton went to work for his father-in-law and learned that the three principal elements in sandpaper were glue, paper, and abrasive. Barton opened his own business in 1876 as a specialist in abrasives. Following the Civil War, America's business community demanded more power machinery. Barton knew that better-machined products would require a better-quality abrasive glass or emery, something more economical than what existed at the time for large industrial users of abrasives.

That is when he remembered the garnet that the stranger had dumped on his counter years before. Studying the old ledgers to see where those garnets had come from, he came across the word *Adirondack*. He looked at a map of the state and located the Adirondack Mountains, an area too large for him to pinpoint the source of the stones.

Coincidentally, a few days later a friend came with an old carpetbag filled "with a rough ragged stone as big as a pumpkin," and he wanted to know if the rock was worth anything.

Barton looked up at his friend and said in amazement, "You got this in the Adirondack Mountains, didn't you?"

His friend said, "Yes, Henry, at North Creek. But how did you know?"

Barton's friend had picked up the garnet during a hunting trip in the mountains behind the village of North Creek. So Barton went to North Creek and contracted with a local man to mine the area. In 1878 he leased nearby Gore Mountain, and in 1887 he bought it.

He pulverized the stone and made some garnet paper by hand. "For two busy years the woodworking industry beat a path to Barton's door, and he sold every ream of abrasive paper he could manufacture" from North Creek garnet.

When the Barton abrasive was accurately identified, "there were a host of imitators, but all were forced to use an inferior quality of garnet." All the other garnet from North Carolina, Virginia, Connecticut, and Pennsylvania was inferior to Hudson River garnet.

Garnet, says the company pamphlet, *Garnet Abrasives: An 80-Year History of the Barton Mines Corporation,* "shares with the diamond the double virtue of being a thing of beauty and utility. . . . Because of the hardness of its sharp crystals, garnet was introduced as an abrasive first in woodworking, then in metalworking, and eventually in the grinding of glass."

I sat with Peter a long while, talking of mining and canoeing. He mentioned his upcoming engagement a few times. He was getting married late as I had done, taking a first step in starting his own family and in carrying on the family tradition of mining. When I got up to go, Henry Hudson's great-grandson was gazing below his office window at the river he loved.

It is only noon, grey and hazy. Jim, Ernie, and I can see Perry Ehlers ahead of us. I've come a long way since that practice run with Ernie last week. Something in the way I look at this river is different now. I better understand Peter Barton's affection for it.

Before we take on little Perry Ehlers, however, we pile out of our boats a few hundred yards below Barton's office and walk with joyful river legs to the North River Country Store. A sign facing the river says, "Dangerous whitewater ahead." But the real dangers are behind us now.

On the road in front of the store, Milda Burns is watering the potted geraniums along the river. It was Milda, who worked with Ernie at the Hudson River Rafting Company in North Creek, who first mentioned Ernie LaPrairie's name. When I walked into the rafting-company building a year ago, Milda said the man I needed to talk to lived in Blue Mountain Lake. Without Milda's recommendation I'm sure I would never have gotten this far down the Hudson.

"So," says Milda, "how's the trip going so far?"

"Just great" is Ernie's short but happy reply.

Milda is a generous and smiling woman in her early sixties, energetic and thoroughly excited about Ernie's and my trip. I visited her and her unmarried, older sister, Helen Donohue, last April at their

12. Milda Burns and Helen Donohue in their father's house in North River.

family home here in North River. The Donohue house, just down the road from the general store, is beautifully maintained with a wide wraparound porch and white pillars. The clapboard has a new coat of grey paint, and the trim is an immaculate white. Red geraniums sit at the foot of the six pillars. The house has a kind of dapper look to it, perky.

On that warm spring day Milda, Helen, and I sat on the porch listening to the timeless sound of the Hudson in spring flood sweeping by us. Milda said, "I practically raised Ernie, you know." Her eyes began to water ever so slightly. She loved Ernie as much as a son.

Milda's sister still lived in this beautiful house where the two women had grown up. Helen, like Milda, seemed extremely generous. But I noticed right away that her generosity took a different form than Milda's. Helen seemed to be less emotional on the surface. She sat a little straighter and with a slightly more severe expression on her face. She was in her seventies, still a handsome woman with deep brown eyes. Her enthusiasm for the river and the old log drives was obvious.

When Helen heard I was writing a book and wanted to include material about logging, she offered her house for me to sleep in when

Ernie and I canoed through North River. "We'd like you to spend the night in dad's house," said Helen.

The sisters had fond memories of their father.

"You know, our dad, Jack Donohue—that's Donohue with two o's—was Finch and Pruyn's river drive boss for the upper Hudson. He ran *all* the logs on this part of the river for nearly fifty years," said Milda.

Sitting on the peaceful porch, surrounded by wide pillars and geraniums, the sisters took turns explaining the process of the drives. First Milda would speak, then Helen, then back to Milda, and so on. The force of their delivery was brought home in a sort of Ping-Pong effect.

Helen passed me old photographs. In one photograph, Jack Donohue looked like a frail, stern old man. He was sitting on a porch, perhaps this one, with a pipe in his mouth and a hard expression in his eyes. He had a rough, no-nonsense demeanor. He had the face of a falcon. Another photograph showed the river jammed with logs during the spring drive. Six men stood on a carpet of logs holding long pike poles like spears. One of the men, I believe, was Jack Donohue.

Milda said, "Dad played an important role in the history and lore of the upper Hudson River drive." At the turn of the century, when millions of logs were driven down Adirondack rivers to the Big Boom and the sawmills in Glens Falls, the genius of the late John Donohue of North River had much to do with the success of the drives. He was superintendent of the Hudson River Boom Association, which handled drives for sometimes as many as twenty major lumber companies.

Helen said proudly, "Our dad could get logs down to Glens Falls in one year. Most drivers took two."

Donohue started with Finch, Pruyn in 1895 and worked for the company for forty-five years. He was away from the family for months at a time on the drives. "We were one of the only houses with a telephone. Everyone in town came to use our telephone. Dad had to keep in touch with the men at the holding dams, where there were telephones, too."

Helen said she might be traveling in Chicago when Ernie and I passed through in late June. Milda added, "But if Helen's away, just walk in through the back of the house. The door is always open. I live nearby if you need anything."

13. Hudson River lumberjack Jack Donohue.

On the banks of the Hudson, after a long, frozen winter in this very home, the children of Jack Donohue eagerly would await spring and the great log drive.

"Yes," said Helen, "Dad would begin checking the weather and one morning early about this time of year, he'd note the direction of the wind. He just knew it was time. He knew the effect the wind would have in thawing the ice in the dams that held back the water and the logs. He'd just pack up and head for Newcomb or wherever the holding booms were. In a matter of hours the first logs would be on their way to the Big Boom, almost 100 miles away."

The trip between the holding dams and the Big Boom, a six-hun-

14. Loggers driving logs to the Big Boom between 1880 and 1890.
Courtesy Finch, Pruyn & Co.

dred-foot-long barrier that held back the logs at Glens Falls, often took as long as two months, said Milda. Occasionally when the winter snows and spring rains were inadequate, the log drive would not be completed that year.

In the early days of Hudson River logging, river drivers ran the large, thirteen-foot saw logs. After 1924 there were only the four-foot pulp logs. Logs would fill the Hudson, bank to bank, in such a jumble of wood upon wood it might look impossible to budge them. But with enough water from the holding dams, it was fairly easy to keep the logs moving. Occasionally they did jam up.

Helen said, "In the rougher water the boatsmen had a hard time breaking the jams in the center. Finding the key log was a specialty. You had to use a pike pole, a harpoonlike instrument, to budge it and break the jam." Then there was a deafening roar as the logs came unstuck all at once, crashing downward. The men scattered in all directions. One of the Donohue's neighbors in North River, Ed Rebtoy, was drowned while trying to rescue a companion.

"Getting the logs down through Blue Ledge was a remarkable feat," said Milda. Helen added, "Our dad never let anyone take the boats through the Gorge in high water. He felt it was too dangerous for his men. So the riverboats were let down through the rapids by ropes." There were so many dangerous areas on the river from the mouth of the Indian to North River, this early form of lining took a long time.

Helen smiled as she recalled the food along the drives. "As girls we joined the driving crew for good meals. The cook was Gerard Arsenault. He prepared 'bean hole beans,' baked overnight in a deep hole in the ground lined with coals. Then there was steak, pickled eggs, fried potatoes, biscuits, 'store cookies,' and apple pie, which was all washed down with great tin cups of hot tea or coffee."

"The conversation was full of tall tales," said Milda as if to punctuate her sister's memory.

The last river drive on the upper Hudson took place in 1950. "People came from miles around," intoned Helen, gazing hard at the river. "People lined the banks of the river to see it. So ended an era in the Adirondacks that will not be repeated."

Ernie and I will run the next twenty-one miles of rapids this afternoon. When we reach "the Glen," we'll be finished with the Hudson's whitewater. Ernie's brother-in-law will shuttle the pickup truck down to the Glen, and Ernie will drop me off in North River at the Donohue house on his way back home to Blue Mountain Lake tonight.

But there are lots of river miles to cover yet before I can sleep in a real bed.

We duck into the general store and with sandwiches and Cokes, Jim, Ernie, and I now sit on a bench in a little park with more of Milda's flowers along the river near a monument erected by Finch, Pruyn & Company, which reads:

In Memory of the River Men and Foresters
who made the Hudson River Drive
from the forest to the factory—
1850—1950.

Sitting in sunlight, I can just picture Milda and Helen standing on their porch on the day of that last drive in 1950, recalling their childhood, knowing that perhaps in a few more years no one would remember Jack or the old river drives. I feel connected to the Donohues. In Big Nasty or the Narrows or the Black Hole, in Blackwell Stillwater or in the ancient slowness near the McIntyre Mine, riding in my canoe has felt like a journey from the Donohue era, somehow old-fashioned and laborious, with no intrusion of loud motor.

Milda told me last April that most residents of North River leave town in May for the weekend of the Whitewater Derby. They escape the crowds of kayakers and canoeists who come to compete in the big races. Thousands of cars line the road along the river. Some residents dislike the heavy drinking and the parties. Milda and Helen were not like some of their neighbors. They said they loved to be right there on their dad's porch during the race. "We like it when new people discover the river," said Helen.

Ernie, Jim, and I finish eating our sandwiches and potato chips and prepare again for the river, for the last long push to the Glen. We are about to pass North Creek, six miles south of North River, where two condominium complexes have recently been built, marring the rustic landscape, along with a controversial motel in the center of town. More and more skiers on vacation are discovering Gore Mountain, and Ernie has noticed a definite increase of traffic on Route 28. I wonder how many of these new visitors know about Donohue and his "mouse."

Across from the Donohue house is an unusually large boulder on the east shore of the Hudson just before Perry Ehler's rapid. In that rock, old Jack Donohue made his living. From the rock he could decide for sure when to drive the logs to the Big Boom in Glens Falls. On the boulder's face is a six-foot black discoloration that looks like a mouse: a head, a body, and a tail that curves down to the water. In the spring, when the river was high, Jack would put his foot in the water and know when it was time to start the drive. But there was one more sign he always checked first: the mouse's tail. Jack knew that when the river first touched that tail, the water would be rising fast enough to drive the logs south. Only a few people these days remember the mouse.

We take Perry Ehlers without effort, with none of my fear from last week, but with only my anticipation of what it will be like when I'm alone a few days from now.

From North River to the Glen, past the hamlets of North Creek and Riparius, the river is a series of Class II and III stairways and rock gardens. This is canoe-racing territory, where Hudson River Whitewater Derby contestants build speed and do not worry about Black Holes and Soup Strainers. The river here has wound itself down into fast but softer music; its former fury is muffled. But dangers still lurk in seemingly simple whitewater.

After North River, comes the first real town on the upper Hudson. A cluster of houses marks North Creek. Next to a lumberyard, we see the old railroad station unchanged since that day in 1901 when Roosevelt boarded his private train to the presidency.

That buckboard ride from the Tahawus Club to North Creek was a harrowing, wet, and muddy ride through the mountains. An article in the *New York Herald* on September 22, 1901, described Roosevelt's reckless trip. The headlines read, "Seated on the Bank of the Highest Lake in the State When He Received Telegrams Telling of Mr. McKinley's Relapse," and "Leading a Charge of Troopers at San Juan Less Hazardous Than Spinning Through Darkness Along the Edge of Great Precipices."

No one, not even the driver of the rig, told Roosevelt that McKinley had died. No one dared add to Roosevelt's anxiety. It was not until he left the Tahawus Club and reached North Creek at dawn, where his train had been fed coal all night for a quick escape, that his secretary handed him a note that read:

Buffalo, N.Y., Sept. 14, 1901

Hon. Theodore Roosevelt
North Creek, New York

The President died at 2:15 this morning.

John Hay
Secretary of State

A man is taking our picture from the bank and calls out to us, "It's a long way to New York!" We shout back, "Thanks for telling us." Ernie says it is the editor of the North Creek paper doing a story on our trip.

When we pass under the bridge at North Creek, I can see the little shed just up from the bank where the pipe enters the water to mark the level of the river. Hundreds of whitewater fanatics telephone this very hut to get a reading on the river before entering the Gorge. Today, back at the North Country General Store, we saw on the chalkboard above the counter that the river level was 3.6. Any less, Ernie said, and "we'd have been dragging that canoe through the Gorge."

In the next four hours we often paddle softly. We take our time; we talk of the future of the threatened Adirondacks.

Jim snaps a few pictures, but like us, he's running out of steam. I look over my shoulder upriver after a particularly technical and difficult set of rapids. All the rocks are strung across the wide river like a convoy of overgrown turtles. It's impossible to believe we have just canoed through those tight channels; there seems to be no way through.

Before we reach the Glen, we come upon two lovers, their pale skin contrasting against colorful bathing suits. We come upon them so quickly, we catch them holding each other on a wide flat rock, kissing. They yell out to us, "Are you the guys coming down from Lake Tear of the Clouds?" Proudly we answer yes. But they add nothing more. Our glory seems ambiguous.

Finally, when we pull out at the Glen to put our canoe on top of Ernie's truck, Jim, Ernie, and I are beat to hell. We are 610 feet lower and roughly thirty miles farther along than when the day began with those shaky knees at Blue Ledge Pool. Today we have dropped one-seventh of the total drop of the Hudson River.

On the way back to North River, Ernie stops for a six-pack of his favorite beer, Labatt's Blue Label, then leaves me at the Donohue house. He'll take Swedberg to Long Lake before driving home to Kimball and to the baby for the night. An unacknowledged bond has developed among the three of us, and now the bond is sundering. I will not see Jim again, perhaps ever, and Ernie and I have only tomorrow left to paddle together.

When Ernie's truck pulls away from the Donohue house, I'm left standing in the shadow of a part of the river I have already traveled. Doubling back just to spend the night somewhere feels weird. But since I'd planned to be here tonight, I had called my paddling friends Scott Overdorf and his wife, Patty, and arranged for them to spend the night with me before they run the Gorge tomorrow.

Scott and Patty arrive an hour later, and we talk about whitewater at the Donohue kitchen table until midnight. These two wonderful zealots of the outdoors leave school in Dobbs Ferry every weekend, and drive more than 200 miles to canoe Adirondack rivers, the Hudson being their favorite. Their marriage is inextricably tied to wild water. They met in Germany in international whitewater competition.

I cannot stop talking about all I've learned since we ran that river in Connecticut last April. Scott has been particularly interested in the progress of my trip. When he grew up on the Hudson near Poughkeepsie he dreamed of canoeing the entire length of the Hudson. Now he's a little envious, but not begrudging, and he has offered more than once to help in any way he can. Perhaps we'll paddle together when I get closer to Dobbs Ferry. I'll probably need some company by then.

Scott and Patty and I sleep the sleep of river people. All night we hear the sound of the gentle river flowing around Jack Donohue's mouse. I'm as happy as I have ever been in my life, in this healthy fun of a new sport and a long trek, with my friends close by who think the same as I do. Of my thirty-eight years, this is perhaps my greatest single achievement to date.

Scott and Patty go off extra early to run the Gorge. Ernie picks me up a little while later, and we drive back to the Glen. It's another silent departure, yet this one is different somehow.

We launch the canoe without Swedberg. Right away when we put the blades of our paddles only a few inches into the river, they scrape bottom. The river broadens. The hills gently slope away and are lost in morning mist.

From the moment Ernie picks me up at 6 A.M. at the Donohue house, there's a forbidding sense of the ending of our tandem run— and a twinge of sadness hangs in the air as we move downstream.

This afternoon when we reach Lake Luzerne, the last village in the Adirondack Park, Ernie will take his truck and the borrowed canoe and leave me with my Odyssey and our memories of these few wild days together.

This good-bye feeling pushes our friendship into uncharted regions. In some sense, it's not until today that Ernie and I really get to know each other at all. We have twenty miles of easy paddling in which to talk about whatever comes into our minds.

We spot a family of mergansers, a mother with her babies along shore, terrified, casting nervous glances back at us. Every gene in her body is poised to protect those little guys who scramble to keep up with her.

The river bypasses Warrensburg, a small Adirondack town. Along the nine-mile section from the Glen to Thurman Bridge, we find log camps, small rustic, unheated structures. But after the bridge, the river grows wild again, and the next section from Warrensburg to Luzerne is perfect paddling territory for canoe-camping. The road is not far away. Civilization is close if you need it, and many swimming ropes dangle over deep pools swirling in the rocky enclaves of the shore.

We make leisurely decisions about which channels to take. As Ernie has told me many times, it is deepest on the outside of a bend in the river. So we take the outside curves. The river is too shallow any other place. Today the North Creek gauge is close to three feet and is dropping fast. In another few weeks, this portion of the river won't be passable by boat.

"I'm going to tell all my friends that Ernie LaPrairie is an Adirondack legend—a legend in his own time," I tell him.

Ernie laughs, but the compliment makes him nervous. I see his body straighten as he paddles. I'm probably the first one to say this to him. There is indeed a flavor of the mythic about the man.

The Schroon River enters from the left, and the Hudson grows even more pastoral. Green meadows lie behind a row of willows that pencil the shore. Gone are the pine stands and boulders. Ernie says every time he's been on this section of the Hudson from Warrensburg to Luzerne, he's never seen any boats. It's as if no one knows the river is still here. (Should I be writing this and giving away one of the lower Adirondack's longest-held secrets?) This has to be the last untouched section of the Hudson. There isn't even a hint of rapids between the Schroon River junction and Lake Luzerne, but plenty of gravel bars, sharp bends, and lovely green islands. The riverbed is dark gravel and the water is dark too. "Tranquil" is the word we use to describe it as we paddle. Ancient and tranquil and ever so gentle. A place to bring Suzanna for a night on the river when she gets a little older.

Tallying up the pollution we have witnessed in the Adirondack Hudson, I ask Ernie, "So what junk have we seen so far?"

Ernie replies, "Well, there were tires at the Upper Works, a television set below Newcomb, a tarp or two in the bushes. Not that bad. The river is self-cleansing. High water in spring washes all that crap down."

"Down to where? The lower Hudson?"

"You guessed it," says Ernie a bit devilishly.

A clump of deer vertebrae sits on a rock along shore. We spot turkey buzzards with red noggins circling some prey in the brush. Ernie says he's not used to seeing these birds in the Adirondacks. Everything is changing, he says. In fact, the northward movement of turkey vultures, which in the 1830s did not appear north of central New Jersey, may be in response to a general trend in the earth's warming.

We hear the loud sound of crickets, too, which are out early this summer. Ernie is not used to hearing them until the first week in July, but he thinks perhaps our drop in elevation accounts for this. We also notice a few spotted sandpipers on shore.

We pass a man in a rowboat at a dude ranch that has a golf course. "Look," Ernie says. "Add golf balls to the pollution list." He points into the water at six or seven golf balls, their unnaturally white glow in the tan water.

"It's a big business, dude ranches. They've got a thousand acres here," Ernie shakes his head. "Dudes pay a lot of money to come and ride horses, play golf, and square dance."

We get out and drag the canoe over a wide shoal. Mink tracks run along the sandy shore. Mallard ducks scatter. We notice more otter slides. Ernie says he's never actually seen any otter on the Hudson, but he knows they're here.

"I'm going to pray you come back as an otter, Ernie."

"That would be great," he says.

The loud sound of our hull scraping along the pebbles of the riverbed interrupts us.

"I'm beginning to miss the rapids already. This is pretty tame stuff."

Our conversation drifts to the difference between old money and new money. Ernie says the land is preserved because of old money and state buy-ups. The big power company Niagara-Mohawk, commonly known as Ni-Mo, has owned much of the land along the river here. Ni-Mo kept the water rights for a time when they thought they might build another dam. (In December 1992 the state acquired the land.)

Approaching Luzerne, the farmland is a secret terrain with isolated farmhouses cupped in the dips between dissembling hills. How strange to see cows and pastures and broad-leafed trees on a river that has been so much conifer and cliffs. Oaks and poplars hang out over the water. Cows stare at us in the hazy sun, the current slowing almost to a standstill.

We talk about how to classify various sections of the Hudson River. This entire process of making categories, of dividing and classifying such a "diverse" river, seems impossible and is related to one's focus. In his book *The Hudson River: A Natural and Unnatural History*, Robert Boyle has written chapters around "The Adirondack Headwaters," "The Albany Pool," "The Mid-Hudson region," "The Highlands," and so on, with a focus on the river south of Albany. His book was first published the same year (1969) in which the Hudson River sloop *Clearwater* set sail launching its environmental campaign to clean up the lower river. Boyle's focus is on the polluted estuary south of Troy.

Ernie's focus is on the north Hudson. He seems to draw an important distinction at the Boreas River, after which the fury and drama of the Gorge—Ernie's rafting passion—abruptly ends and the river gradually softens, rapid by rapid, until it reaches this last liquid poetry leading into Luzerne, where the river is punctuated by Rockwell Falls, a twenty-foot-wide sluice of Class V killer white spume. This is the narrowest stretch of the whole river. After Luzerne it's another river altogether. It is no longer Ernie's river when it leaves the park.

Classification systems are established with specific goals for making them. For me, I suppose, the upper Hudson is four rivers. First, the Feldspar-Opalescent madness, then the short, almost Canadian wilderness along the mine tailings, followed by a climax of long violent rapids to the Glen, succeeded finally by a twenty-mile aftermath, this easy, sociable paddle before the departure of a good friend.

"Ernie, we've only got a few hours left for you to teach me how to guide myself after I leave the park."

"Sorry, Pete. I don't know how to do that."

"I guess I'll need an industrial guide from here on."

Ernie shows me how to paddle in the shade of the trees along the shore to avoid the hot drill of the midday sun. I put on sunglasses and sunscreen, and we pump, pump, pump, this hard work of the long distance now impressing upon me my stupidity for not taking anyone along to help after Ernie departs today. It's nearly impossible to imagine being alone. I've come through a difficult part, but the harder part is just beginning. I can tell by the feel of the hot, lifeless day that there is danger of great loneliness ahead.

Without the rush of wind and the feverish current of rapids, the river is as long and sultry as the dog days of late August. Every bend should reveal Luzerne but does not. The frustrated child says: "When are we going to get there, Ernie?"

No answer.

But I hope this tedious paddle will never end, even as I wish it had never begun. The truth is that all this humid day I have the feeling Ernie has already left me. His job is done.

The narrowest part of the Hudson River is a twenty-foot chute called Rockwell Falls. We can hear the roar as we land near a restaurant called Papa's. Tourists eat on the back porch overlooking the river above the falls. As we paddle to shore, we can feel the pull of the great south-moving river as it tries to shoot us through Luzerne. We draw the boat up into the foul-smelling muck of civilization. There must be a bad drainage problem here. Perhaps some houses still dump raw sewage into the river.

We try to walk through the brush and seven-foot reeds to the steep banks of private backyards, but we fail at first. We are watched casually by the clients of Papa's.

We find a steep trail that leads to a village street. We leave the canoe in the reeds and walk past Papa's, to stroll on wobbly legs to a diner in the center of town. It's an odd feeling to see cars and people. We order coffee, and I pay Ernie his guiding fee of one hundred dollars a day, plus an extra hundred. I'd like to give him much more, but I cannot. He folds the money and places it in his pocket without counting it.

I say, "Now that the trip's over for you, Ernie, I have to agree with your wife: you really should charge more money for guiding. You're worth ten times what you charge."

"Maybe next time." We laugh.

Ernie is happy to be finished with the work, but sad to be leaving the journey. I know he would like to go the whole distance. Perhaps he has grown as fond of me as I have of him. Of course none of this will be discussed. It is a peculiar fondness, this dangerous and rugged travel that makes bonds between us.

The journey of this tandem partnership is complete. From the time we first put our canoe into the Hudson just below the McIntyre furnace, together we have dropped around 1,200 feet in about eighty miles of paddling.

But for me the river stretches out, and my trip is far from over.

PART TWO

Dams and Locks

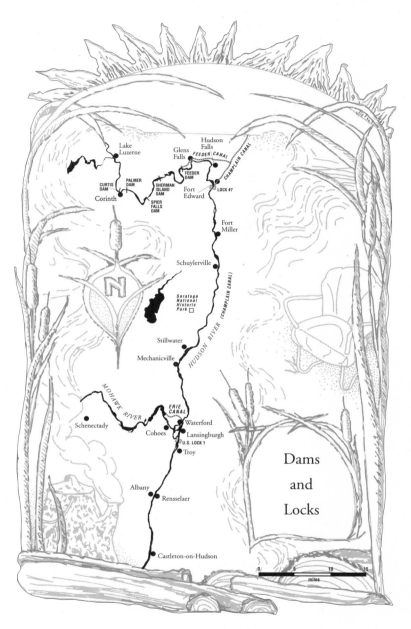

Lake
Luzerne

Glens
Falls

Hudson
Falls

FEEDER CANAL

CHAMPLAIN CANAL

CURTIS
DAM

PALMER
DAM

SHERMAN
ISLAND
DAM

FEEDER
DAM

Corinth

SPIER
FALLS
DAM

Fort
Edward

LOCK #7

Fort
Miller

Schuylerville

N

Saratoga
National
Historic
Park □

HUDSON RIVER (CHAMPLAIN CANAL)

Stillwater

Mechanicville

MOHAWK RIVER

ERIE
CANAL

Schenectady

Waterford

Cohoes

Lansingburgh

U.S. LOCK 1

Troy

Albany

Rensselaer

Dams
and
Locks

Castleton-on-Hudson

0   5   10   15

miles

2. From Lake Luzerne to Troy.

7

A Forgotten Town

In the middle of a river journey, to find my own father waiting for me over a leisurely 8 A.M. cup of coffee at an outdoor table on the street-side of Papa's restaurant in the soporific village of Lake Luzerne is slightly apparitional. The fact that it's Father's Day, June 17, was not planned although I did know when I left home that he would rent a summer camp on nearby Sacandaga Lake, and we had agreed to try to meet when I was passing through. But *here* he is, not thirty yards from the Hudson. *My* Hudson River.

I order coffee and look at his aging but enthusiastic face. He doesn't look like a man who is legally blind. His blue eyes gaze directly at me when I tell him about my trip. Of course I talk mostly about the rapids.

Even though his blindness (from an inherited disease of the circulatory system) gets worse every year, my dad still loves adventures. He has done a lot of traveling since he left business, but when he was my age he was moving rapidly up the corporate ladder at a mining company. He wore a suit and tie every day and was connected to New York City. He did little of what I am doing now. Yet today he seems to understand why at the age of thirty-eight I have come this far, and why tomorrow, after a night at his rented house on Sacandaga Lake and a small reception at the local museum, I must continue downriver alone. I think if he were young again, he too might be in a canoe on the Hudson.

"Are you eating enough?" he asks.

"Sure, dad." He orders me a big breakfast, and within an hour we've talked all we can. His third wife, Selma, meets us at the restaurant and drives us to their rented camp fifteen miles away from the Hudson.

The night is cool and full of stars, but I have an uneasy feeling I've misplaced my canoe somewhere. Canoes, which do not lose their value over the years, do get stolen. Tonight the canoe is resting up against the side of Mr. Butler's house on the other side of the falls. Butler is the director of the local historical society, which has organized a reception for me tomorrow morning. He's invited some journalists from the Glens Falls paper in honor of my "historic visit." I just hope Butler keeps an eye on my Odyssey.

After dinner I do laundry and lie on a big bed with a road map of New York State and a book. I cannot bring myself to read. I would much rather study the map. In fact, this is the only map I could find that actually shows the whole river. I've cut out the western half of the state, and I've been marking the places where I have camped or stopped for the day along the river.

I notice the names below the Blue Line are changing. No longer quaint-sounding Newcomb, North River, North Creek, and the Glen—here come the army names, the machine names, the European names: Fort Edward, Fort Miller, Schuylerville, Mechanicville, Troy. It's a different river indeed, a river with iron in its syllables, a river forged by the American and Industrial revolutions.

The moon is coming up crisp, half-full, and waning. I thank the moon for waning during my journey. The less full the moon, the less violent will be the upcoming tides below Troy.

In the morning the Hadley-Luzerne Historical Society has gathered at the local history museum. A grandfather clock ticks on the wall of the tiny building that is situated not far from the river. I wonder if Mr. Butler sees my visit and my journey through Luzerne as a way to bring attention to his forgotten town. The society's director is a quiet man, with hangdog shyness, and long stringy red hair falling in a few lines over a slightly pockmarked forehead.

Fifteen members of the historical society have come to hear me speak about my trip. My father joins them as they sit in a circle around me, and I begin, nervously, by telling them how one day I looked at the river in front of my house and was curious about it and also how I needed an adventure close to home. I speak about the rapids and explain how I am looking for towns and people along the river where there is forgotten history to be remembered.

Luzerne is such a town, not only forgotten, but, as I discover now, quite depressed in its soul. Butler wants me to write about Luzerne, to help polish the old luster of his faded village. From the 1880s to the 1920s, luxury hotels in Luzerne attracted summer-long residents from far away. But the hotels have long since burned or been torn down. Even the train has stopped running. "The rich and famous used to come here," Butler tells me as he shows photos of the rambling Victorian structures with names like the Wayside Inn and the Rockwell Hotel.

Niagara-Mohawk is guilty of buying land and tearing down at least one of these old hotels. Butler says Ni-Mo bought much of the land on both sides of the Hudson and once talked about building a power dam at Rockwell Falls. The idea began in the 1940s. "But," he complains, "around 1952 they started working on another project and said they were coming back here to build the dam. Nothing ever happened. It would have made our area great for recreation."

And this was not the only dam the power companies had had plans to build on the Adirondack Hudson. An article in the *Albany Times-Union* from July 28, 1968, said there was a major threat to the wilderness of the upper Hudson when an engineer's report was released by the New York Water Resources Commission proposing that the Gooley I Dam be constructed a short distance below the confluence of the Indian River with the Hudson at a cost of 57 million dollars. Such a dam would have required 16,000 acres of land, 14,000 of which would be flooded. The twenty-five-mile long reservoir above the proposed dam would have been used for industrial and municipal water supply, power, and "recreation." But Gooley was effectively stopped by the APA (Adirondack Park Agency) Act of 1974, along with the Wild, Scenic and Recreational Rivers Act.

The bitterness of Luzernians because they did not get their power dam, and their crushed expectations, remind me of an isolated colony of settlers I once stumbled upon in the high jungle on a muddy road in the foothills of the Andes of Ecuador. Those colonists, too, had been waiting twenty years for the delivery on a promise made by the Ecuadorian government decades before. A paved road was to be built from the Andean spine down into the Amazon. The road would have meant prosperity and fortune. The long, terrible wait had seeped into their speech, into their rags, even into the bent barrels of their old and useless shotguns.

Overshadowing this general Luzerne depression of an opportunity unrealized is dangerous Rockwell Falls itself, an eighteen-foot drop. Called Jessup's *Little* Falls when Lossing hiked through town, the narrowest part of the Hudson has killed a large number of Luzerne's youth through the years. For children, the falls are attractive but deadly for swimming.

Jessup's *Great* Falls are the falls on which International Paper has constructed two dams in the town of Corinth six miles downriver, my next destination. Both falls were included in patents granted to Ebenezer Jessup, who settled in this area before the Revolution. E. Jessup, a relative of the Jessup I met at the Tahawus Club, was sympathetic to the king. According to Lossing, his family "held intercourse with the loyal Scotch Highlanders, who were under the influence of the Johnsons and other royalists in the Mohawk valley, and acted as spies and informants for the enemies of republicanism." Unable to capture the traitors, republican troops laid waste the royalist settlement of Luzerne. (Nelson Jessup and the members of the Tahawus Club, too, were modern-day royalists doomed by a revolutionary age.)

Outside on the lawn after the reception, an Abenaki Indian named John Bennett, a descendant of a tribe that came to the Adirondacks from neighboring Vermont, tells me about Luzerne the way it used to be before the coming of the Northway, built from Albany to Montreal, the superhighway that, as he says, *"poisoned the region."* He also talks about the dangers of kids dropping into the pool below the falls from ropes hanging from the bridge.

John is a stocky man, all torso, thick hands, and wrists, probably as strong as anyone in the North Country. He walks with a limp and is slightly bowlegged. His silver hair is thick and curly. His face is bronze with deep lines creasing his forehead. He doesn't smile much. His lips clamp around big ivory teeth when he talks, and he

15. John Bennett of Lake Luzerne.

has a kind of sad look. One tooth is gold and it gleams in the hazy summer light.

John seems a self-assured man but an angry man, too. He's angry about Governor Cuomo's interest in preserving the Adirondacks, a policy that keeps the region poor. He's angry because the Indians never signed a treaty with the white man. He believes the Indians still own these mountains. He says he loves the woods. In this he is like Ernie, but unlike Ernie, who has an ancestral home in Blue Mountain Lake, John exhibits the restlessness of a man without land. His home was the farm, but the farm has gone. His home was the woods, but the woods are disappearing. He seems trapped between a desire for economic growth and a yearning for the untouched forests.

He says he was a farmer for years, and now he's a security guard for fifty-two camps "up on the mountain." His mom was full-blood Abenaki "from Saratoga-way" and his dad was from the North Creek area (pronounced North *Crik*). John used to work many jobs logging. He drove teams in the woods, cut logs with the old cross-cut saws,

peeled pulpwood, loaded logs by hand, and rolled them right up on
the trucks. He used to cut logs when he was not farming. He cut
wood to sell, cut wood for sugar houses to boil sap. I ask him to talk
about the Hudson.

"Well," John says in a deep Adirondack accent, "it can be a kinda
sassy river at times, and then it can be very very calm."

"Sassy" is a mild word for that time in May 1972 when the Hudson flooded Luzerne. The water formed a tidal wall as far down as
Northumberland below Hudson Falls. Pulp wood that had been sitting on shore for twenty years since the last log drive suddenly came
loose, ramming boathouses and docks for miles and miles downriver.
The floodwaters measured almost 40,000 cubic feet per second. In
many areas, just the tops of trees were visible. At the dude ranch
Ernie and I passed the other day, only the tip of the flagpole could be
seen out of water. The deluge roared through Rockwell Falls, forcing
water up forty feet to touch the bottom of the bridge. Several camps
below Luzerne were tied down with cables to prevent them from
floating away.

"Used to have good farms on the sides of the river, too. This here
area is what you call general farming, not the big dairy farms you got
down Saratoga-way. But all our farms are dying out, and people is
going to be sorry. They got to eat."

John talks about the demise of farming: "You got so many government regulations now, it ruins it. You can't do this, you can't do
that. You got to be careful about the streams, and a lot of this other
nonsense. Rules and regulations made by someone sittin' behind a
desk."

These are the sentiments of a whole nation. Our country has
grown angry and bitter in its ripening. Imprisoned in regulation, we
beat at the bars of our jails. Armed renegade posses hide out in the
Rockies. Guys like John Bennett are angry everywhere. They've seen
what the twentieth century has done to our freedom, and this national anger thrives in Luzerne.

As if the river mirrored his anger, Bennett says, "Rockwell Falls is
real dangerous right down in there. It's real deep, and you got a lot of
current underneath that bridge."

"Anyone try to run it in a boat?"

"Some's tried. A lot of people got drownded in there. Kids are foolish. They hang a rope under the girders and swing off there and dive. You don't know what you're going to hit. One kid cracked his head on a rock and had to have the emergency for him. There's lots of things you can get tangled up in. When they put the new bridge in, they dropped the older bridge in the water, too. It's down there still! And a cement mixer's down there too."

Butler has joined us on the lawn, so I ask, "Has Luzerne changed a lot since you were kids?" From hearing their raucous laughter, you might think my question was downright lewd.

"Oh Jesus, cricket, you wouldn't believe it," John says, shuffling his feet.

"It's getting too darn citified. Too many people comin' in. Just *cartourism.*" The way he says it, "car tourism" becomes one word. "*Cartourism* is no good for the North Country, we can't live on it. The people who used to come for the whole summer came by rail. But these here new *cartourists*, they just pass through. You used to have farmin' here and a tannery before the turn of the century. Now you've got this here Northway. People zip up and zip back. It was the Northway that hurt us. I remember when it was built. All them politicians said, 'We'll open up the North Country.'

"Yeah, and they did, and now you got everythin' coming up from the city with it, too. People you don't want. Bad influences. I don't care for the cities. I love the mountains, I love the woods. Of course, I got Indian blood in me, and Indians got to be free. Indians can't be cramped up."

"Some say Luzerne was called Jessup's Landing in the old days. Is that true?" I ask.

Butler says, "Nope. That was definitely Corinth, six miles downriver."

When the French and Indian War came to a close in 1763, the upper Hudson was safe again for settlers. Ebenezer Jessup built a log home in what is now Luzerne. He and his brother Edward, the first to lumber the area, gradually claimed large tracks of the southern Adirondacks. In those earliest days of Adirondack logging, to get their logs downriver to the sawmills, the Jessups floated their logs on large rafts fastened by chains. Before learning to run individual logs through the rapids, the Jessups skirted the falls in present-day Corinth by loading the logs onto carts at Jessup's Landing, now a public beach just above Palmer Dam. Today in Corinth the rapids are gone, replaced by dams. The Great Falls have vanished, but here in Luzerne the Little Falls survive.

Butler says, "I wished they'd kept this town's name instead of Lake Luzerne."

John adds, "It was changed for tourism. That's the only reason. 'Lake' draws tourists, like *Lake* George. But we don't want anything like Lake George. We don't want to be dependent on *cartourists*. Everybody's now worrying whether we'll get enough snow in the winter. Everybody gets bent out of shape 'cause we're not makin' money from *cartourists*. We get poor weather in the summertime, and we don't have the beaches, and not enough people don't come in for ice cream. Nothin' but worry worry. When we had city business in the old days, we didn't worry so."

Butler adds, "The main thing for me is that *Luzerne* is the town and Lake Luzerne is the lake. The two need to be defined."

"So," says Butler, getting to the point of my visit, "It seems like every time someone writes about the Hudson River, they skip right over Luzerne. They write about North Creek above us, and then there's nothing about the river until you reach Glens Falls. Now *we* got the narrowest part of the river *right here*, and the *most beautiful* falls. So why don't somebody write about our town, eh?"

"But some writers have," I say. Burmeister has written: "The Lake Luzerne-Hadley region is exceptionally scenic. High wooded points, delightful lakes, the wild lower Sacandaga . . . , and the magnificent Hudson River trough assure a selection of pleasing landscapes *deserving more attention*" (italics mine).

I ask, "Why do so many other writers bypass Luzerne, then?"

"Maybe it's a little more glamorous upriver, in the North Creek area, closer to the source. You got whitewater derbies up there. But really, you know, it was all one river as far as the logging went. From up there all the way to Glens Falls at the Big Boom, the history of logging is the history of Luzerne, too. I can remember at least two times when logs wiped us out."

"So what went wrong here?"

Butler's eyes shift back and forth, to and from the ground. He says, "For so many years, even now, the politicians in this town had their own businesses. *They* were content. Anytime some outfit wanted to come into town and set up shop, they made it hard on newcomers. Because the politicians were satisfied; they were making money. They said, hell with these people, let them find work elsewhere. So industry shied away, 'cause the people who run the town wanted to make it a *tourist town."*

I know what Butler is getting at. The idea is to bring in growth, bring in jobs, bring in industry. I decide not to tell them who is sponsoring my trip. They might take me as one of the enemy. I'm canoeing behind the DMZ here, and I better paddle silently. But why shouldn't I speak my piece and tell these people I too favor trees over cement, even if trees keep an area poor? I favor the river as it is rather than the river dammed and flooded into a recreational lake. Better poor than ruined. Trees and the natural flow of the Hudson will make us richer in the long run. Even as I think it, I know mine is the idealism of an outsider, a canoetourist.

I wonder how happy Luzernians would really be if Ni-Mo had gone ahead and made its dam and changed the configuration of the river, letting condos spring up along its banks and powerboats buzz north of town.

Perhaps Luzerne is the saddest town I'll find on the Hudson. Rockwell Falls will continue to kill Luzerne's children, and the past here is a kind of yoke around the town's future. I wonder if this abandoned feeling, this hopelessness, along the Hudson will grow more pronounced as I proceed downriver.

Butler says, "Below Glens Falls, God only knows what you'll find."

It's time to get moving. I have seventeen solo miles to paddle today in order to reach Glens Falls, not to mention many power dams to skirt. The total drop in those seventeen miles will be only 22 feet, compared with last week's daily drops of 600 feet or more.

I lead my father up the road to my canoe on the other side of the falls near Butler's house. Dad slips me a $100 bill. "I don't need this, dad," I say. He says, "Here. Come on. I know you can use it. For a hotel. Or an emergency. You never know." He's smiling a father's smile, and I pocket the money.

Coming out of his front door, Mr. Butler takes a few last photographs as I climb into my canoe, which I haven't paddled since Ernie and I switched to the sturdier Wenonah above the Tahawus Club bridge. Come to think of it, I haven't ever paddled this canoe alone with all my gear, which weighs the Odyssey down nicely into the water. I shove off into the light river chop where the Sacandaga and the Hudson meet, into what Burmeister calls a "a huge, restless pool."

"Well, good-bye," says Butler who walks across the street and vanishes into his home. Selma too says her good-bye and graciously gets into the car to give my dad and me a private moment. My loyal father stands there on the bank waving. I see an old sadness in his eyes as I pull away from shore.

8

Dams

8 A.M. Monday morning. Motorboats appear on the Hudson below Luzerne. Alumacrafts and Boston Whalers are moored at the many docks that pierce the river. The Hudson has become as groomed and straight as Florida's inland waterway. Only two days off the Hudson, and I feel I've been landlocked for weeks. But now the blood starts to churn as I paddle. I'm a sailor returned to the sea, happy spray in the beard as I round the bend on my six-mile paddle to Corinth, old Jessup's Landing.

I dig hard at the dark water. The wind is straight on. There is an old canoeist's maxim: "When you're in a canoe, the wind is always against you." Solo, this boat is far less controllable in the wind. I sit on the cane seat Ernie dropped just aft of center, and my hands scrape on the rivets in the gunwales, drawing blood. I tape the rivets with first-aid tape, but the tape comes off when it gets wet.

Preferring to hug the lee shore where the wind is a bit less fierce, I follow not ten feet from a busy road. The sound of people going to work, so many cars, and the sight of all these moored motorboats are intimations of increasing river activity to come. The land is flat, and the camps alongshore are modest. American flags snap in the wind everywhere. I'm not sure I agree with Burmeister that this part of the river is pastoral.

When the wind gusts I am blown backward. But if I don't paddle

131

with all my might, I could easily give up my trip altogether, for surely there will be many days like this. I must find a successful stride.

Ernie suggested I take out the yoke that runs from gunwale to gunwale right under my kneecaps so I can bend my knees and get more comfortable. I had planned to remove it in Luzerne, but have chosen to wait until after this long day of portages around dams. When I reach the Feeder canal at Glens Falls, I'll unbolt the yoke and get more comfortable.

About the next town, Butler told me, "We say Ker-INTH, but its real name is COR-inth. The story goes that when they were looking to name their town, someone in church once handed a lady a Bible and said, 'Go ahead, pick a name.' She flipped the pages and let her hand come down on Corinthians. So its real name is COR-inth, but we call it ker-INTH, among other things . . . "

The tone of community rivalry was unmistakable. Corinth, after all, is home to the *Great* Falls; Luzerne, only the *Little* Falls.

Perhaps the surrounding towns begrudge the region's major employer, the International Paper mill in Corinth. Workers come from Warrensburg, Glens Falls, and even Saratoga to work at the mill, the only place around that pays well. Last month on reconnaissance, I drove through the village. Corinth is a tough town. Out-of-work kids laze about on street corners. The pavement in the streets needs repair. The houses have a parched, leached look as if the cold winters have neutered them. Everything about the town seems tattered from harsh times and no money. Corinth makes even Luzerne look prosperous.

For me, entering Corinth after the Adirondack Hudson is a milestone. Just before the town the river opens out, and I can see bridges and industry before me. With about 5,000 people, this will be the biggest town I've come upon since I began my trip.

From here on I'll read Burmeister religiously. Although I've been warned by more than one Hudson canoeist that Burmeister's figures are not exact, he nevertheless has good advice on how to handle the dams ahead. For example, his book covers fifteen "Danger Points" on the Hudson. The first six, which take us from the river's source to Luzerne, are natural dangers. The next eight are dams, what I might call human booby traps. If I'd thought the rapids were tough, perhaps I should have waited until this day was over and the dams were behind me.

At the Corinth beach I take out before Jessup's *Great* Falls, which Burmeister accurately describes as the river's first "barrage." Actually, there are twin dams here, a double barrage, down which the Hudson drops 100 feet. The Curtis Dam was built in 1905, and the Palmer Dam in 1915 after the flood of 1913. Both are owned by International Paper and are the first of nine power dams that blockade a twenty-mile stretch along the Hudson, below which there are no more dams. Lossing in 1859 did not see the dams, but he drew a picture of Jessup's *Great* Falls (the highest natural falls on the Hudson), which, he said, were known to the Indians as *Kah-che-bon-cook*, formerly known as Hadley Falls, and afterward called Palmer's Falls, "the land on each side of the river being in possession of Beriah Palmer and others, who there constructed extensive works for manufacturing purposes." Lossing says the water power even at low water was estimated at "fifteen thousand horse-power" and that by 1858 a village had been recently established with a public square and fountain. Preparations were under way for "industrial operations far greater than at any point so far up the Hudson."

My first impression of dams on my journey is dams be damned. Dams tamper with nature and frustrate canoeists. They're cement blockades to a boater dreaming of freedom. They are like iron doors slamming and locking behind me as I enter a prison. The dams have eliminated nearly all the natural rapids and falls along this section of the Hudson. After each one, I'm farther from the Hudson River Gorge, from the wild outdoors of the headwaters, and now there's no turning back. Worst of all, dams like the International Paper Palmer dam transform the river forever. Millions of gallons a day of Hudson water at IP are used in the pulp process. That means the water below the dam is never quite the same. Still more than 200 miles from the sea, already the river gets mauled, man-handled, and tainted not only by chemicals but by human arrogance. The demarcation between the upper and lower Hudson is defined by where the river gets *damned*.

These barrages scare me. They force me to invade corporate property. No longer do I fear rapids and natural rock. Beginning at Corinth, I fear angry plant managers. I fear walls of concrete. I worry whether or not I'll be able to get out of the way of the mammoth turbines that spin underwater sending electric power to the cities.

Truth is, I don't know what to expect anymore. The rules of the river are changing. I just hope the dams are well marked. I hope I don't accidentally topple over one of the spillways. I wonder if I'll actually hear the dams as I approach, or see them, or notice the water speeding up, or discover any warnings along the shore.

Last month I drove to the guard house at the International Paper plant and asked to speak to someone about getting permission to portage around the dams through IP property, which could save me from at least a mile carrying canoe and all my gear. But the guard gave me an exasperated, "Jeessuuus. Damn canoeists. Last week a kid got stuck between the two dams. Had to get Rescue to *fish him out.*"

So forget it, I thought. "Never mind. I'll manage," I said and drove off cursing.

Forrest Hartley, the local journalist who was at the Luzerne museum get-together this morning, told me in Luzerne that he would help any way he could. He lives right in the center of Corinth and has some contacts at IP.

Exhausted by a mere six-mile solo paddle, I come ashore at the public beach, formerly Jessup's Landing, and Hartley is here as planned to help drag my canoe up the sand. He says, with only a slight remnant of a southern accent (he was raised in Florida), "I just drove down the river looking for an access point. But I don't see where you can put in. I can't figure any place unless you go through IP. But I guess you've made other plans?" He shakes his head, looking pretty doubtful.

"Well, not really."

"I could have set it up with IP on a little more notice, but they tend to be suspicious on the fast stuff. Come on. My house is near," he says in a soft voice. He's a slight man with light blue eyes and a delicate disposition. A two-day stubble shadows his chin. His arms are thin. There is something ethereal about Hartley, who is a horticulturalist and a beekeeper, and only recently a journalist.

"We'll make some phone calls after coffee. Let's see if I can get you permission to put in just below the second dam, near the water-treatment plant. That should save you a heck of a portage."

Taking advantage of his interest in my trek, I ask Hartley if he wants to paddle with me for the day. I sure could use the help around these barrages, and I'm feeling lonely already without Ernie. He says, yes, he would like that very much, but unfortunately he has some stories to cover. He looks about as disappointed as I feel.

Hartley carries my Bills bag and paddles. I follow with my eighteen-foot Kevlar helmet, watching his feet. Thank God for his help. Strolling my canoe through the depressed streets of the mill town after fighting a river wind is, to say the least, unreal. Logging trucks, top-heavy with timber, heading for the mill, turn corners carefully, their engines grinding low.

We leave the canoe propped against a nearby municipal building, and after dropping my Bills bag and camera inside his apartment, his wife Maggie joining us, we head out for breakfast at the greasy spoon on the corner. Hartley and his wife write for the Glens Falls *Post-Star*. Maggie, who is the business editor for the paper, drives every day to the main office in Glens Falls, but Hartley works out of his home as a stringer.

"Sure looks like a rough town," I say.

Hartley laughs, "It's beyond that."

At the U-shaped counter, unshaven men drink their coffee in silence, some with baseball caps embossed with IP logos. They watch us sit in a booth along the wall. Maggie, who's very quiet, says in a low voice, "Supposed to have thunder showers today."

"Hope I can reach Lock 7 before that."

It's probably crazy, but I've chosen Lock 7, at the end of the Feeder canal as my destination today, perhaps twenty-six miles of paddling and hiking around dams. I wonder if I can make it in thunder and lightning.

Maggie studies her husband when he talks. Her gaze is intent. They seem to be from two different worlds, she from a northern city; he southern, from deep Dixie country.

Hartley says he fits in with hicks. He grew up around them. He doesn't mind them although he's "not of the same mindset." He's about thirty-two.

His dream has always been to take a regional approach to beekeeping, he says. "You have to have your apiaries in different places, some here, some there, so if one gets wiped out, the others will be okay. I realize this kind of beekeeping depends too much on fuel, though." Hartley cares about the environment.

He squints and shrugs his shoulders. In seeming contradiction to his love of nature, he has a passion for motors, any kind of motor. "I've got a lot of motors out back behind the house." He looks guilty about this, but smiles. Maggie studies him, smiling, too. The intensity of her gaze makes her quite beautiful.

A graduate of Wesleyan, Maggie used to be an editor for a world wire service in New York City. She took quite a step down in jobs when they came here from New York to be near some land they own in Hadley, across the Hudson from Luzerne.

Maggie says, "This town's very depressed. We left Brooklyn to come here. We were shocked by all the noise at night. The kids don't feel like they have any future. They hang out on Main Street all day, all night."

There's some heavy drinking in this town, she says, logging-style. One night the Hartleys saw a fight start outside a bar. Out came the broken pool cues and a shovel from someone's truck. Then one guy fired up his chainsaw. "It was a real war with two battle lines, Napoleon formation. It looked just like a peasants' revolt. A couple of people got beaten bloody."

Hartley shakes his head and smiles, "But when the fight was over, everyone said, okay, see you tomorrow. They waved and off they went. Maggie and I couldn't believe it!"

So why doesn't International Paper hire these kids?

Maggie says IP has been cutting back during these tough times. "The old assumption in a mill town that you grow up and get a job at the mill is no longer valid. In fact, it's gotten so bad, the people in town say 'Oh, IP won't hire anyone from Corinth.'"

Last year there was a single entry-level opening at the mill. "Four hundred people lined up for the job!" Before Hartley started writing for the paper, he too was in that line. Maggie says that it's a tough life, mill work. "Every old guy in town has the ends of his fingers missing from some sort of mill job. They're deaf, too. The safety standards have improved a lot since the old days, but . . . "

As a side income, Hartley mows lawns with his tractor.

"They make fun of all the safety devices I wear when I work. They yell at me, 'We never used to do that *at the mill.*'"

Hartley seems better suited as a writer. He says he likes writing for the local paper—everyone in Corinth knows him now—but, like many beginning journalists, he's frustrated by how little some people read. "People like to read the headlines," he says. "Never mind the article. If they like what they see in the headlines, they're happy."

"But it's tough to make money as a correspondent," he says. "The paper works me hard and pays badly. You have a situation where everyone wants a reporter's job. So you've got skilled people lining up for a job that pays $15,000 a year."

Paid up, we saunter out of the greasy spoon under the wary eyes of men who've been in barroom brawls. We hike back to Hartley's apartment to call Forrest's contacts. Maggie goes off to work, and Hartley picks up the phone. In a polite, gentle voice he says "I have this guy here who's canoeing down the Hudson and would like to get around the dams, but he needs a place to get back in the river. Can he go into the town sewage treatment plant? Yeah, he's coming all the way from the top, from Lake Tear. . . . Yeah, I've got a truck. I could drive him. Yes. Yes. Thank you." He hangs up.

"The town says you've got to get IP approval." He makes another call, this time to the head of IP public relations. "I have a request. I have a friend here who's working his way down the Hudson in a canoe. Yeah, a canoe. Is he a writer? Well, yes, sir, but he's not writing about any ecological impact on the river. . . . [silence] . . . yeah, I just thought I'd help him. He spells his name L-o-u-r-i-e. He's got a canoe, a pack, and a camera, but he won't take any photos. Okay, thanks."

Hartley hangs up. He says, "They're pretty cautious."

We wait while IP checks my story. I wonder exactly how they do "check" me out. Perhaps they have a list of trouble-making environmentalists.

"If they knew about the Riverkeeper, they wouldn't let me through, would they?"

"Nope. They're pretty worried. But at least they *talk* to me. Finch, Pruyn won't even talk to anyone. IP lets me into their plants. They want honest press, and they're pretty up front with their problems. They took me through their operation last year. They said straight out they weren't perfect, that once they had a bacteria problem and for a little while they were discharging bad water into the river, but they fixed it. I even wrote about that. We get along pretty good."

"What does IP do here exactly?" I wonder.

In 1869 the Hudson River Pulp & Paper Company bought the property in Corinth; then in 1898 it joined with nineteen other mills to become International Paper.

"This mill grinds wood for newsprint," Hartley says. "What they make here is coated newsprint like catalogue paper with a glossy finish. It actually requires fewer chemicals than making fine white paper." He says that Maggie often writes articles about the paper industry in the region, but has had a tough time because most companies just won't talk to her. They're afraid of lawsuits and losing their competitive edge.

"Just make sure you don't take any pictures in there. They don't allow that."

Waiting for a call from IP, I pick up a big map of the Adirondack Park and see that the actual border, the Blue Line, runs from Luzerne right along the river and then through Corinth, most of the village being inside the line, and IP just outside and below.

Hartley and I sit in his living room, books and papers scattered everywhere.

"Hartley, you've lived here for a while. How does the Hudson change from here down?"

Hartley has thought a good deal about an answer to this question. He has written stories on the power companies and on the mills and on the water supply stations, too. He seems to love this section of the river, an odd section to love, I think. But he has a corner on the subject, since no one writes about this area much. Since he loves motors, he's particularly fascinated with the turbines in the power company dams. With great enthusiasm he says, "They're state of the art." When he does a story on them, he gets to go under the river into big control rooms.

Holding his delicate hands together as if in prayer, he says, "I'd say that once you get past this series of ponds between the dams, the river becomes navigable for the first time. That's a big change." He means navigable for commercial boats, not canoes.

Ponds? "Did you call them ponds?"

Hartley stands up to explain, "Even before industry came here, there were ponds, large pools of water, separating the waterfalls where later the dams were built. They really are ponds of a sort." Hartley won't leave the phone, which should ring any minute.

"From Corinth to Fort Edward the Hudson is *used*. That's a change. The river is now used for power and drinking water. This first pond above IP is used for power. The next pond, above Spier

Falls, is used for power *and*—for the first time—a water source. People drink the water out of the next pond."

"What do you mean 'used'"?

"IP uses the river to generate steam, and also to process paper. Then the water's treated before it goes back into the river. And right after the IP treatment plant, comes the first town sewage treatment plant along the whole Hudson. After the first sewage plant, you get the first drinking water coming from the river. How about that?"

"So that means Hudson water is completely different after it leaves IP?" Again, this idea of the river now so affected by human industry disturbs me.

Hartley leaves the phone for a quick moment to fetch a few articles he and Maggie have written on the area. Then he's standing close to the phone again.

"Yup. It's pretty interesting. Alum is used to settle the paper sludge out of the water. The settled stuff from the bottom of the tanks is taken out to be processed. The rest of the water goes through a trickling tank with microorganisms that consume the water soluble sugars and starches. Then it goes into another settling tank and the bugs are taken out, after which the water spills out over the top and back into the river. You can go to the Department of Environmental Conservation and ask what are the discharges of this plant. They have to be within certain guidelines. That's what some of the dispute is about."

Finally the phone rings. Hartley waits for three rings, picks it up, says a few things, then hangs up smiling I think, to help me out: "They say it's okay. Let's go."

We leave by the back door. The yard is scruffy with weeds and old motors. Hartley will drive me through to the river below the sewage treatment plant. We load the canoe onto the bed of his pickup, the canoe's end sticking out lawlessly without a red flag. The canoe bounces as if on a trampoline as we hit potholes down through the mill. Miraculously it doesn't fall out. When we pass the guard house, I look for the man who was so nasty last time I was here, but I don't see him.

A man in another pickup waves for us to follow him down into the plant.

"Boy, I'm surprised they let *any* writers in here."

Hartley says, "At first they never called me back when I tried to come in to write stories. At other IP plants and mills, journalists can't get in at all. First, they called me to cover some public service events. And only now, after half a year, have I really developed a rapport with these people. It was hard work."

Hartley believes executives and environmentalists must learn to work together, or nothing will get accomplished. Corporations are thinking more about media manipulation, but that isn't all bad, he says.

Over the Delaware & Hudson tracks, we pass abandoned box cars and piles of junk metal and huge stacks of pulp wood. The smell of sulphur used for the pulp processing is so strong I'd like to escape—to make a quick dash for the river—but I don't want to get shot by any suspicious sharpshooting IP guards. We pass lots of pickup trucks with hard-faced men behind the wheels. The scene reminds me of the lead mines in Missouri that dad and I visited years ago. Something raw is going on here, too, something having to do with the earth. Some mysterious extraction of the elements.

Riding through the IP compound, we pass the town high school. Also old buildings, old bars, closed down, from some former, busier age. Hartley thinks this is the oldest of the IP mills, dating back to around 1890. Then we bump and jog down to the big settling tanks where front-end loaders are moving sour-smelling sludge. Men in hard hats stop work to peer at my canoe, an oddly graceful and delicate thing in so rough a landscape.

The guy in the pickup that we've been following hops out and slams his door.

I say to him, "Thank you so much. This'll save a lot of walking." I'm a little obsequious, but I really am thankful.

A smile softens the man's hard face. He says, "I used to have a canoe. How long you been canoeing?"

I say, "What day is it?"

"Monday."

Strange, but I haven't thought in calendar time since the day Ernie and I left for Lake Tear.

I say, "One week, I guess. But it feels much longer."

The IP man nods. He says, "From here you go just a little ways to

16. The International Paper Company dam at Corinth.

hit another dam. It's called Spier Falls. Stay to the right, so's you catch the boat ramp right there."

Hartley says, "Good Luck," and the two pickups drive slowly up the rough road and out of sight.

I push the Odyssey into a huge pool, what Hartley calls a pond. With a few strokes I glide out from shore, the loud bleeping of backhoes and dump trucks and the roar of the plant's activity fading behind me. The strong sulphur smell lingers.

Eerie transition. Suddenly the river grows as quiet as it was before I reached Luzerne. There are no docks here, no humans in sight, and the pool, the river, is much wider now. The water looks darker, different. I wonder if there are any fish in here.

Mine is an ambitious plan. If I hustle, perhaps I can make Glens Falls by evening. I'm supposed to hook up with Joan Patton of the *Post-Star* at the Feeder Dam and then canoe with her through the seven-mile Feeder canal. She is an avid boater herself and wants a good excuse to run the Feeder while doing a follow-up story on the one she ran on Ernie and me the day we set out for Lake Tear.

From the foot of the second IP dam to Spier Falls Dam will be just over five miles. From there to the Sherman Island Dam will be about four miles. From the foot of that dam to the backwater of the Feeder Dam is about two miles. The dams below this I can avoid by taking the historic Feeder canal that parallels the main river. I had never heard of the Feeder canal until Kunz told me it would be a nice way to avoid four of the nine dams. The Feeder, he said, runs right through the center of the twin cities of Glens Falls and Hudson Falls all the way to the Champlain Canal above Fort Edward. The Feeder was built in the early 1800s literally to "feed" the Champlain Canal so that the Champlain, which runs from Whitehall to Troy, would have enough water to run its two uppermost locks.

I also hope to talk to the Feeder Canal Alliance, a group of historically minded citizens in Glens Falls who are in the process of restoring the canal, which was so important to the industrial development of the area. No one has told me, however, if it's possible to canoe the whole seven miles of the Feeder. Even Joan Patton, who lives in Hartford, New York, about twenty-five miles from Glens Falls and who is a correspondent like Hartley, doesn't know for sure if we can get through, or if there's enough water. I don't know anyone who has traveled it since Kunz and his Boston University group back in the '70s. He told me the canal was in such disrepair in places, they had to take their kayaks out.

So I may end up camping somewhere between here and Lock 7.

A duck and her ducklings follow along shore. The stillness of the river here after Corinth's industry is unsettling. Perhaps the land remains undisturbed because the power companies guard, defend, and protect it under threat of death. But this is beyond quiet, really. The water itself, the surrounding woods, everything has a stillborn feeling about it.

Even the sky is a wounded grey. Hartley had said it was not only going to rain today, but that the thunderstorm would carry hail. Hartley advised me, "If a storm comes in over the river, just get off the water as fast as you can. Storms come in real quick here."

There's a scuffle along the right bank. I can't see any animal, but it sounds like an alligator taking some prey under. A mile downriver from the dam, the smell of sulphur, a typical mill smell, is as intense as it was at the mill itself. Perhaps there are no homes here because no one can stand the smell of rotten eggs.

A jet overhead, high and safe.

This is not the Hudson I paddled through the Gorge. The former Hudson is a memory distanced by what I have witnessed in Corinth, bad smells and rattling backhoes. I'm paddling fast now with so many miles to go, and the wind picks up—a fetid, south wind I hate, bringing in pollution and bad weather from metropolises. Hot and hazy. In three days it'll be the summer solstice, and the direct rays will reach the Tropic of Cancer; then they will turn around and flee southward. But before the days start to shorten, the solstice will mark Melissa's birthday. I must remember to send her flowers.

I pull ashore and put on sunscreen. Being on the river, I have no idea what's happening in the world. I have no idea what's happening even in Glens Falls. I have a touch of news about Corinth, that's all. But there is no rush. Slow it down, Pete. Time on a hot river stretches out before me, and there are moments I feel like Camus's *Stranger*, who in prison learns "the trick of remembering things" and who in solitude finds "that the more I thought, the more details, half-forgotten or malobserved, floated up from my memory. . . . So I learned that even after a single day's experience of the outside world a man could easily live a hundred years in prison. He'd have laid up enough memories never to be bored."

What I would love right now is the north wind, bringing in the cold clear weather of the Adirondacks. I pray for north wind, but fear this trip is doomed in south wind. I push my paddle to drive me forward, but the south wind makes me lazy. I sit on my life vest—no need to wear it. My pack and other gear are not tied in; my camera sits outside its waterproof case. I won't tip over in this easy water, and it sure doesn't look like rain yet.

Strange sight—a motorboat carrying two men approaches, cutting up the silence of the pond. No camps, no docks, no roads, nothing but trees in sight, yet here two fishermen in a motorboat head upriver toward the IP dam to fish. They must have put it in the river at some invisible launching site alongshore. The boat passes at a good distance. Then comes the boat's wake. My Odyssey rolls easily up over my first motorboat wake of the journey, suggesting that much bigger waves from barges, tugs, and container boats will come my way soon enough.

Twenty minutes later I paddle up close to a lone fisherman.

"How's the fishing?"

"Pretty good," says the middle-aged man, his face darkened by the brim of his fishing hat.

"So what are you catching?"

"Mostly rock bass. A couple of black bass, too." This could be a fisherman anywhere in America. His clothes are grey. He's a private sort of fellow. I don't think he wants to speak to anyone much, but I cannot say nothing.

"Is it a pretty good place in the river to fish?"

"Yes."

"Well, see you later." There is no reply.

Paddling on, I will not say over my shoulder what's going through my mind—water water everywhere and I wouldn't eat fish out of this pulp-processed river if you paid me. If I'm thirsty I'm not going to drink it, either, unless my plastic K-mart, five-gallon water jug runs dry, and my mouth goes parched like papyrus.

I heave, lean into it, bathe my paddle deep into black water. When the wind gusts, I throw my whole body forward like an oarsman in a racing scull, drive my body back, its full force behind the paddle, feet braced against the sides of the hull. When I take three strokes on the left, the boat swings around right. I take three strokes on the right, and the boat swings to the left. Take three more strokes, the boat swings. Take three more strokes, the boat swings. Watch the wind, watch the wind. Don't let the boat swing too far in any one direction. That's more work than I could bear.

My feet are hot and sweaty. Today I left my hiking shoes on because there is dam-climbing ahead. I've been hugging the right shore ever since Luzerne. Feels good on the right shore, but it might as well be the left.

Freedom. This is a feeling I haven't felt since I was a child. On a river in a canoe alone. When the Hudson opens out before me like a prairie, I realize the river connects me to every single port on the high seas. I could literally keep paddling from here to Bali or to Sidney or to Bora Bora.

But the Hudson between the dams is not entirely free. It has a strangely restricted feeling. The river of the dams is forgotten or ignored by the general public. Even Robert Boyle's classic book *The Hudson River* jumps from a chapter on the "Adirondack Headwaters" to the subject of the Hudson below Fort Edward. He says little to nothing about this twenty-five-mile section from Luzerne to Glens Falls Feeder Dam, and then he has only a short chapter on the Albany area. Boyle gravitates to the effects of industry on the lower Hudson's ecology. By page 100 he is already taking the reader into what he calls "the mid-Hudson" area not far from my house in Beacon, which is only sixty miles upriver from Manhattan. I wonder what happened to the actual mid-Hudson region, this pond-dam-lock area—this is the ignored mid-river.

Reading Boyle's arguments against pollution makes me realize how much I miss the Adirondack clarity already, and I'm sure glad I am not here at night on this ghostly river between dams. I imagine Ni-Mo monsters emerging at midnight, turbine fish creatures crawling out of the dead water onto the midnight land, into this transition nature, to terrorize naive canoeists in unsuspecting Sierra Design pup tents.

Ann Brewer told me that her children used to send toy boats into the Hudson's headwaters at the Tahawus Club hoping they would sail for 300 miles and reach Manhattan at some future time. But the toys never had a chance after the dams were built, that's for sure.

I search the shore for old logs from the drives, but no remnants can be seen from the river. Lossing, who walked here with his wife 130 years ago, found "the stream was choked with thousands of logs that had come down from the wilderness and lodged there. They lay in a mass, in every conceivable position, to the depth of many feet, and so filled the river as to form a safe, though rough bridge, for us to cross."

Daring duet of husband and wife.

Just before Spier Falls Dam, the river heads east and even north. Aside from the Gorge, this is the only other place in the predominantly arrow-pointing, south-flowing river where the water travels east.

In fact, I am now heading east northeast, the stiffening wind suddenly behind me. Here is the dam ahead, too. I wish I had a sail. I remember at canoe camp how we lashed ponchos together around our paddles and joined three or four canoes on upper Ontario lakes to catch wind and lean back and forget the work of paddling.

Rolling hills rise on either side with grey-blue mist lingering in the trees. When I paddle sideways to the wind, the wind catches the canoe, and for a moment, if the canoe is aimed just right, the canoe itself will act like a small sail giving me a meager forward thrust.

I must get all the way to the right bank in order to take out on the road and hike 700 yards around the dam. During one of Kunz's trips in the '70s, someone spotted his kayaks headed for the dam spillway and came screaming through the woods, "The falls are ahead, pull over. Pull over for Christ's sake!" But Kunz had topographic maps and knew all along exactly where to take out.

"Caution: Dam Ahead. Keep Away" says the old sign hidden in the trees. I take out just before the intake channel, which is roped off with big logs. It's a twenty-foot climb straight up. I stumble back, fall into the river, get wet up to my belt, push up again, and finally get all my gear up, including the paddles, then hoist the canoe, ramming it into some trees, almost puncturing the side. I sure could use Hartley now.

The dam is deserted. The strange hum of high voltage wires numbs the air. I'll make this portage in two steps; first the canoe, then the gear. Along the road with this canoe, I might be on another planet, no cars, no people, just this feeling that the world has come to an end and the machines we've built will hum along forever. In fact, the power plant looks really old and rundown. It's difficult to imagine today that at the time the dam was constructed, it was the largest power dam ever built with private capital and the fourth largest dam in the world. It's also hard to imagine how this deserted plant can be one of Niagara-Mohawk's largest hydro facilities, providing electricity to Troy, Albany, and Schenectady, as well as to nearby Glens Falls.

Originally completed in 1903, the first dam was built of stone. Only three dams, the Aswan across Egypt's Nile, the Croton reservoir dam that helped provide water to New York City, and a dam at Clinton, Massachusetts, were bigger than Spier Falls, which took three years to build because the terrain was so mountainous and rugged. The site was ten miles from Glens Falls. All the materials had to be dragged by horses. Sometimes one load needed a team of twenty. The spring floods nearly ruined the project, and in 1901 an unexpected large pothole was discovered in the riverbed. The construction company halted work for lack of funds until William E. Spier, a Glens Falls entrepreneur, came to the financial rescue.

Burmeister says the hike is only 700 yards around the dam but that it is not so easy to put in below the dam. I have to travel a good distance below for safety. Under the ninety-foot barrage, huge rock ledges are exposed. The water is being channeled to the turbines beneath the dam, and it empties into the river below the rocks in a swirl of whitewater with an underhand twist to it. Black water boils up and bubbles from way below the surface. I have never seen a river do this before. It's as if the river were coming up from some cavern or as if huge turbine manatees were fanning their fins furiously from the deep.

Children's swinging ropes hang from trees along the bank below the dam. I've seen maybe fifty of these ropes since I began my trip. It is only June 18 now, and the kids are not out of school yet, but the ropes make me think of long summer days on the Mississippi and of Mark Twain.

The river looks dirtier in Pond 3. Rocks look browner, filthier. No boats, no people, just that eerie feeling increasing as I sink deeper into the realm of the dams. Next stop will be Sherman Island Dam, also run by Niagara-Mohawk. According to Burmeister, it will be a bitch of a hike around it.

Looking at the map, I see that the road distance from Corinth to Glens Falls or from Corinth to Saratoga is only fourteen miles. But because the river moves so far east on this one section, I will have to travel about four times that distance by river. Lossing and his wife were able to cut down on the miles they traveled here. "We did not follow its course, but took that nearest road, for the day was waning."

I wish I could take a short cut, too, but I'm committed to the river, even though I'm getting pretty tired worrying about Sherman Island just ahead. Between the dam and the power plant there's a canal that might be runnable with permission from authorities, but I'll try to get around the monstrosity of Sherman Island all by myself commando style—without talking to anyone. Built almost seventy years ago, this dam has been rebuilt in the last few years.

That storm of Hartley's might be coming. The leaves turn upward. The sky darkens behind me as I paddle faster through blackest water. More swinging ropes on shore, forlorn and idle. I really don't think I can make Lock 7 today. It's just too late in the afternoon.

The first houses since Corinth come into sight as the sky lets out a light sprinkle. Sherman Island Dam is awesome looking, a huge, box-like, iron-brown barrier stretching across the entire width of the Hudson—an audacity of metal and concrete. I see people up ahead, too, little dark figures scurrying along the rocks to the left of the dam. They seem to be working fast. Perhaps the media has come to witness this historic paddle, or maybe Joan Patton of the Glens Falls paper has alerted some TV station. Yes, by God, they are setting up cameras on tripods. I comb my hair in anticipation of publicity. The storm races up behind me.

Burmy, baby, you have written your book for whitewater people, haven't you? You've forsaken the cowardly canoeist like me. You did a lousy job prepping me for Sherman Island. Panting like an old dog after the hardest carry on my entire trip, I'll tell you what happened.

First (and this was not your fault, Burmeister), those men ahead disappeared just before I landed near the mile-long sluiceway at Sherman Island. They were not from the press, but were simply workers on the dam trying to beat the storm. They probably didn't even notice this little canoe racing toward them.

Second, when I pulled ashore, not only was there no one around, but I found myself *inside* a high wire fence, in a place I obviously did not belong, and with no one around to give me permission. I threw my Bills bag over my shoulders, my canoe onto my head, and raced all hundred pounds along the dirt road that parallels the canal and the river, praying at each rest stop that no one would spot me and tell me to get the hell out of there. I ran and stopped so many times I couldn't breathe. When I got to the end of the road, I had to duck into the bushes to avoid trucks passing down to the power plant, and then gather my gear and canoe in two separate trips, and also run through a field well past the plant along the high bank of the river and down a steep and long hill to the water way below the dam. Once, I fell sixty or seventy feet, my Bills bag and I turning somersaults into a patch of thorns!

When finally I got to the water's edge with both the canoe and the gear, I listened to the roar of the power plant for a long time before I had the energy to shove out into the river again, cursing power dams.

Why I wasn't spotted I'll never know.

After Sherman Island, the sound of cars grows loud from shore, and the river makes some wide bends. Docks with pleasure boats begin.

I lean back and lie on the gunwales as it starts to sprinkle. The rain is warm and I won't bother to put on my $200 fancy Gore-Tex Eastern Mountain Sports rain gear that I bought especially for this trip. I don't need rain gear. Besides, I like to get wet.

So let the rain come. I've made it over my last big dam.

Just before the Northway bridge (so that's where the sound of traffic has been coming from) I pass a very wide bay in the river. This is the Big Bay that leads to the Big Boom. Finally I am here where the great river drive boss Jack Donohue brought his logs after a season of river driving. I imagine him and his men standing on top of a million logs blanketing this wide bay. They hold their long pike poles over their shoulders. They are tired from months of cold, wet work, but the boss is happy because this year he made it the 100 miles through the Gorge to the Boom. He knows of course that every spring brings different weather, and perhaps next year because of a drought the drive might take him two seasons. But for now I imagine that he's smiling, too, because very soon he will return to his home in North River, to his family.

Under the Northway bridge (I've driven over this bridge a thousand times but never noticed the Hudson before), a big old ragged armchair sits near the edge of the water on a pebbly beach facing the river. Some man or woman sits here fishing or just takes in the Hudson while a zillion cars and trucks race stupidly overhead. Where is that guy today? I want to give him a hug. This chair is like the chairs around Newcomb, assembled along the bank when Ernie and I first came out of the wilderness of Tahawus to those hunting cabins— chairs for congregating at the river's edge.

It has been five hours since I left IP. I pull under a big maple while the sky dumps its rain. I watch two boys playing with a golden retriever in the water with a stick; then I paddle in more drizzle. As I round the gentle bends and move through swampy islands (with a kind of southern feeling), I see piles of dark-brown slag in the middle of the river. Trees grow right out of the slag. Gulls have taken over some of these slag islands. No motorboat could run in here because the slag piles are just under the surface. I cannot see them until I'm upon them. My canoe scrapes so easily. I wonder what these piles of slag are doing in the river.

Then finally—Yahoooo—the Feeder Dam lies dead ahead past many more piles of slag. A dam was here in Lossing's day. One hundred and thirty years ago he referred to the nearby village as State Dam.

We were now fairly out of the wilderness in which the Hudson rises, and through which it flows for a hundred miles . . . The dam was about two and a-half miles above Glen's Falls. It had been constructed about fifteen years before, to furnish water for the feeder of the canal which connects the Hudson river and Lake Champlain. It was sixteen hundred feet in length; and the mills near it have attracted a population sufficient to constitute quite a village, named State Dam. About two miles above this dyke was the Great Boom, thrown across the river for the purpose of catching all the logs that come floating from above.

I pull up to shore just left of the dam. A man with a baseball hat says there was a journalist here not ten minutes ago and that I just missed her. She waited for three hours, he says. She left a note. He hands it to me. The note asks me to call Joan Patton tonight if I'd like her to go with me down the Feeder.

I'll set up camp here and see if I can arrange it by phone, perhaps at that little building up the hill there. Tomorrow I'll paddle the seven miles through Glens Falls, paralleling the main river, and into the Champlain Canal, then a few miles down the Champlain to Lock 7, where the big canal joins the Hudson.

Lossing realized State Dam was the dividing line between the wild and the tame. This is true today. "We have taken leave of the wilderness," he wrote. "Henceforth our path will be where the Hudson flows through cultivated plains . . . by the cottages of the humble, and the mansions of the wealthy; by pleasant hamlets, through thriving villages, ambitious cities, and the marts of trade and commerce."

I too now take leave of the wilderness. From here on, it's people people people, and their marts of trade and commerce.

9

The Feeder Canal

Brian Kunz and his outdoor friends in New Hampshire last winter had described for me their love of river trips. Addicts for solitude down nature's watery byways, they were similarly addicted on long canoe journeys to the camaraderie of meeting strangers en route. When Kunz told me about his trips down the Hudson, it was as if he had made those three trips not twenty years ago but only last week. He could still smell the river, see the faces, and recall in loving detail the kindness of the people who gave him drinking water from their taps and told him river stories.

I liked what he and his friends had said about transporting all their gear with them, food, water, a change of dry clothes, and choosing a campsite wherever they decided to halt for a night. With a canoe, they were like snails carrying shelter on their backs. I, too, am like a snail in my desire after today's hard strokes and dam-busting carries to find a resting place, get cozy, drink a bucket of coffee, pitch my tent in dwindling dusk, drive away mosquitoes with a powerful night fire, then drop to sleep and let the final curtain of darkness descend.

I pull my canoe into some bushes and walk up a short, dirt road to a tiny cinder-block building. Behind the building is a house with a nicely mown lawn sweeping down a steep hill to a dock jutting into the Hudson. Chairs of all kinds sit facing the river: wire patio chairs, winged Adirondack chairs, canvas-backed director's chairs, and a few old car seats, too.

A handwritten notice pegged to the front door of the building says, "Closed Daily between 12 and 1," which indicates this is a commercial building of some sort. If I weren't so tired, perhaps I wouldn't knock here, preferring instead to hike up the road to someone's home.

The door opens. The light inside is artificial. My eyes have been leached by the hazy paddle from Sherman Island Dam, and they hurt as they adjust to phosphorescence. I see maybe four or five people bending over what look like Bunsen burners on counters littered with—is this right?—teeth: human mandibles, maxillae, and loose molars cluttering the counters. Everyone is dressed in a white lab coat, each busy, squirrelishly scraping and scratching at human teeth. The place has an odd smell, chemical and caustic. The buzz of whirling grinders is the unmistakable sound of a dentist's office.

What's going on here? I want to ask, but instead I inquire about a phone. Everyone seems friendly enough and not particularly surprised by my appearance, almost as if they've been expecting me.

"The phone's right there, but it don't work too good," chuckles the oldest man in the room. He has a big bald head, thick glasses, and a wide grin of pearly teeth. He is leaning over an immense magnifying glass attached to a bare lightbulb. He's short and thin, perhaps seventy, and he's wearing thick safety glasses, which add to the overall Martian effect. He holds a dentist's pick in one hand and, yes, a set of false teeth in the other. He goes on scraping those teeth under the magnifying glass. Then he turns to the grinding wheel spinning next to him and grinds the outer edge of an incisor. All around the room there are quick movements, heads bowed intently over intricate work, an occasional glance up at me. Everyone appears to be in some hurry.

I haven't even taken off my bright yellow life vest yet. If they were to take note of me, perhaps they would think I looked a little bedraggled myself with this week-old beard and sleepless eye sockets, all my clothes sopped from the rain.

"I'm the guy canoeing the river." The voice in my throat sounds hollow.

Everyone glances up from busywork; then their eyes return to the teeth.

"Yup. We heard you was coming," says the old man still working hard under the bright light. "Read about you in the paper last week. Expected you earlier."

He stops work, takes off his safety glasses, says his name is Pete Bishop. He shakes my hand warmly, then introduces me to his two sons and his daughter-in-law. "It's a family operation," he says, then puts his glasses back on and goes back to work.

When he talks, I get a glimpse of something pink in the corner of his mouth, as if his own false teeth don't fit him quite right.

"Want a beer? I was about to take a break anyway." This time he gets up and leaves his workstation.

"Thanks, but I don't drink."

"I'm too old to worry about it, I guess. I've got Coke if you want."

Pete Bishop disappears into a back room, brings out a can of beer for himself and a soda for me and waits for me to make my call to the *Post-Star*, which I do, all the while feeling uncomfortable in the presence of hundreds of half-finished mouths. I have stumbled into, of all places on this earth, a false-teeth factory, what Bishop calls a dental lab, and not just any dental lab, either, but apparently one of the most productive dental labs north of Albany.

"There's another guy in Glens Falls who works all alone, and a few places that do crowns, but our lab is the only place in town that does *removables*."

Bishop and his family work for dentists all the way from Saratoga to Plattsburgh. He does work for nearby prisons and for people up and down the Hudson. He himself is in the process of retiring and has given the business to his family, but he keeps coming into work anyway. "I guess I just can't stop. Force of habit."

"So," says Bishop's daughter-in-law, "Why do you want to go to Manhattan?" This is a popular question. (Suppressed laughter comes from the bowed, studious heads.)

"Well, I'm not really sure. I guess because it's never been done before."

"So where do you live?"

"Beacon."

Silence, except for drillers and grinders.

"It's near Fishkill. South of Poughkeepsie." Bishop has no idea where Beacon is. I add, "It's on the river."

17. Dave and Pete Bishop.

"Naturally," says Pete. "You're *supposed* to be on the river. Everybody should live on this river. Anyone who likes this river is okay with me."

He tells me he's spent his whole life on the banks of the Hudson and he knows every "setback, nook and cranny" from here up to Sherman Island. These are the nine miles of river he loves most of all.

"This is *Pete's River*, you know," says Bishop. It turns out the Bishop family has been here for quite a few generations. Pete's father, his grandfather, and his uncle were all carpenters in this area.

The "pond" above Feeder Dam, he says, is the "Bishops' playground." In fact, Pete's grandfather helped build Feeder Dam, and just before the war, Pete's father operated a trout hatchery along the river until one day in a thunderstorm, the rising river sent the two- and three-pound trout over the top, and he lost nine thousand of his best fish. After that, he gave up the trout business altogether.

Pete's oldest son says, "When I was in the navy, dad sent me pictures of the river. And it'd always be the same picture. Right from down there, a Hudson sunset. Every time my friends picked up a package or letter for me, they'd say 'Well, Bishop, more pictures of the river, eh?'"

Pete's brother Rod, who is "rigging up a program for the lab" on his computer, walks in and says, "You should live on the river, that's right, unless you got PCBs in your river, like I have." Rod is almost as genial as his brother, but he has opened up a can of environmental worms, for now I have entered PCB territory. It was Bob Boyle of Cold Spring, in an article in *Sports Illustrated* in 1970, who sounded the first warning about PCB-contaminated fish. Boyle found PCBs in fish from the East, West, and Gulf Coasts, but the striped bass from the Hudson River were the most contaminated.

Between 1946 and 1975, a few miles below Feeder Dam, the GE plants at Fort Edward and Hudson Falls deposited about 600,000 pounds of PCBs into the river as waste products. PCBs (*polychlorinated biphenyls*) are complex chemicals used, among other things, as insulators in the manufacture of heavy electrical equipment. In 1976 they were barred as toxic.

The Fort Edward area was the site of the Hudson's biggest environmental disaster. The Niagara-Mohawk Power Company decided in 1973, without much forethought yet with the permission of the DEC, to take out the dam below Baker's Falls in order to build a new dam. What they hadn't considered was that the PCBs that GE had thrown into the river for almost thirty years had found a resting home on the upriver side of the dam, and when the dam came out, the carcinogenic PCBs went washing downriver. That spring, a flooding Hudson spread the contaminants all the way from Glens Falls to Manhattan, 200 miles away. But the "hot spots," the places of the heaviest PCB concentration, were on the forty-mile Champlain Canal section of the Hudson River between Fort Edward and Troy.

Since 1973 the fish feeding on the contaminated plants and bottom deposits have become inedible, ruining—among other things— the ancient fishing industry on the lower Hudson. In 1975 the state banned fishing on the upper Hudson River. In 1976 General Electric and the state's Department of Environmental Conservation (DEC) agreed to spend $7 million to assess potential remedies to the Hudson contamination. Some dredging has occurred, but GE and many locals think dredging is the least desirable alternative and that it might be more effective to destroy the PCBs biologically instead, or simply to let them lie where they are. In 1989 a renewed $280 million plan to dredge PCB-laden sediments was announced, but more evaluation will have to happen first. Some dredging has taken place since, but mostly what is happening is talk, debate, argument, and planning. Dredging of the canal has stopped until certain difficult questions are resolved. Bridges have been closed, and anger is flying high.

"So how does it feel to have those PCBs so close to you?" I ask Rod.

How could I *not* ask the question? I've been concerned about traveling the next forty miles of river, a section that has gotten a lot of press in the past few years as a highly poisoned part of the Hudson. I've feared pulling my canoe ashore in the toxic muck. The Hudson River has had bad press all over the world. A friend from Australia told me that school children study the Hudson as an example of what might happen to all the rivers of the world if we let pollution reign.

Rod says, "I'm too old to worry about it. I been here for so long. I didn't *catch* anything yet." (This is said as if a PCB were a virus and not a chemical.) His determined nonchalance reminds me of the asbestos mine workers I once interviewed in Morrisville, Vermont. I met a handful of angry men at the fire station in town, who had all been laid off because the Eden mine was closing down. One man threw a piece of asbestos at me and said, "There, does that stuff look like it could kill you? You're not afraid of *that*, are you?" I said no and handled the silky fibers gently.

The Vermonters said, "No one ever dies of asbestos. Tom here worked forty years in the mine and he's fine." But it came out that one man who also had worked for decades in the mine was indeed in the hospital with what might be asbestosis of the lungs. Like those miners, many people in Glens Falls, Hudson Falls, and Fort Edward have a similar anger about "outsiders" coming in to announce some environmental disaster that must be cleaned up.

Pete Bishop says, "We disagree with dredging the PCBs. I think they should be left alone. You only make things worse when you stir it all up." This is the Glens Falls debate: to dredge and make leak-proof landfills to store the stuff, or not to dredge. Tomorrow I will pass the first big PCB landfill, where the Feeder joins the Champlain Canal on the other side of Hudson Falls.

Adding mysterious fuel to this already explosive debate comes the latest news. Recent studies are showing that fish are much more contaminated in this stretch of the river than they were in the 1980s— indicating there is another, unknown source of PCBs. As I write, the *New York Times* is reporting (July 18, 1993) that GE has agreed this week to "stem a new flow of PCB's into the Hudson . . . that the company was committed to correcting any damage caused to the river" and that "A company investigation found that 1,500 cubic yards of sediment contaminated with PCB's had been deposited at some point in a now-abandoned paper mill near the General Electric site . . . [and] were being carried through groundwater into the nearby river."

Pete's son Dave is leaving with a delivery of teeth. Dave is the runner, the driver for the family business. He's a restless young fellow with long scraggly backwoods hair and a ragged mustache. His dad says Dave should go with me tomorrow when I paddle the Feeder because he's done it before a few times and he might be able to help.

Dave, like his whole family, talks with that north-woods accent I love, sounding vaguely French Canadian, like John Bennett from Lake Luzerne. He says, "I been as far as the toxic dump, almost the whole way. It took about five hours, and we had to take out at least three times. Some places you can't take out, and you got to go back then hike around some old locks in the barge canal. Last time, my dad picked me up at the PCB dump, or toxic whatever it is. It used to be a regular dump. In them days it wasn't fenced off. I used to walk on the dirt road right past the dump."

The Bishop family, it turns out, are perhaps the friendliest people I'll ever meet not only on the Hudson but anywhere on the planet. Others tell me the same thing: the Bishops are famous in the region for their loyalty and generosity. Especially Pete. It's as if that constant smile on Pete's face derives from the same kindness genes he has passed on to his family. Within a few minutes I feel as comfortable here as I do in my own kitchen.

"So how long have you been making teeth?" I ask Pete.

"As a teenager I worked in a dental lab before the service. Doing what? Same thing I'm doing now. Making teeth, bridges, and crowns.

"My real name is Leroy, but the guy I worked for called me Pete. I don't think he liked the name Leroy. That's how I got my name. I been making teeth as a living since 1946."

The only kid who didn't work in the dental lab for long was Pete's daughter Sue. Why did she quit?

"She found the work boring."

When Pete makes even the most simple statements like this one, he jerks his head back, casts his eyes to the floor, and smiles.

Pete works only from a dentist's prescription. It's the law that he can't "work for the public directly." In fact, when I ask him how much it costs to get a set of these teeth, he says dentists won't tell him how much they charge. The only way he knows some prices is when patients tell him what they paid. But he thinks a set of uppers will be $800 or so.

"Some people think the family must be making a mint because the price is so high." But Bishop is forced to keep his prices low so dentists will not find other labs.

How many of these dentures can he produce in a day?

"Each one of us can do one or two, but we're more likely to be doing many sets of teeth at any one time. And we've got to charge as much as we can for this work, or we'd be doing such workloads we'd never have time to enjoy our lives." It seems Bishop works all day and into the evening. Retired or not, he is a devilishly hard worker, but he also knows how to play.

"The dentist sends us an impression." Pete lifts the pink plastic cast of a mouth with holes where the teeth will go. "This," he says, "will be a full upper. This man's got his lower teeth, but we're going to make him some uppers."

Pete reaches down and pulls out a drawer of teeth neatly arrayed in rows. He has boxes and boxes of them: "We got all different shapes, all the way from the whitest and a real light color, down to an ickier brown color. Depends on what kind of teeth we're trying to match. Some got little lines in 'em. We make 'em look as real as possible. We even got teeth here that look cracked and old."

Pete's older son shows me a set he's working on, upper and lower. He snaps them together, dentures snapping in midair suggesting an entire skeleton.

"Here's what the guy's got in his mouth and here's what we're adding. He'll try 'em on [here he snaps them open and shut so they click in the air] and he'll say, 'Ah, them's is good,' and then we're in business."

Pete's brother tells me that he and his son went through the Hudson River Gorge one time and nearly died. Of all the canoes that day, his was the only one that made it through. He says they had "a hell of a time." The canoe got turned around and went backward. They tipped over a few times, hit sandbars and ricocheted off rocks. From his description it sounds as if he and his son are lucky to be alive.

When I began this canoe trip, I never thought I would stroll off the river into a nether world of dentures, of artificial light, magnifying glasses, Bunsen burners and beakers, teeth and plastic jaws of all sizes lying about the cluttered tables like paleontologists' specimens, so many sets of teeth in various stages of being fit to order for the food-chomping populace of the North Country. If it were not for the smell of chemicals, this scene could be another lab from twenty years ago when I worked for Margaret Leakey at the Centre for Prehistory and Palaeontology at the Nairobi Museum in Kenya. About to study anthropology, my apprentice's job was to sort the exhumed skeletons of Mau Mau victims, rather gruesome work.

The sky loses light fast. Pete insists I camp on his lawn down by the river. I ask him how close the nearest grocery store is, and he says, "You going to get groceries just for something to eat tonight?" I say I need to stock up on some supplies.

"Heck, I'll drive you up to the Price Chopper later." He says this as casually as if I were just another one of his sons. "And I don't want any of your lip, neither," he jokes. "You're eatin' supper at my house tonight, and that's all there is to it."

"I'm a bit of a mess right now, but I could use a good meal."

"Well, you're comin' over to my house and take a shower, do your shit and shave . . . and whatever."

His older son says, "But he's trying to camp out, dad, and you're making it very difficult for the guy."

They laugh. The son continues, "When a buddy of mine got out of the navy he was traveling around the country. He came here to camp out, but we made it pretty hard for him. He kept coming in for dinner and everything."

"Listen," Pete says, "You're on *my* river now . . . "

"Okay, okay, I'm not arguing," I say. "Thank you very much."

"Tomorrow," he says, "You can go down the Feeder with my son."

The rain has stopped. I take a long shower. Pete's house is air-conditioned, which feels nice in this muggy evening. Pete's wife, Shirley, grew up in Glens Falls and says it's getting too big. There's just too much development now. It's gotten so you don't know anyone anymore and you have to shop at the malls. It's the old story in America.

Over a spaghetti dinner, Pete asks me how I got around the dams in Corinth, and I talk about the day. He wants to know the details of the day's twenty-five-mile paddle, which he thinks is a "good chunk of river" considering how much I had to go through with all those dams.

Then he talks about his river. He says he hopes people aren't dumping so much raw sewage into his river anymore. He knew a guy who used to hang his privy right out over the river. Pete's own father used to hate the smell from the paper mill sludge.

"The sludge was so thick, it could almost stop a motor dead in the water. My father would be heading downriver when the methane gas building up in the sediment would rise and pop on the surface and nearly knock him over."

Pete thinks the river has gotten much cleaner since they stopped dumping the paper sludge in it. He admits, however, that there are occasional oil spills from the Niagara-Mohawk power plants. Recently, a thousand gallons of oil spilled out of the turbines at Sherman Island. When that happens, the ducks get black with oil. Pete thinks there are many more spills from the dams than people know about.

"I suspect it's only because of new regulations that the companies even report some of them." Pete also thinks when the power dams change the level of the water, it's hard for the fish to spawn. "Bass just don't lay their eggs in deep enough water to survive the drop."

Perhaps no one in America relives the days of logging in the Big Boom as much as the Bishop family. They live right on top of the old lumbering operations. Pete shows me *Glens Falls Today: A Regional Commentary, Spring 1987,* in which I read that Big Bend, Big Bay, and Big Boom are "wonderfully alternative terms tossed around by area residents" but "are most mysterious to the uninitiated."

It has taken me six days from Newcomb to Glens Falls, but in the days of the big drives when the spring floods broke the ice and the river was running well, under the best of circumstances a log might take only two days to complete the same journey.

Pete doesn't remember the days of the big thirteen-foot logs; he recalls only the more recent, smaller, four-foot pulp logs. These are the logs (the last pulp logs came down to Pete's house in 1950) that people today remember piling up behind the Big Boom.

The bigger logs have not come down the Hudson since 1924. That's when loggers used to cut trees into what was known as the "Adirondack" or "Glens Falls Standard." This standard was unique to the Hudson River. The dimensions were nineteen inches in diameter inside the bark at the small end, and thirteen feet, four inches in length.

In those days Glens Falls was the lumber capital of the East. By the early 1830s, however, the trees around Glens Falls had all been cut, and rather than move the mills upriver, logs were floated down to the Big Boom, which used to cross the Hudson at the very beginning of the slag piles I saw today just after the Northway bridge. Logs collected in the river for two or three miles above the Big Boom, which was constructed from huge timbers bolted together in fours like rafts connected by chains. The Boom was 600 feet long and 4 feet wide. It could hold 2 million logs. In 1851, its first year of use, lumbermen guided 25 million board feet of lumber through the Boom. In 1871—its peak year of operation—214 million board feet of lumber passed through the Boom. The Boom survived many floods, but in 1859 it let go, and 500,000 logs were scattered the forty-five miles down to Albany.

The Boom held in the flood of April 1869, but then came the 1913 flood, remembered now as the Great One, when the junction boom, where the sorting of the logs was done below the Big Boom, broke and sent a mass of logs downriver that took out many bridges. Some of these logs were found in New York harbor with the Finch, Pruyn mark still on them.

In the days of the Big Boom, when the logs piled and jammed for miles upriver, each log had to be separated from the logs of other companies by sending it down one of a series of chutes below the boom. This way, the logs would end up at the right sawmills. The loggers separated the branded logs with pike poles. Like the Boom itself, these smaller chutes were built from chained logs anchored in the river on the slag I saw today.

Since the days of the Big Boom, winter ice has sheared off the tops of the slag piles, which makes Pete especially fond of this section of the river. Unsuspecting boaters use his private shoreline near the Feeder Dam to launch their powerboats. He keeps erecting signs, and the motorboaters keep taking them down. In a fury of ignorance, they fire up their engines and head straight out into Pete's River full bore. In a matter of seconds, they shear the pins off their propellers on the submerged rock. Not only are there five invisible slag piles just off Bishop's dock, there are also piers and buried machinery of all kinds. Pete likes it this way. He says the slag keeps things nice and quiet.

Apparently, the supervisor of Queensbury (that is the township that wraps around the city of Glens Falls, a town, by the way, that has doubled in the last ten years from 18,000 to 36,000 people and which draws its drinking water from the pool above Sherman Island Dam) came to Pete and asked if he thought the town should invest in taking out the slag piles. Pete thought it was a waste of money. "Besides, this is historic slag!" he says with delight.

No wonder Pete calls it his river. He lives at the very center of what made the upper Hudson so profitable in the nineteenth century. Where his house stands, there used to be a boarding house for the rivermen. The rugged history of the region vibrates in Pete's stories.

Shirley tells me how they used to swim in the Feeder. She would drop her little son into the fast-moving water at the start of the canal after tying a rope "onto the little nine-month-old bundle," and Pete would catch him a few yards down-canal. Pete adds, "My grandfather and grandmother—everyone—our whole family always swam in the canal."

"Nine months old?" I doubt I'd dump my one-year-old in the canal. "Did your son like to be dunked in the canal?"

"Oh yes," says Pete. "We were always throwing him in the river when he was in diapers, ha ha ha."

Pete adds, "Shirley and I often talk about parents nowadays. They let their kids go right by 'em. We always did things with our kids. Today, parents don't care. We always went camping with the whole family."

Shirley asks, "Are you married, Peter?"

"Yes. But I took my wedding ring off."

"So you could have a little fun along the way?" She laughs her deep throaty laughter.

"And canoe better," I say. "The ring rubs on the paddle."

"Heck," says Pete, "Rod and I used to climb those logs piled up at Big Boom, and then we'd find a hole and dive under them logs and come up another hole. It was great."

After dinner, Pete walks me through mosquito swarms down to the river to my pitched tent. Here's my noble canoe turned on its stomach by the river, paddles beneath, the loud Hudson rushing over Feeder Dam. When I leave my canoe for a few hours and then come back to it, I'm surprised how much I missed my sleek companion. Seeing it again always makes me feel good.

Two woodpeckers drive their beaks fiercely into a dead tree.

Pete has been smoking a cigarette. "I shouldn't smoke these things," he says with a grimace. He has brought a big bottle of kerosene down from the house, which he now dumps on top of a few logs from a nearby shed. The logs are placed carefully inside a wide circle of stones; obviously there have been many Bishop campfires here.

The night is black, the bugs bad, and when Pete throws his cigarette onto the wet logs and the fire jumps up like a red, hot jack-in-the-box, those six swinging ropes hanging side by side from the big old tree near the dock are suddenly visible like orange snakes or jungle lianas. On the whole river, I will never see so many swim ropes in one place.

In a blaze of kerosene, Pete's head is illuminated. The dry logs catch easily. Pete and I stand back, then stand closer around the sobering fire. He can talk about the river forever. "My mom still tells a story about them old logging days. When she was a girl, she and a friend up in Big Bay in springtime went swimming and afterwards sat on what they thought was just a bundle of junk under a tarpaulin. Well, what they was sittin' on was a dead logger who'd fallen in and drowned and was just lying there along the river waitin' for the coroner to come pick him up and get buried."

The night frogs make a kind of screaming sound, not like frogs I've ever heard before. A few miles in the distance, the Northway trucks whine the night through.

Ten minutes after Pete leaves, his son Dave drives up in some

18. Camping on Pete's River at Feeder Dam.

muffler-less car. He's had dinner with his wife, and he's drinking a beer. He is a little wired and says he "don't want to talk about his lady," who is pregnant, and with whom I suspect he has just quarreled.

As the second-youngest Bishop, Dave is in his early twenties. I can tell by the slightly manic joy in his eyes that he drinks a good deal and probably has gotten into some trouble as a kid. Maybe still does. He keeps coaxing me to go *over the dams* with him and not down the Feeder as I planned. He says, "Everything's all fenced off above Cooper's Cave, but if you want some adventure, we could . . . " and proposes an intricate scheme to get over the dams and over the falls. He says, "No problem." He has climbed all over this dam and the next one down, too, and no one ever hassles him. But I remember well what Ernie taught me about the dynamics of dams, and I worry about Dave's plan.

Just outside the lab entrance, Dave's old motorcycle sits forlornly on cinder blocks. Rundown and rusting trucks and cars in various stages of disrepair lie in the dark, waiting to be fixed. Dave is a wild, kind kid, who will most likely never finish work on his vehicles, never get them on the road, and one day they will be carted away to the junk heaps of Queensbury. He is the kind of son you love but you worry about because that bright energy in his words and all those manic good ideas can lead to real trouble when it's partying time. He reminds me of an Adirondack version of myself twenty years ago. He's the kind of young man who might head out for Alaska or the Yukon on some gold rush if that were something reckless-hearted people still did. He helps dredge up my wilder days, making me happy I am not so wild anymore. There is peace in settling down. If I were still drinking and I had no family at home, I would be standing here by this fire with my own six-pack ready to hightail it out for Alaska, full of that restive anxiety, hair-brained schemes, and indecision.

Dave is really excited about going with me tomorrow. He says, "I wish I could do what you're doing. And my father wishes it, too. He loves this darn river."

My trip must look pretty glamorous. But I'm not really a nomad. I am a temporary schemer, a fugitive, a responsible refugee, a nomad for a month. No longer is it a world of endless choices for me, no matter how fortunate I am to make this journey that most people only dream about.

Dave seems lonely. The night, the frogs, the fire draw his sadness out.

But I love campfires, and this is my first campfire since Ernie and I were together on the trail to Marcy. How wonderful are the orange flicker, the bright cinders dying into the cooling air beside the great river, the smoke stinging my eyes not far below the Great Boom, a hundred yards from the site of one of the many old sawmills that used to run along this shore. I feel so alive, in tune with something I don't get a chance to feel when I'm at home.

Dave Bishop calls the Feeder canal the "barge canal" for a good reason. Today I'll re-create the old barge routes through the adjacent towns of Glens Falls and Hudson Falls and then move into the more substantial Champlain Canal, through Lock 8, a summit lock, down to Lock 7 where the canal rejoins the Hudson River in Fort Edward. Kunz had said I might want to take the Feeder not only because it would save some difficult carrying around four mammoth power dams but because "there's so much wonderful history associated with it."

It is about nine in the morning when Pete and Dave walk me and my Odyssey and Dave's heavy green plastic kayak the few hundred feet from the lab to the start of the Feeder canal. On the north end of Feeder Dam, not far from the dental lab, is a high cement structure with valves that control the flow of water into the Feeder. Two boys are jumping into the spillway, letting their pale bodies be carried by the frothing water rushing into the Feeder. They climb out on a ladder perhaps fifty feet down the Feeder, then run back to the cement wall and jump in again, screaming.

Joan Patton of the *Post-Star* is here with her light, one-woman cedar canoe. Like Forrest Hartley, she's a correspondent for the paper and works out of her home. She too is fairly new to writing, and today's excursion excites her because she loves canoeing and will enjoy writing this follow-up article to the one that was published the day Ernie and I left for Lake Tear. Joan is a large woman with a ready smile and kind, Flemish face. She has had a bout with cancer, but her excitement about today's paddle outshines any lingering horror of chemotherapy. I'm a little nervous because she says a photographer is supposed to take pictures somewhere along this seven-mile barge canal. Unlike those false alarms at Lake Tear when I heard an anonymous airplane combing the sky behind the clouds or at Sherman Island where the men with no TV cameras vanished from the beach, this will be my journey's first real coverage.

In certain places on either side of the narrow canal, I find the old towpaths for the mules that pulled the barges. Before the age of engines, a team of mules or horses would pull the barges while the line driver walked along the towpath and tended the animals. Pete's wife's mother's uncle used to be a horse driver for Feeder barges.

To understand the Feeder, I had to grasp the history of canals in

New York, which begins with the construction of the more famous western branch of the Erie Canal in 1817 from the Hudson River city of Waterford to the Great Lakes near Niagara Falls. This western route opened the interior of the nation and stimulated economic development in the state. Less well known was the simultaneous opening of the Champlain Canal from Whitehall on Lake Champlain to Waterford, just north of Troy, where the Mohawk joins the Hudson. Like the Erie, the Champlain Canal also was begun in 1817. Boat traffic passed through in 1823, two years before the Erie was complete. The relatively short Feeder canal was built in Glens Falls so the Champlain system could function.

From the beginning of the Champlain Canal project, it was hard to keep up the water level in the summit of the canal, a twelve-mile stretch roughly from Fort Ann to Fort Edward. So a channel was dug from the Hudson River to divert water through Glens Falls to the section between the canal's two highest locks. The Hudson actually "feeds" the whole Champlain system enough water to run all the locks north to Lake Champlain and those south to Troy.

To understand why this is necessary, I had to imagine that for a boat to travel from Fort Edward to Whitehall, it would first have to climb a hill and then gradually float down the other side of that watery hill. It was not possible, so a series of locks had to be built to lift the boat up and back down again along the way. It was hard to keep enough water in the stretch at the highest or summit level. So the water had to come from a high place on the Hudson River, which would insure a good supply of water for the canal even in long periods without rain.

When the Feeder was first built, it was simply that, a channel to feed the Champlain system. Area leaders soon recognized the value of opening the Feeder to canal boats that could bring in supplies and, more important, take local products like lumber, stone, lime, fine black marble, and paper to market. By 1830 the first boat traveled on the Feeder from Glens Falls through a system of wooden locks into the Champlain Canal, and on to the cities in the south.

In 1834 the Feeder was improved to make the canal more serviceable. Feeder Dam was raised and strengthened, and the locks were rebuilt of hammered dressed stone. A complex system of underground bypass culverts was designed to maintain a flow of water to

the Champlain Canal even when the locks were closed to allow boat passage.

In recent years residents of Glens Falls and Hudson Falls have joined together to restore the old canal by forming the Glens Falls Feeder Canal Alliance, which hopes to preserve the land around the Feeder as a public park.

Dave says there are thirteen mini-locks or combines on the canal that will be hard to get around. The short carries around them often are difficult because the towpath has been obliterated by thick vegetation, and in some places we'll have to hike our boats through people's backyards. The hardest part will come at the end of the seven-mile canal, just after the PCB dump, before we reach the Champlain Canal itself above Lock 8. Even Dave does not know what we'll find down there.

Pete shakes my hand and says good-bye. He starts to walk off but turns and says, smiling of course, "What's your last name, anyway?"

Pete has brought his camera. He takes a photo as our three boats launch away down the gentle canal. Not since Ernie's leaving have I felt such a pang for a departing river acquaintance.

Paddling along the narrow canal away from Pete Bishop and his river and suddenly finding ourselves within a matter of a half hour deep into the city of Glens Falls, unable to see the city and only hearing it in the distance from this channel of wild vegetation overgrowing the nineteenth-century stone walls, is truly like entering some enchanted version of my river trip. Birds chirp ebulliently from thick trees overhanging the bank. The day is fresh, although it will turn muggy and fetid by noon. I could be punting on Oxford's Cherwell River in July, or walking along the pond in Saint James Park. There's something vaguely civilized about this part of my journey. Yet ragged too. In fact, canal paddling is a nice combination of urbanity and rudeness. The water is slow but steady as it heads for the Champlain Canal, seven miles away.

At one point I try to turn my eighteen-foot canoe around mid-canal to look back to see why Joan has slipped behind. I must make sure I'm standing quite still before I sweep hard on the right and pry quickly on the left. Then I alternate these two movements fast enough to spin the canoe. If I don't perform this fast enough, any momentum I build up in the way of forward movement will slam me into the stone walls of the canal. Joan's light, little canoe and Dave's kayak are much better suited for this kind of narrow-channel paddling.

Joan has stopped to take a photograph; then she races up to meet us, and we continue. Dave has taken off his shirt. His chest and arms are bronze. When I take off my shirt, he says, "Man, you're pale. Don't you ever take off your shirt?"

Great piles of logs sit along the canal, and old cranes rust in the slanting morning light. When we reach the center of the city, the busy traffic seems muted somehow from down here in the canal. Just before Glen Street, the very center of the city, we find a little path and pull our boats out of the water. We leave them beside the canal in the parking lot of the Finch, Pruyn office building. This is the most historic section of the canal perhaps because it was right here that Abraham Wing, the city's original settler, established in 1763 the area's first sawmill.

Unsteady legs carry us along the concrete.

Free of the canal, we stop to view a fifty-foot dam structure above a terrace of dry rock ledges and potholes leading to caves in the heart of downtown Glens Falls. Embedded in these falls, which Native Americans called *Chepontuo* (hard place to get around), is one cave that appears in James Fenimore Cooper's *The Last of the Mohicans*. In Cooper's novel, Hawkeye, hiding from his enemies in the cave, describes the beauty of the place before industry altered the terrain.

All around the falls, which are now nothing but dry cliffs with trickling water here and there, Glens Falls is ablaze in activity, this first real city of my journey. Lossing, you were so right: we have decidedly taken leave of the wilderness as Joan, Dave, and I stand here on Glen Street that crosses the Hudson just below the famous falls. The bridge is jammed with cars. Pete Bishop told me how he used to climb spiral stairs right down into Cooper's Cave, but, for whatever reason, they took the stairs out and stopped people from going down there.

White men first called the falls Wing's Falls in honor of Abraham Wing, who had settled here after the French and Indian War under a grant from the King of England. When Wing died, his son took possession. One day Wing's son and a man named John Glen were drinking heavily in a nearby tavern. As Lossing says, "The wine circulated freely, and it ruled the wit of the hour." Wing agreed to change the name of the falls to "Glen's Falls" if Glen would pay for everyone's supper. "For a 'mess of pottage' the young man sold his family birthright to immortality," says Lossing, who passed by the town of Glens Falls when it had a mere 4,000 inhabitants, nearly a century after John Glen bought the falls for a supper.

Today Glens Falls is like some South American city with aspirations to culture, an ambitious outpost of urban cowboys. It is a raw city at the edge of a threatened Adirondack forest.

Joan, Dave, and I walk the mile or so to the Hyde Museum. The three of us feel slightly out of place. I look back at Dave, who is straggling behind. His steps falter on the asphalt. We pass historic buildings, the history gutted out of them, piles of junk in the yards, bedsprings, and torn mattresses. Even the brick is crumbling. The streets are deserted except for logging trucks. The pavement is potholed from the catastrophe of winter.

Just behind the Finch, Pruyn mill with its sulphur-spewing smokestacks and mountains of logs and bleeping backhoes, there are three "houses" adjacent to each other that were constructed by Pruyn himself for his three daughters. One daughter married a Mr. Hyde, and her "house" has been converted into a museum, a sort of mini North Country version of the Vanderbilt estate in Hyde Park.

Dave chooses to wait for us outside. The day is hazing up. "I just don't feel right going inside looking like this," he says, meaning shorts, tee shirt, and sandals. From the rather condescending reaction of the museum staff to our casual visit, I'd say Dave made the right choice. The derision and superiority of the cashier and the ever-eyeing guards in this established symbol of Glens Falls' pride and culture is not something to recommend a return.

But what paintings—Caravaggio and Titian. It is like coming upon some rubber baron's private stock of Rembrandts in a palace built in the heart of the rainforest. There is even a Winslow Homer Adirondack scene of a man fishing in a lake from a canoe at the Northwoods Club, not far from Blue Ledge Pool.

After an hour of the Hyde, Joan and I step outside into the heat where Dave is smiling, glad to have us back again. We hike vigorously to a lunch shop a few blocks from our canoes. I buy everyone sandwiches.

Dave remains quiet as Joan and I talk about the region and my

19. Jeremy Frankel on the Feeder canal in Glens Falls.

journey. Then Jeremy Frankel joins us. He is from Britain, and his hair is dark. He has a handsome, almost boyish face, and he's such an energetic man in his thirties or so, he seems he might explode with enthusiasm. Jeremy has been appointed waterway consultant for the Glens Falls Feeder Canal Alliance. He seems to me a good choice because of his passionate knowledge about canals. To a large extent it is Jeremy who will make the major decisions in restoring the old barge canal to a functioning waterway and public park.

As soon as Jeremy sits with us and orders his sandwich, the

mood of our group changes. He loves canals, a love that evolved first in England but has spread to all canals all over the world. I find his enthusiasm infectious. His main argument for turning this canal and its surrounding land into a park is a belief that society needs desperately to preserve open spaces. Glens Falls is growing fast and without much provision in its zoning laws for open space, he says. Jeremy thinks the Feeder is a natural choice for a park and will leave future Glens Fallians a place to play in the spreading concrete.

Jeremy speaks with a slight lisp. He speaks fast but clearly. "New York State owns all its canals. Unlike the land on the Hudson owned by IP and Ni-Mo and the many other private power and railroad companies, this state land has a better chance of becoming a park."

Jeremy loves canals in part because he loves people. "Canals," he says, "bring people together. I don't know if this happens so much in the States, but on our 2,000 miles of English canals, I can meet someone, have a drink, say 'au revoir,' and know I'll meet that same person a year from now on some other canal. And we'll just carry on as if nothing happened in between. I've met so many people in the fifteen years I've been on canals."

Although Jeremy arrived late, he has finished his sandwich long before any of us. He looks like a man with a perpetual appointment to keep.

"Canals," I interject, when there is a break in Jeremy's excitement, "aren't something most people think much about these days. At least *I* hadn't thought about canals, until today."

"You're right," he fires back. "It's not a high priority, but I like to say to people, 'Hey, this is an important part of your heritage.' Without canals we'd be nowhere. Every single civilized country in the world has used canals to make the transition from an agricultural-based society to an industrial-based society. England, France, Germany, Holland, China, India—everywhere. Canals were the first nationwide system of transportation for industry. In the United States, to reach the hinterlands, from Maine all the way down to Georgia, canals were used to develop the nation. Then the Mississippi and the Midwest. Without the opening of the Erie Canal, New York City would still be a second-rate port."

Canals go hand in hand with the birth of the nation, he says. George Washington himself was a surveyor and canal engineer before he became a soldier and statesman. Acclaimed as the father of American canals, Washington, before peace was declared at the end of the Revolution, left his Newburgh headquarters (right across the river from where I live in Beacon) and journeyed through central New York State to consider the possibilities for inland navigation.

Phillip Schuyler, a provincial company commander in the French and Indian War, was perhaps the first to conceive of a canal between the Hudson River and Lake Champlain. After the Revolution he helped design a part of the canal. He was aided by New York State Governor De Witt Clinton, who also had a dream of opening up the western part of the state by canal, but who was opposed by many. Called "Clinton's big ditch," the idea for the Erie and Champlain Canals seemed like a dream in those early days of the nation. The proposed canal system was the moon shot of the times. Although largely forgotten now, it was a huge undertaking in the evolution of our country. Clinton was right, too. Before the canal was built, Philadelphia had been the nation's chief seaport, but after the Erie Canal was finished in the early 1800s, New York soon took the lead. The value of real estate in New York increased more rapidly than the population. Personal property was nearly four times its former value, and five times the number of people followed commercial pursuits in New York than had done so before the completion of the Erie Canal.

Jeremy orders a second dessert and says, "The engineering of canals taught engineers how to build railways, which quickly took over as the major industrial transport system in this country. In fact, civil engineering didn't exist until the coming of the canals. It was an amazing feat of construction at that time."

The Erie Canal and the three chief branches of the state system— the Champlain, the Oswego, and the Cayuga/Seneca Canals—were ten times the length of the Panama Canal and were considered the world's greatest waterway system. The success of the Erie Canal led to a frenzy of prospective canal building in New York, and the pace of commerce along the canal increased so rapidly that the Erie had to be enlarged often. Finally, in 1903 the state decided to upgrade this "ship canal" into a "barge canal."

Formerly only twenty-five feet wide, now widened and deepened, the Erie Barge Canal could take much larger barges. There are a total of fifty-seven locks on the Barge Canal with drops varying between six and forty feet. Some of the lock gates weigh as much as 200,000 pounds and can be opened and closed in thirty seconds. The greatest series of these locks are the five lifts on the Mohawk at Waterford near Troy, just off the Hudson River, with a total lift of 169 feet, which is twice as much as the total lift from sea level to the summit of the Panama Canal. There are 306 railroad and highway bridges crossing the canal.

"The Champlain section of the Barge Canal is just a small part of this great system," says Jeremy, who, if we didn't have to get back to our canoes, might easily go on talking for days about his blessed canals. But he looks anxiously at his watch, and up he jumps.

"It's been great," he says.

The day is dwindling, and I have to get moving, too. It's still a long, unknown way to my first lock. After talking to an impassioned canal person, I can't wait to paddle the big canal. I'm growing a bit weary of this Feeder pip-squeak. Bring on the barge canal!

Onward.

Joan, Dave, and I positively bound back to the boats. This feeling is the antithesis to those moments in travel when I feel myself sinking in quicksand. I have felt great lassitude when I linger too long in one place, on land, in museums, in lunch shops—it is the deadly procrastination of a sailor who cannot get himself back to sea.

But now fresh paddling invigorates. We pass alongside the Finch, Pruyn pulp mill. Low-hanging pipes cross the canal. They make us duck as low as the gunwales so we don't smash our heads. Men driving log trucks wave.

I shout to no one in particular, "I love industry."

Passing through heavy industry on an artificial canal feels right. I like waving at the guys in the trucks.

We pass a great chalky-white building on our left, lime dust everywhere. Jointa Lime is one of the canal's few remaining lime operations. Years ago there were as many as eighty-three lime kilns along the Feeder. Then we come to Portland Cement Company. Linden trees overhang the bank. The current is swifter now. We pass old abandoned factories and spot a muskrat under the brush.

Only a few yards from the main river, we can neither see nor hear it. The canal is so far above it, set into a bluff, that it seems a separate world. Not far down from the Finch, Pruyn mill, the Hudson, which

20. On the Feeder canal with Joan Patton and Dave Bishop.

has been running parallel to the Feeder, veers abruptly south while the Feeder continues east, then southeast a few miles over to the main canal. When we reach the canal, we'll have to paddle a few miles south through Lock 8, then on to Lock 7, before joining the Hudson again.

We float past the abandoned Ciba-Geigy chemical plant on our right, where the canal is suspiciously lined with black plastic. The canal then crosses Cold Spring Brook via a small stone aqueduct. There was once a narrow-gauge railroad from this section down to the sawmills on the Hudson River. We pass a patch of wild raspberries. From his kayak, Dave picks a handful then passes them out to Joan and me. Suddenly a trailer park sweeps its shoddy field of ugly metal boxes right to the edge of the canal. Refuse layers the canal bottom. Chain-link and stockade fences line the banks. Dogs bark.

We pass under Route 4, the main road along the Hudson from Troy.

A newspaper photographer is waiting ahead at that little culvert there. I comb my hair, and he shoots me paddling boldly by. Then he wants me to back up and paddle boldly again. I pass him three times (each time a little less boldly) to make sure he has the "natural shot" he needs for Joan's article.

Another half mile ahead we must paddle fast across the heavy spray of the Glens Falls Fire Department. They are hosing canal water 300 feet into the air over a long section of the canal. We dash one by one through the artificial rain.

This part of my journey is hard to describe, passing through a messy city on a soft-flowing, quiet canal. The channel is very narrow, the current picks up quickly, and the terrain alternates between thick vegetation, industry, and backyards. The water fills with old tires, hubcaps. This half-urban, half-pastoral gliding is a paddle I've never dreamed of before. The day is a steam box, the sky bloated with future rain.

Just above the PCB dump, at Pearl Street in Hudson Falls, we reach the impasse that Dave told me about at the combined locks— five huge stair steps for a giant. In fact, at Griffin Lumber, we reach the first in this series of thirteen locks that long ago dropped barges into the old Champlain Canal a few miles east of here.

We hike around two locks, but there is no path around the combines.

Joan heads off in search of help. She grabs the first man with a truck she finds in the nearby Griffin Lumber Yard and comes back to us in the cab of the truck, sitting beside a big German-looking man who says, "Throw 'em on here."

Dave and I throw kayak and canoe on the back of the flatbed, hop on, and hold tight. But Joan must leave us to file her story. It's getting late now. She's had a wonderful time. She says she'll carry my Bills bag down to Lock 7 so it will be waiting when I get there in a few hours and so I won't have to lug it through the unknown sections ahead.

Dave and I keep on. We're getting awfully close now to our goal, our shirts off, our boats bouncing through the back neighborhood streets of Hudson Falls, a view of the city no tourist will find unless he's lost.

A few blocks away the truck plunges past the plastic-lined dump on that little dirt road Dave described before. The road quickly ends at a fallen tree trunk. We thank the trucker, who then nods and begins to back out carefully.

We carry our ships a hundred yards down a small path and drop them into the old Champlain Canal, a small section that runs north before we can go east and then south on the new canal. Two boys fishing are startled by our sudden appearance. "Where you guys headed?" they manage to ask before we vanish.

"New York City," Dave says proudly.

The old canal is so run-down, it seems more like a river than a canal because the stone along the embankments has crumbled and the vegetation has lease. In the swampy terrain an old car lies on its side, crushed under a stone bridge abutment. I wonder if Kunz actually paddled here, too.

After a short hike through a cow pasture around a small set of rocks in a narrow channel, and then across the Delaware & Hudson tracks, we paddle the Feeder out into the sixty-foot-wide Champlain Canal proper and head south in the clay-brown water.

Dave says, "This is the highest part of the Champlain system," as if to say, "We did it by God." If we turned left and headed north, we'd hit Lock 9, which drops a boat toward Whitehall and Lake Champlain. But going south we'll come first to Lock 8, a temporary lock, which will drop us down sixteen feet toward Troy. Sitting here in my ship—looking up-canal and then down-canal—I really do understand the Feeder idea. Except for perhaps natural springs or small brooks, this canal system would have no water if not for the Feeder. Even with the Feeder, the two highest locks must operate on a schedule so they don't drain all the water in this slow-filling summit pool that lies between them.

Dave says, "So where are the tugs and ocean liners?"

We have entered a major shipping lane. The afternoon glare off the wide canal is ferocious.

"Let's get out of here, and keep our eyes peeled for big boats," I say, and we head off like the cavalry over the open plains. "Forward Ho."

A sign on the canal bank says, "10 Mile Per Hour speed limit." Perhaps it should read "Canoes Beware."

10

Lock 7

We glide past farms, cattle, and horses clustering on the cropped hillsides. Open fields slope up to the horizon, and the wide-open country refreshes the spirit after the claustrophobic Feeder. In this new farmland and battlefield territory, hot and sunburned now, we are happy. We are buddies-for-a-day.

Huge metal gates lie open for us ahead as if someone knew we were coming. The lock tender waves us into the lock chamber and says, "How far you going?"

I yell back, "To Lock 7 tonight. Maybe Manhattan." He shakes his head with a smile as if to say, "To each his own." He disappears into a little gatehouse at this end of the lock.

Identical gate houses painted white with neat blue trim sit on each end of the chamber. The chamber itself is 44 feet wide and 300 feet long, big enough for a barge to pass. Dave and I paddle our craft up to the concrete sides, and the lock tender advises, "Hold onto the metal rungs when the water drops."

A sign beside the lock says, "Upper water level: 140 feet. Lower water level: 129 feet." It seems odd to be only 140 feet above sea level, for I have come all the way from Lake Tear's 4,300 feet. And now, with so many miles of paddling left on the river, I'll drop only another 140 feet, 11 of which will take place in this lock chamber alone.

21. Dropping in a lock on the Champlain Canal.

Dave's kayak is on one side of the chamber, and my Odyssey is on the other. We don't speak. We sit in the gurgling water in a kind of stupefied awe as the gates hydraulically close behind us. When the big doors come together, the lock tender walks to the other little gate house on the far end of the chamber. He is in no hurry. His heels click on the cement.

Quickly the water bulges and boils beneath my hull as it drains from the huge chamber, millions of gallons displaced from the highest level of the Champlain Canal for our two tiny boats.

A kind of deep sucking sound comes from way beneath us. As the canoe drops, I pass my hands from rung to rung, slimy with algae. Dave and I look up eleven feet to the top of the chamber where we have just been. Then we glance at the huge doors behind us where the canal water is spurting through seams in the metal. Those doors are holding back millions of pounds of pressure. I notice, too, that both sets of closed doors, in front and behind, point in a V facing upstream, so the pressure of the natural flow of the water itself keeps the doors closed.

Inside his hut, the lock tender works his levers. Magically, the doors in front open ever so slowly. Canal and chamber water mix freely in swirls of liquid adjustment. The lock tender leans out of his hut, says something I cannot understand because it echoes off the huge wet slabs of concrete around us, and waves us on.

Cautiously we paddle out, casting nervous, unbelieving glances backward at Lock 8. Then onward the two miles to Lock 7, which is only a few yards above the confluence of the Hudson.

We paddle past something dead floating in the murky water, bloated and insect-infested beyond recognition. We have escaped the city. Only pastures and land here, no people, nothing but farms and cattle and horses and lots of quiet.

A big rain is coming up fast behind us, though. A storm wind blows up, and we hardly have to paddle because it blows directly off our sterns. Our bodies catch the cool air, our backs acting as tiny sails. From the north this ominous, premature darkness and the thunder-cloud make us paddle harder than we'd like to after a long day. I want to make Lock 7 before the sky breaks, so I can set up my tent on dry land.

At the gates to Lock 7, we haul our boats out. Dave calls his brother. I set up my tent quickly. Rain and dark come in fast now like a storm over the Great Plains.

When Dave's brother arrives, his car has no roof rack, so Dave leaves his kayak locked to the side of the canal house. He shakes my hand and says he'll be back.

I feel great. No more carrying the canoe from here all the way to Manhattan. Just a few locks to pass through until I get to the tides at Troy.

No more dams, no more carries, no more goddamn dam worries.

No more dams, no more carries, no more goddamn dam hurry.

These locks are beautiful.

Facts and figures about the Hudson River's Champlain Canal:

Lock 7 to Lock 6 = 7.24 miles
Lock 6 to Lock 5 = 3.64 miles
Lock 5 to Lock 4 = 14.3 miles
Lock 4 to Lock 3 = 1.83 miles
Lock 3 to Lock 2 = 2.53 miles
Lock 2 to Lock 1 = 3.9 miles
Lock 1 to Troy Lock = 6 miles.

For a total of 39.44 miles from here to Troy, where the tides begin.

I'll spend most of tomorrow here and leave in the afternoon to paddle the ten or so miles to Lock 5, which is in the town of Schuylerville, on the edge of the Saratoga National Park, a major battlefield of the Revolution where the Americans had their first great victory of the war. On my way up to Ernie, I drove along this part of the river on Route 4 from Troy to Fort Edward. It is a terrain of historic landmark signs. Standing in front of a trailer, some run-down old cars, and a pile of firewood, one sign said, "Headquarters of General Gates."

Each of the Champlain Canal locks has its own little grassy park with barbecue grills and enough open space to pitch my tent. Kunz suggested I use these for camping while I descend the forty miles of canal Hudson from Fort Edward to Troy, which he thought would be a three-day paddle.

Most people never think of locks and canals on the Hudson. Few know much about the lock tenders themselves. Kunz had said, "Those lock people hand down their jobs from generation to generation, and they're just very different, very nice folks. Sometimes they wait to run the locks at planned intervals, or they'll run them for you right away. You should talk to them. Tell them what you're up to and why you're doing what you're doing. They love the river. If you show genuine interest in the river, they're going to be happy."

"Yes, sir. Those lock tenders treated us well." Kunz repeated himself in his enthusiasm. "They asked us to camp with them. In the morning, they'd radio ahead to the next lock so that guy would have his lock open waiting for us. Sometimes we'd screw up and stop for lunch and a nap. The lock tender down the line would say, 'Hey, I left the lock open for you for a long time. Where were you guys?'"

The rain breaks just after I get my tent up in the neatly kept, mowngrass park beside Lock 7. The lock tenders sit in a little house nearby. About a hundred feet from the lock itself, the lock house is covered in wood planking. Built of metal during the First World War to house the guards who watched over the lock, it functions now as an office and storeroom.

In the driving rain I run into the house to find Alexis Nadeau, one of the two full-time lock tenders at Lock 7, sitting in a swivel

22. Camping on Lock 5 in Schuylerville.

chair at a desk listening to AM radio. He is a heavy-set man with a rather big belly and sturdy face. His easy smile and brash French Canadian accent belie his rather timid nature. Alexis is from the small Hudson River farming village of Northumberland, just north of Schuylerville, twelve miles south of Fort Edward. "I grew up right on the canal," he says. "Tomorrow you'll go by the back of my house." Alexis's father built most of the houses in Northumberland.

He says the spelling of his name is something he's always made a joke of. "I always said N-a-d-e-a-u is low class. If it was high class it would be N-a-d-e-a-u-x, with an *x*." He says seriously, "When the French came to this country, they changed their names to be more American."

I cannot think of anyone more American than the Bishops, and I tell Alexis so.

"Nice people, the Bishops," Alexis confirms. "One of the kindest families in the North Country. Loyal, too."

"Have you seen my gear? Joan Patton was going to drop off a big blue bag today, and there's another one from a few weeks ago," I say.

"Your bags are right over there, safe and sound," he says as he

23. Alexis Nadeau.

swivels on his chair and points. "No one's going to touch anything here." Aside from my Bills bag, I can see the big brown duffel I dropped here on my way to Ernie's. I planned Lock 7 would be my way station, so I had stuffed the bag with topographic maps (which I know now I'll never use), extra candy, quick-energy food, packets of dried Stroganoff to cook tonight, and all sorts of odds and ends, including a sail and mast I rigged for the canoe.

Alexis says, "You can use the barge hut for cooking, to get out of the rain, if you want." This is a little wood structure, like an ice fishing hut, with a wood stove on one side, a picnic bench in the middle. Parked next to the campground not thirty feet from my tent, the cabin is a sort of portable makeshift unit that gets lifted by crane onto a barge when the men work on the canal in the winter.

Alexis says he runs both Lock 7 and 8, which are about two miles apart from one another. This gets kind of hard when the canal gets busy, starting this month. The state is cutting back on staff, and whereas there used to be twenty-four-hour coverage of the locks, now he will go home at eleven at night and there won't be anyone here until seven in the morning.

Last summer, he says, was really difficult. Alexis gets worked up just thinking about it. Leaning forward on his swivel chair, he complains in a soft voice, "I had ten boats in the lock and ten waiting below. I'd run up to Lock 8, let out the ones going north, then lock the south ones in, then run back down here and let the north ones in and then the south ones in and then there'd be more north ones to come in and then I'd have to run back to Lock 8. Gosh darn!

"It can be tough work, but I'll tell you the worst. I came down from 8 one Sunday afternoon about two o'clock. It was hot, a real warm one, a heavy day. Boats all lined up. I came in with a state van, and some guy was walking along the wall. He said, 'Mister, are you running this lock?' I said, 'I also run Lock 8. It's been busy.' He said, 'Do you know it's *hot* down there in that boat?' I said, 'I realize that. I have a boat. I know how hot a boat can get.' And the day *was* hot, really miserable. 'Well,' he said, 'I could have had a *heart attack,* for *Christ's sake!*' I said, 'Yes, it's hot, and you could have had one. I agree it's hot, and I'm trying to be nice to you and do my job. And I *am* going to be nice to you, but the thing is, you'd have to join the same club I joined ten years ago, because I've *had* a heart attack. But I don't feel any worse for it.' I says, 'No problem. I'll work as fast as I can. Then after I lock you through 7, when you get up there, I'll be at Lock 8 waiting for you to get you through faster. But if I stay here and argue with you, it'll hold me up, and somebody else will be waiting.'

"'Well,' he says, 'I'm sorry I held you up, and I apologize.' Some people are just hard to take care of. I'm French, myself. Some of these Frenchmen come down here and they don't even know you, but they start talking bad about you in French. And I understand French. 'Be careful,' I say, 'I speak a little French myself, you know.'"

Alexis shakes his head. With Alexis I don't have to ask any questions. Information just flows. He answers just about any question I could possibly think of, and he goes on and on, explaining his job.

"Oh, it's bad, all right. But I ask you, what have I done to these people for them to get all worked up just because I can't run two locks at the same time? I wonder."

My first impression of Alexis is that he is terribly insecure. But two things tell me different. First, he offers to drive me in his fancy, secondhand van to the laundromat in Fort Edward and then to the Grand Union for supplies. Second, when he drives this van, which has wall-to-wall carpeting, he is extremely relaxed and confident at the wheel. The van has every creature comfort: TV, sink, bed, refrigerator, fan, and so on, and whenever he goes somewhere in it, the multiple speakers engulf him in FM radio tunes.

Another thing about Alexis is that he is extremely confident with his young girlfriend, Tammy, who walks in and throws herself on one of the counters flirting with him like a saloon girl in the gold rush. She is from Fort Miller, a few miles down the Hudson.

Alexis is also very kind, like a big bear. He has offered to take me out tomorrow for breakfast. He is, I will soon discover, a much-loved man in Fort Edward and Hudson Falls.

His busiest time starts next week, he says, and will run all summer long. If Alexis had a choice, I think he would work only during the off-season months. He seems to be dreading the June-to-October pleasure-boat season.

"Where do these boats come from? And where are they going?" I want to know.

"Well, what they'll do is come from New York and go up the Erie along the Mohawk from Waterford, and for a shortcut they'll go up the Oswego River into Lake Ontario. There's beautiful boating up there. Then some will go up the Saint Lawrence Seaway and up around Nova Scotia and then back down in open water back to New York. Or they'll come into Montreal, down the Richelieu River into Lake Champlain and then right down here through the Champlain Canal into the Hudson."

Tammy comes over and sits on Alexis's lap, and I decide to leave them alone.

"Alexis, do you mind if I make some phone calls?"

"Go right ahead. There's a public phone on the wall," he says.

When I check in with the Riverkeeper office, I discover that *USA Today* will be running a small article on my trip and that CNN is planning to put a television crew on the George Washington Bridge.

Next, I call Melissa, who says the baby is okay. I can hear Suzanna babbling in the background as Melissa reports on what's been happening. Then Melissa puts the phone up to Suzanna's ear, and I babble words unintelligible to adults.

Feeling lonely, I say to Alexis, "See you tomorrow. I'm going to cook some dinner." He and Tammy will pick me up in their van at 9 A.M.

The rain pours loudly on the roof of the barge shed as I cook my coffee on the little stove I prop on a picnic table. I get to thinking what I love about this trip. After a long day, I love boiling up coffee. There is freedom in preparing coffee—Old-West, prairie freedom. Up here in this wild part of New York State, it's still free. I know this because I am boiling coffee sheltered from the rain at Lock 7, where the Champlain Canal meets the Hudson River. Perhaps to some it might seem like a small thing, but boiling coffee on a long camping trip is darn important.

Ernie taught me how to make "cowboy coffee," boiling the grounds with the water. Ernie is a free man; the Bishops are free; Joan Patton is free; these lock tenders are free. Even at the Tahawus Club, Jessup and Ann Brewer in their enthusiasm for the land of their old club are remnants of the free. John Bennett in Luzerne used to be free, his freedom now highly endangered.

I say the word ten times, free free free free . . . , and speaking it makes me feel on-top-of-this-world free, too. Huddling around a little stove in the barge hut out of the rain, I see three identical brand-new houseboats heading for French Canada in the pouring rain. They move in eerie unison, slowly, into Lock 7. Now I hear a screen door slam and watch Alexis walk slowly out to the lock. All three houseboats have swim slides on them, and radar. They're made from some slick-looking, blue fiberglass, not at all like real houseboats, not rickety, not old, never lived in. These are the playpens of the rich Quebec middle class.

Letting the coffee boil and donning my expensive Gortex rain gear, I head over to Alexis. We stand together in the rain on the lock wall as the boats nudge up to each other way below us deep in the trench of the lock, and I ask him, "How much do you think those cost?"

"I'll bet they're in the $60,000 to $70,000 range. Mine is only a little twenty-seven footer."

"You have a houseboat too?"

"No. But I spent $44,000 for my little boat. That's how much boats cost. It's crazy." Alexis likes gadgets.

I feel comfortable enough already with this man to say: "You own some pretty good machinery. I didn't know lock tenders did so well. You running drugs from Bolivia or something?"

"No. I only make twenty-three grand a year. But I was in construction. I built a lot of homes. And I still would be making homes if I hadn't had the heart attacks."

I am disappointed to hear that Alexis is not one of the lock tenders Kunz had spoken about, those who worked as lock tenders all their lives and who came from generations of lock tenders. Alexis says the old lock-tender families are gone.

Alexis enters his little pagoda, the downstream gatehouse, where he pushes levers that close the gates; then he saunters up to the gatehouse on the north end and fills the chamber. I can tell why people might take offense at Alexis: he seems to move to his own time; he does not appear rushed, nor bothered by the rain.

The houseboats slowly rise up up up until they are no longer in the pit of the lock, but are flush with the ground where I am again cooking and eating my meal. The up-canal gates open, and the boats head north, like canal phantoms through the wet falling dusk.

8 P.M. and still some light out as the rains begin to ease. What I like about this trip is just meeting people and cooking dinner. At home, dinners pile up like airliners on a Friday night runway. But out here on the river, it takes a long time to boil water, and there's time to think.

I like Fort Edward. People are nice up here. It's wild, too. And you know what? It's only *day nine*—June 19. It is 11 P.M. when I hear the screen door slam, and through the mosquito-proof mesh of my tent window I see two dark forms hop into that plush van and drive slowly away.

I'm alone here.

The night comes down on my tent with its soft, but everlasting summer landing. The sky has cleared, and the fireflies sparkle by the thousands through the crisp night air; they are like visiting stars come down for a closer look.

When Lossing and his wife passed through Fort Edward in the mid–nineteenth century they found a busy town of 2,000 inhabitants with its "chief industrial establishment . . . an extensive blast-furnace for converting iron ore into the pure metal." Lossing found a picture of the town from the 1820s, thirty years before his own journey. Only six houses and a church stood here then.

Before the 1970's hoopla about the Fort Edward PCBs, the town's real fame came not from the canal, but from the death of a beautiful seventeen-year-old girl, Jenny M'Crea (or Jane McCrea), "described as lovely in disposition, graceful in manners, and so intelligent and winning in all her ways, that she was a favourite to all who knew her."

In 1777 Jenny was visiting a friend in Fort Edward. General Burgoyne was camped nearby, and his army consisted of a motley crew—British regulars, mercenary Germans, Canadians, French, and Indians. "Burgoyne had found it difficult to restrain the cruelty of his Indians," writes Lossing. So in order to give them purpose during idle times, he offered them bounty for prisoners and scalps. One Indian entered Jenny's friend's house and captured Jenny and her friend and fled. Soldiers chased them, firing muskets, but no one was hit except for Jenny. "She fell and expired, as tradition relates, near a pine-tree." The Indians scalped her and "with her black tresses wet with her warm blood" they went back to camp.

The story's horror grew in the imagination of the Americans. General Gates who had just taken command of the northern army from General Schuyler "took advantage of the excitement which it produced, to increase the hatred of the British in the hearts of the people." He accused Burgoyne of hiring savages to "scalp Europeans and the descendants of Europeans," and said Jenny was "dressed to meet her promised husband, but met her murderers" instead, all of which had the desired effect of inflaming the people against the British.

Jenny's fiancé, Duncan Campbell, retired to Canada. Some said he had changed dramatically. A naturally talkative and happy man, he now began to mope and to avoid people. He never married, and when "the anniversary of the tragedy approached, he would shut himself in his room, and refuse to see his most intimate acquaintances; and at all times his friends avoided speaking of the American revolution in his presence."

In the morning I hear activity at the lock house. Bob Smith, "Smitty" to his friends, has come to work the morning shift. Smith is perhaps

24. Bob "Smitty" Smith.

in his seventies, with a round face and the Midwestern look of a
farmer. He wears a grey button-down shirt not tucked into his navy
pants. In his shirt pocket are three pens and his glasses case. He is
one of the oldest old-timers of all the lock tenders these days. He's
been on the locks for thirty years, he says. His father was not a lock
tender, yet Smitty knows these locks as well as anyone. He even remembers Kunz's coming through here twenty years ago.

"In them days, the old-timers were still around," he says. Yes,
they used to pass their jobs from generation to generation. "But those
guys have died, and some with forty years service just retired this
year."

"But," Smith tells me, "there is one guy on Lock 2, Lester Moll. Moll's father and grandfather worked on the locks. But he's the only one left who comes from a lock family."

I find this information depressing. I had come looking for continuity, but once again I find that typical breakdown in continuity that I always think of as a modern phenomenon and that frustrates my love of history. In fact, the old days are gone, and even in the old days, former old days were already gone, and the sooner I get used to this, the better for me.

The days when the big boats used to come through the locks, too, are gone. Now it's just a few barges and tugs. Mostly it's pleasure boats. "Why," Smith says, "they used to load scrap iron right out there on the other side of our lock, but that's gone too. That's called Roger's Island over there. You heard of the concrete canal barges? Nope? Well, they were strictly experimental, and they were made right there." Smith points across the canal.

"Are all the Champlain locks the same size?"

"Yes. All but U.S. Lock 1, which is bigger. That's a Federal lock," Smith says. "But our state locks, like 7 here, vary in drop between sixteen and twenty-one feet. You know, they used to all be run by hand, and sometimes in winter, two men will open and shut the valves by hand even now." He figures the amount of water displaced here at Lock 7 is close to 1 million gallons. When the Feeder is running low, the locks up here go on a four-hour schedule, he says. The boats will wait four hours for the Feeder water to fill the canal between locks 8 and 9. Then the whole canal system can work again. Without the Feeder, he says, it all breaks down.

Did the Feeder ever dry up completely in the summer and prevent boats from using the Champlain Canal? Not that Smith can remember, not in his day, he says.

"Hey, you want to meet some real canal people, come back around eleven this morning. Jim Nichols, he's a friend of mine. He comes round every day and we chat. He was an engineer on a tug in the canal for, golly, more than a hundred years, it seems. Jeees. And so's this other fellow. He's a tug captain, Fred Godfrey. I can get him over here at the same time, if you want."

I tell him that would be great.

"Fred even wrote a book. Have you read *Tugboats I Have Known*?"

"Nope. Not yet, but I'd like to."

"Cripes, Fred *grew up* on the canal. *He's* the one you need to talk to."

So Bob Smith will arrange for me to meet an old-time tug captain who actually does come from a canal family, and also a tug engineer. First, though, I'll have breakfast with Alexis.

At 9 A.M. Alexis and Tammy pick me up. We stop at a newsstand. Alexis says, "Let's get a paper."

Tammy opens the *Post-Star.* "Hey—look here—you're famous. What a picture!" She passes me the paper. Joan evidently filed her story in time. Here's a picture of me canoeing the Feeder. "Canoeist Navigates Feeder," Tammy reads as we pull up to the restaurant. "A week ago, Pete Lourie stood high on the slopes of Mount Marcy. . . . Lourie, in his 18-foot Kevlar canoe, set out on a silent voyage through the heart of Glens Falls, unseen by most, until he pulled his canoe out of the water on Glen Street . . . " And on and on.

Alexis feels proud to take me to breakfast in a local spoon. Walking past the table of some friends, he flashes the newspaper and says, "Here's the guy right here."

I'd like to deflect my new-found fame onto this nice man. I want to bury my own face in the sand. I suppose Ernie, too, is reading the paper this morning up in Blue Mountain Lake. Now he'll know I've come this far. I'll bet he's been wondering how things are going. Perhaps he's kicking himself for not coming the whole way.

Alexis introduces me to a small weathered man with a dark blue leprechaun's hat, much too tiny for his head. His name is Winchell, and there seems to be some dispute about the island he's squatting just south of Lock 7. He looks like my Scotch grandfather. Alexis says he has cleared the island and built a house there but that people are trying to move him off.

Before we leave the restaurant, Winchell comes over to our table and invites me to stop and visit on my way downriver later this afternoon. His island is in the heart of the most polluted PCB territory. He'll be on his island all day, he says in a deep, raspy voice.

"Thanks, I'll try to stop. But it depends on time."

After breakfast, Alexis and Tammy wave as we leave their friends. We hop into the carpeted van and drive across the canal down Route 4 through future PCB dump territory. Alexis drives casually and talks constantly.

The value of the land here has plummeted since the state decided to dredge more of the PCBs and to put them in dumps "right up there where those farms are." Tammy and Alexis point. One farm, they say, bought by developers, is now being broken into lots with an uncertain future. Another farm is a racehorse breeding farm.

Shaking his head, Alexis says, "It's a real shame. They ought to just leave the stuff where it is. It'll only make it worse to dig it up. They're going to dredge what they call the 'hot spot,' from Fort Edward right on down the canal. They even estimate a certain tonnage, but how, I want to know, do they figure the tonnage!"

Back at Lock 7, Alexis and Tammy drop me off. I probably won't see them again, so I promise to send a card and news about whether I reach Manhattan. Alexis has a great big smile as they both wave and drive off. I cannot tell whether he believes I'll do it or not, reach Manhattan, send a card.

Godfrey and Nichols are waiting inside the lock house with Smith. They chat even as I enter the room, but their talk seems self-conscious. They know I want to interview them, and they probably wonder who the hell I am.

Godfrey strikes me right away as a spartan, ex-marine, no-nonsense kind of fellow. He is stiff and serious like one who has known many responsibilities. At first glance he looks like any elderly man in retirement, somewhat sour in his tight-lipped face. He wears a white tee shirt and light blue slacks. Nichols, on the other hand, who is also in his seventies, exudes an ingenuous warmth. There is nothing sour about his looks. He has a big round nose. When he smiles, which is most of the time, his mouth opens more to one side than to the other. He is wearing a short-sleeved shirt, tucked neatly into his navy-blue pants.

Godfrey says stiffly, "So what's your purpose?"

I reply that I just want to hear some stories about barges and tugs and the canal, that I'm writing about the whole river, and that this part fascinates me. Not many people know that the Hudson River is part canal for forty miles.

Silence. Nichols grabs the tip of his Yankees cap. Smitty, a genial man, helps me break the ice with his friends by asking me a simple question. He wants to know how I got my canoe up to Lake Tear. I tell him the story about Ernie and me. Godfrey shakes his head and finally smiles. That loosens everyone up a bit.

The puppy-faced Nichols has a powerful Bronx accent. I find it surprising that he has settled way up here because he strikes me as a quintessential New Yorker, the kind of loyal New Yorker who might never want to leave his native town.

Nichols was an engineer on a tug for forty years. He says he rarely saw the river the same way captains did; he was always down in the engine room. He lightly touches his hat and says, "A captain looks at the river 360 degrees, but engineers look at one side of a river through a portal. To see the other side, we have to climb across the engine and look out the other portal."

Godfrey is still holding back. He hardly moves in his seat. He won't really look at me. I say, "Mr. Godfrey, I understand you've written a book."

All of a sudden, he sits back on Alexis's swivel chair, the springs squeaking as they tighten, and says, "It's available just over the bridge here in the first house on the right. It's $10.95 and has forty-eight pictures in it. It's out of print at the moment, but they might have a copy left." In fact, he says, he'll drive me across the canal to the Fort Edward Museum after this interview.

The introduction to *Tug Boats I Have Known* reads: "My parents were running a barge canal boat in 1915. Mother went ashore to visit her mother in Glens Falls and to give birth to a baby. . . . No doubt I saw tugs at that time and perhaps that is when I first became attracted to them." And chapter 1 begins, "The first tugboat trip I made was aboard the TRITON, though I must confess I do not remember it. . . . The vessel was tied up for the night and, as I was only four years old, I was asleep in Dad's bunk in the pilot house. A fire broke out and my father gathered me up in the blankets and laid me on the dock. The fire was extinguished and I was returned to bed, still asleep, and unaware of the excitement."

The book goes on to describe all the tugs he traveled on, and the escapades of a tug lover and soon-to-become tug captain. But today Godfrey is no captain. He begins to speak more freely. He becomes the historian of his own life and likes to talk about the past.

Smitty gets up to check if any boats need to be locked through. The screen door slams when he returns.

Godfrey says, "I'm a fifth-generation canaler. My great-grandfather operated a canal boat. His daughter, my grandmother, was

25. Fred Godfrey of Fort Edward.

cook for him. She was married to a printer here in Fort Edward and they had four sons. Her husband, my grandfather, developed consumption and couldn't work. In order to survive they bought an old canal boat. She and her four sons made a living on the canal pushing freight."

Godfrey says canaling was a family affair. As each of the boys reached age sixteen, "they'd get a few bucks together, buy an old leaky canal boat and off they'd go into their own business." Some operated with more than two or three boats. "My father operated at least two boats for the Griffin Lumber Company."

In fact, only one or two relatives were not canalers. Godrey's mother's father, for instance, was a logger in the logging camps. When Godfrey was four years old, this grandfather got killed in some kind of logging accident.

"I wasn't actually raised on the barges. Come school time I was in school," he says. "My father and all my uncles moved up from barges to tugboats. They became tugboat captains and had nothing to do with barges." There is a clear but unspoken hierarchy implied in his tone: tugs are worthier than barges. After all, they had engines in them. Barges are pretty helpless creatures.

He thinks tugs came onto the canal up here around 1915 or so. Before that, mules pulled the barges. But there aren't many tug captains left, says Godfrey. He himself was a tug captain for forty years and worked New York harbor as well as all the canals.

"Something I found very hard to understand when I started was how you could leave New York on low water and travel all the way to Albany on a single flood tide. If you could make a fifteen-knot boat go from New York to Albany you'd carry one ride. Never buck tide. All the way up. Because the way the tides work, for every fifteen miles you travel upriver, you make the tide last one hour longer. The six-hour tide schedule just keeps getting extended. It was hard for me to visualize. And going downstream, you'd think with the force of the Hudson River behind you, you would have an advantage, but you don't because for every fifteen miles *descending* the river, you have an hour *less* tide. Why? Because in effect, you're running out of it." Godfrey shakes his head.

"But you could come north on a flood tide, against the current of the Hudson River, all the way to Albany on one tide. Imagine!" Godfrey seems amazed at the phenomenon even today. Smitty and Nichols sit silently watching their friend.

"What you're saying is that if I make any progress at all going downriver with the tides, I'll have only four hours of canoeing instead of six?" I ask.

"Well, you might not have a problem. You'll be so close to shore, the dynamics of the river are different there. And also, you don't draw any water."

"I read many years ago," adds Godfrey, beginning to warm to my questions about this curious river, "that whaling ships used to sail from the Hudson River as far north as Hudson, New York. Also that the Hudson River sloop, which was quite a vessel, was used in the old tea and silk trade to China. And the old-timers claim that the best water to put in barrels came from the river right off Esopus Island just north of Poughkeepsie. When I was eighteen or nineteen, we filled our water barrels there one time, to try out the water. We all

26. Jim Nichols.

survived it, nothing happened to us. But I wouldn't want to drink it today."

I turn to Nichols and ask how he came to work on tugs. He answers in his thick New York accent. His father was an engineer on a tug before him for nearly forty years. Nichols started on a Moran tug when he was sixteen. "Mostly I worked in the harbor, but I worked the canals, too."

With a smile and a glance at Godfrey, Nichols says, "Captains are always sipping coffee while engineers do all the work in a hot engine room." Godfrey laughs at this old rivalry between captains and engineers.

Smitty has left the lock house again to lock someone through while the others keep talking. Rummaging through his memories of the river's beauty, Godfrey says, "In spring it all comes out green. In the fall you get all sorts of colors, and the old lighthouses are beautiful."

"I first noticed the beauty," I say, "before teaching school one morning in Dobbs Ferry. I took my canoe out at six-thirty. The sky was blue, the water calm. A tug passed me. It was pulling a barge. I could see the city in a pink mist and all around I could hear the distant whine of the cars on the Tappan Zee Bridge and the highways, millions of people going to work. But out there on the river, it was peaceful—a secret."

Godfrey smiles sternly. "I'll tell you a story about another canoe in Dobbs Ferry. It was a beautiful Sunday afternoon. I was a young man, a deckhand. I was steering the boat, going about one or two miles an hour. I saw an empty canoe drifting down the river and I thought, gee, maybe I can veer over and pick it up. We used to pick up rowboats and so on. But then I saw a man's head come up. And I thought, just somebody taking a nap. But then a woman's head came up under his face. [laughter] I couldn't get over close enough after that. . . . Everyone on board wanted a look."

Not trying to top his story, but reminded of something I heard in Cold Spring, New York, years before, I say, "I know the story of a man who was in that same situation with a woman out in the Hudson when a wave came and the little boat swamped and the man died. But the woman lived."

Illicit sex on the Hudson seems to be dangerous business. Our conversation has rounded a corner toward the prurient, and Jim especially looks a bit embarrassed. Godfrey describes a place along the river that was a great lovers' lane. He'd take his tug up close to the bank and then suddenly throw his spotlight on the lovers. "Oh, we was really jealous of them," the captain says, shaking his head. "Heck. We hadn't been home in three months."

"You know," says Smitty steering the subject on a more decent course, "they used to run eel boats down through here years ago."

"What's an eel boat?"

Godfrey looks at me as if I'm stupid, "A boat fulla eels."

"It was one odd-looking boat, very small and rickety and frail, built with a screen around it, and there'd be a little shack that looked like an outhouse. They'd come down from Canada. One of them used to stay all summer catching eels up in the Province of Quebec and throw them alive in the holding tank. And the following year they'd contract with our tug, and we'd take them all the way down to the

Fulton Fish Market, where they'd sell eels out of their boats all winter long.

"Eel boats would go in tow with other barges. Maybe along with them we'd be taking barges loaded with hay and lumber, maybe as many as five or six or even eighteen and twenty barges all in a row."

I interrupt the captain to ask how many barges could go through the locks at once.

Godfrey answers, "You could take six of the small barges. These were remnants from the old canal. They were real small, a hundred feet long and twenty feet wide. The old canal was extremely narrow. Well, it was as narrow as the Feeder canal."

"What is the *old* canal?"

"The original canal was built *beside* the Hudson. It didn't use the river at all. It wasn't until 1913 that the *new* canal was open. The new canal is the canal you're canoeing—the Hudson River itself. In fact, these locks you're using weren't built until it became the new canal.

"You can still see the old canal if you look for it beside the Hudson. It isn't used anymore, but it's there." Of course I'd seen a tiny piece of it when Dave Bishop and I had made our way to the new canal from the Feeder.

Working the canals was rough work. I want to know what it felt like to be away from home for months on end. It's a simple question, but the three old men giggle like boys.

Smitty says, "Lock 7 was the good spot for drinking. There was a gin mill right here on top of the little hill. Some guys'd be so anxious for a drink, they'd tie their tugs right there on that wall and run up to the gin mill. I'd have to go up there and get them down to their boats, then through the lock and out of the way."

Godfrey adds, "Troy, Albany, every place had a sportin' house. And all the bars had girls working in them. Then there was Goose Island. That was a street of bungalows, each with a small kitchen and living room downstairs and two little bedrooms upstairs. Two girls worked a bungalow, and we'd be taking the tug by real slow in the middle of the day and the girls'd be out there waving at us. Ha."

Nichols says with the quiet resignation of a man who has lived close to water, who has suffered some hard times near water, and who perhaps has taken his blows well: "It's a tough life. I remember my father would go away in April and I wouldn't see him until December. Eight months. That was the time he'd work on the canal tugs. He'd get two weeks off for Christmas, then after New Year's he'd be working the harbor tugs, until April, when he'd go off again. And that lasted until the thirties when the unions came in.

"There was no time off, either. You just lived aboard the boat. The only recreation and enjoyment you had was to go ashore and get some *fuel* and sometimes it got a little out of hand."

I can just imagine the lust for women, weeks on the water, the desire for affection, the longing for family, the loneliness, the insufficient all-male camaraderie in the hot engine rooms or in the captains' houses, and in the ports of call so far from home-cooked meals. I too have felt a growing need for affection on this river. It builds up inside me in so many small increments I don't even know it's there, until suddenly I see Tammy kiss Alexis, a little warm hug, and I am thrown into a tailspin of hunger for touch. There is something about working on the water, floating all day long in the sun and sky that makes me crave tenderness. In the lengthening of the scruffy beard and in the toughening of the arms, I'm ready to lie down on a soft clean bed.

As if reading my mind about hard work and loneliness, Godfrey says, "In those early days, you worked six hours on and six off, eighty-four hours a week. There was no such thing as overtime, and when you left the boat you were still responsible for it. Often I'd take other guys' six-hour shifts, work twenty-four hours two or three days in a row, so they could have some time home. When I was finished, my wife would come pick me up. Or I'd take a train or bus to get home."

Interviewing a captain, engineer, and lock tender all at once allows me to see in almost three dimensions what canaling was all about. For now, Smitty adds his perspective; or, rather, layers it on top of Godfrey's.

Recalling the old days, Smitty looks directly at Godfrey when he says, "The tricky part of tug work here on the canal section of the Hudson is when we get high water and the tugs get going pretty fast. Current can be a problem in the new canal because it's a river. In the old canal you didn't have to worry so much, and the barges were smaller. But now, if a tug captain don't get over to the locks on the side of the river, he can drive his freight *right* over the dam. And you got only eighteen inches on each side of the lock to maneuver. That ain't much."

Smitty sums up the mystery of this whole canal system when he says, "How many people know that the Hudson River, part of it anyway, flows north into Lake Champlain. The Feeder, which *is* Hudson River water, flows north as well as south when it reaches the canal. It's amazing but so many people don't even know the Feeder canal is there."

Godfrey asks me as if giving a quiz, "Have you been to Rondout yet?"

"Rondout? What's that?"

His eyes are severe. I would hate to work on a tug for Godfrey and screw up. He says, "You mean you live in Beacon and you've never been to the Rondout? That's Kingston's port. You better stop there on your way down. More men who worked on the Hudson River—riverworkers on the Day Line, the Night Line, and the White-hall Steamboat Companies—were from Rondout, more than any other town along the river. Long before there was any canal, the river workers came out of Rondout. The canalers were from up here and from Whitehall, but Rondout was the center of all water transportation below. It's changed a lot. There's a museum down there. Men with the most knowledge of anybody on the Hudson River were from Rondout Creek. And they have their own canal right there, too. The Delaware and Hudson Canal comes into Rondout from the coal fields of Pennsylvania."

It is time for me to go, but first I ask if I can take a photograph of the three men. The canal veterans joke as they step out into the light. Godfrey looks more hesitant than the others. Jim Nichols puts a comb through his hair. Smitty just shuffles out onto the lawn.

They come over to my canoe and ask what it's made of. Godfrey bangs it and pushes at it. He says, "The vessels I knew were a lot sturdier than this," and his laughter is hearty. They inspect my Bills bag. These canal veterans, with more than a hundred years of canal service among them—this tug captain of responsibilities, this man of the motors, this man of levers and dropping water—are by now genuinely interested in my journey.

Nichols says, "I would have thought you'd be using a double-bladed paddle."

"Canoeists have a saying for kayakers. 'Half the paddle, twice the man.'" Which is something my friend Scott Overdorf taught me. I don't mean to sound macho, but I've never even tried a double-bladed paddle, and it's too late to start now.

In the feeble sunlight and the returning haze, they try to smile for the camera. I take their picture as they stand on green grass near a big "Lock 7" sign. They look like three older men you might run across on the golf course in Florida.

Smitty says as a warning, "Your next lock will be in a channel on the left side of a big island. Then you'll hit Lock 5. Watch the buoys down there or you'll be in trouble. A lot of people don't even know the dam is there. Can't see it, really. So stay inside the buoys."

"Thanks for the tip."

I poke the long canoe into the mud and quickly load it. I've lingered too long, it seems. The sun is setting. I step into the canoe and push the paddle into the PCB muck and head out into the canal that instantly widens into the Hudson River. A north wind picks up, and I try to catch it with my sail, but I get all tangled up and cannot steer the canoe properly, so I repack the sail. A mile downstream I see Winchell on his dock waving at me to come over. When I'm tired, I am an amazingly incurious traveler. I'd like to keep moving—it's getting late, and the sun is ready to drop behind the hills—but I will stop for a minute or two, I guess, and check out what a Hudson River squatter's life is like.

11

~~

The Hudson River Champlain Canal

It is odd to paddle way up here and to be thinking about New York Harbor. But I'm dreaming of the sea because Nichols said when I reach the Battery, I will come across the old fireboat from the thirties, the most powerful fireboat in the world. Tied to the pier at Battery Park, the boat still puts out fires. He also said I should watch the wind as I canoe my last stretch of river down the Hudson along Manhattan's shore. He said the old piers for boats like the Queen Mary jut way out into the river around Forty-second Street. "Piers all run down now," he said shaking his head.

That talk of New York makes me want to paddle harder in this brown water. I don't want to stop here on Winchell's island. I want to keep moving and put some big miles behind me even though the day is shot and already it is late afternoon.

One thing is for sure—it's good to hold a paddle again after a day of interviews. There's nothing like this instrument of steerage and power, this weapon of grace, this javelin of homecoming. A paddle in the hand is a friend, a utensil of self-control. I like what veteran canoeist Paul Jamieson has said: "Time and place are at the will of the paddler."

I pull out on Winchell's flimsy dock. An American flag flutters on a nearby flagpole. I follow the tiny old man up a path cut in a scruffy island. He says he's been here about ten years. He's got a home in

Fort Edward, but comes here whenever he can. He loves this little mangy patch of grass. An old lawn mower sits beside a sort of hunting shack, and a small fire burns in a ring of rocks. Chairs are scattered everywhere—chairs of all discarded kinds, big ones, little ones, wire ones, wood ones, a greater variety of chairs than I've seen along the Hudson so far, where chairs seem to be the big item for enjoying the river, sitting and watching the sun go down over the water.

Winchell's three-acre island is at the epicenter of the PCB contamination and controversy. Smitty told me some Japanese scientists had been catching fish and cutting them open here in this "hot spot." General Electric was taking water samples, too, he reported. But as far as Smitty could tell, the river itself was much cleaner than it was in the old days. "In 1964," he said, "you could drop a flat rock into the canal and it'd practically float in human excrement." There was no sewage disposal in those days. On a muggy day you couldn't stand the smell. "A lot has changed since them days."

As forgiving and optimistic as Smitty was, Winchell is the opposite. He is angry and hard in his anger. He's also like a pack rat fighting for a secret cache of nuts. Some guy in town claims to own the island. And now, according to Winchell, after ten years the bastard is trying to reclaim it.

"He says it's his. But it ain't," says Winchell. Winchell is a scrapper, a fast talker in an almost unintelligible North Country accent.

"I traced it back. Two hundred years ago Colonel McGreggor owned all this frigging land. He's dead and ever since then it's been vacant. So I got squatter's rights since ten years ago."

He leans over the fire and plucks a coffee pot out of the coals, then picks up an empty tin cup, casts out its leftover grinds, fills it, and passes it to me. The smell of smoke in the setting sun on a scruffy squatter's island in the north woods is not unlike an Amazon ambiance—a third world, rudimentary olfactory experience. Grubby, but wonderfully grubby. There is something really appealing to me about all this scruffiness.

"Want some sugar? Hell, I got everything. I even got cream up in the refrigerator. It's a gas refrigerator."

Winchell does not come out here in the winter but has been known to visit his island with his wife as late as October.

27. Don Winchell on his island in PCB territory.

"If that guy thinks he's going to scare me off my island, he's crazier than a bedbug."

We sit on chairs, and he asks me where I started from. Soon he's back to the subject of his island.

"I love this frigging river," he says, sipping his coffee in the setting light.

"This frigging guy isn't going to get *me* off, no sir. By the time he gets me off this island I'll be dead."

It is unclear exactly who "he" is, but perhaps it doesn't matter. To Winchell, "he" is just all the bastards of the world, the victimizers, the oppressors and dominators, the United Fruit companies, the multinational enemies, the guys in the next town who are to blame for goddamn everything.

"Hell, I put a lot of work in here. Christ, when I come here, it was all brush and ferns and all poison ivy. First year we just sat on the ground. Jesus Christ, it rained and we got so frigging wet. Then I said, fuck that, and I decided to make a platform. Then I started hauling stuff over. It was tough. I got hurt when I worked with the state. Five years ago a steamroller tore my legs up. Christ, I got thirteen screws and all metal all the way down this leg. My ankle is shot, there ain't no pulse in it, and it aches all the time. It was smashed all to hell, like mush. I love it over here. My wife works. When she comes home tonight we'll both be down here. I go home and grab my mail and come down here. I love my island. I'm always cleaning it out, cleaning the brush and leaving it on shore and when it's high water, the brush is carried off."

I ask Winchell why this other guy wants suddenly to reclaim the island.

"The land was cheap here. Contaminated, they said. But now the PBCs [*sic*] are going, and the river is getting cleaner. Now *everyone* wants land here. This sucker probably thinks he can sell it off and make some money. But after ten years, squatters got *rights*. It'll be ten years next month."

Winchell is going to go to a "fucking lawyer," he says, and get "some of this shit," meaning some legal advice. "Hell, I ain't that fucking smart. I only went to one year of school and I quit."

"Are you Scotch?"

No, he says, "French and Indian. Family been here forever."

Secretly, I pour Winchell's coffee into the dirt behind me.

Bird feeders of all kinds hang from many branches. Some are tall, some wide and fat, some with metal perches, others all made of wood. They're full of seed, but I don't see any birds, until suddenly a cardinal flashes its crimson in the bushes. Winchell says his grandchildren often come over to play. He burns wood found on the island. They have big bonfires. The island is low, and it floods sometimes. Like this spring, a real wet one. The whole island gets flooded.

"What about the PCBs around here. People worry about that?"

"Heck, no. PBCs don't worry *me*. I been swimming in this river all my life. I swam near the paper mills when the river was so full of paper sludge, you couldn't hardly see. Jesus Christ, I ain't dead yet. But now it's a lot cleaner. You can see the bottom of the river now. All the trouble started when they took out that dam and they dredged all that shit from the bottom of the river. Now they want to dredge again. I say, leave it frigging alone."

This visit is like a glimpse into an earlier America. Later I will remember the chairs, the bird feeders, the gas refrigerator, everything secondhand and grimy looking. His little shack took six years to build.

"I got a door to the outhouse now, so when it's raining you don't have to go outside and get wet. And I got a Port-a-Potty, too. Just take it home and dump it. Didn't have to do no raking this spring, either. Flooding just took all the leaves off my island."

At the end of the movie *Papillon*, Dustin Hoffman, after so many years of trying and failing to escape from prison, has finally capitulated. He makes a little life for himself on Devil's Island, a modest but orderly existence with his chickens and tomatoes. Maybe he's gone crazy. Maybe Winchell is nuts, too. This is Winchell, short with a tiny blue hat, French—a little human chipmunk happy in this scruffy existence on his own Devil's Island. I like him.

"Everything come over by boat. Did it all by myself, too."

"I've got four or five miles to go to get to Lock 5 tonight," I say apologetically. "So I better push on. You've got a nice island."

We walk to the river.

"Bye. Good luck with your island."

"If you get on TV down there, tell 'em you stopped on Don Winchell's island, okay?"

"Okay, I'll do that." And I pull away from Winchell's paradise. I've met many squatters in the Amazon of Brazil, Ecuador, and Bolivia. But now I have visited their northern cousin, my first American squatter.

Most maps of the Hudson are highly detailed from Manhattan to Troy. This is the great route of commerce. Some even cover the forty canal miles above Troy to Fort Edward. But I have yet to find a good map that renders the details of the whole river from Lake Tear down to the sea. There is the New York State road map I have in my Bills bag, but I cannot find anything else that will help me. I wonder if this is because the river is so compartmentalized, so cut up and so diverse, that no commercial reason exists for a cartographer to make a good map of the whole thing. Perhaps the upper Hudson especially needs a new perspective, a better focus in relationship to the entire river.

The channel before me is marked by red and green buoys. Since I draw only a few inches of water, I can take short cuts from side to side and ignore the commercial markers. Of course when the dams approach, I'll follow the buoys religiously. But canoeing between these channel markers now adds a new restriction to the freedom of my trip.

Nichols had said, "And some guys don't even know you're supposed to stay inside those buoys!"

It is hot and muggy. I'm thirsty, and my arms are sore. The land is open with farms on either side. Even in Lossing's day there was a road down the western bank of the Hudson from Fort Edward to Troy. "A carriage-ride . . . down the valley of the Hudson . . . affords exquisite enjoyment to the lover of beautiful scenery and the displays of careful cultivation . . . and the traveller seldom loses sight of the noble stream. . . . The shores of the river are everywhere fringed with beautiful shake-trees and shrubbery, and fertile lands spread out on every side."

With the heavier load I picked up at Lock 7, the canoe tracks better, so I don't have to switch sides with my paddle as often. At times when I'm paddling along, suddenly an inescapable stench will rise up from the river, a dead fish or some cesspool, but it passes fast, and there's not a lot of this. Not nearly as much as I was led to expect. But, I wonder, what exactly a PCB is, and if it kills by radiation or can harm through skin contact, or if it has any odor. Perhaps I had hoped I might recognize it. Maybe, like cancer, it's an abstraction until it makes you sick and kills you.

People wave from motorboats racing by. Friendly motorists stop cars on nearby roads to wave eagerly, as if seeing a man paddling the river connects them to the water.

Then there are long stretches with no houses at all, very calm portions, followed by a Great blue heron startled in the reeds, its seven-foot grey wings flapping awkwardly into the sky.

This trip is all about meeting people like Winchell, Bishop, Nadeau, and Godfrey. People along the river cut the journey's tedium and break the miles into human components. It's no longer a journey of distance, but of humanity. A trip like this one, if you squint at its specifics, is not a long journey at all. The distance between people along the Hudson is not so far. Good people are everywhere. They dot the river like buoy markers. If I look at the channel markers, I see commerce, I see tugs or barges. But if I think about whom I've met along the way so far, I see a river full of stories and history, living still.

The difficult part of the trip is to be showerless for days on end, unable to use the river for a bath. In the upper Amazon of Brazil, we bathed at least four times a day in the river (the piranha only went for your flesh if you were bleeding!). The Brazilians were forever asking me, "Don't you think, Dom Pedro, it is time for us to take a bath?—*tomar banho.*" And I would slip with them into the brown river like a muskrat to cool off.

In Troy, I have decided, I will hunt down a motel, blow my money, and clean up. This will be my treat before I face the tides. It will be my shore leave. I might call Melissa and ask her to drive up to spend the night with me.

The main part of the river moves to the west of the island at Fort Miller and falls over a dam. In Lossing's day the ships occasionally would miss the channel and dive over the rocks. "When we visited the spot," says the traveling Victorian, "a large-class boat lay wrecked in the rapids below, having gone over the dam the day before."

I'm glad I follow the buoys correctly to the left of the island. The town of Fort Miller is hidden away off Route 4. You have to take a bridge to the island to find it. I pass great clapboard houses here in Tammy's town. At the end of the island, sheep graze near Lock 6. I paddle into the chamber—gates open, gates close, water drops 16.5 feet—and I am now only 102.5 feet above sea level. Another million gallons of Hudson water are displaced for a canoe. Lock 5 is still 3.64 miles away.

At the bottom of the lock chamber, the lock tender's voice startles as it echoes against four slimy walls, "How long you think it'll take you to reach 5?"

"Probably an hour or so," I say. "Will you tell the next guy I'm coming?"

"I *am* the next guy. I work both locks. I'll see you in an hour." He waves and disappears.

I paddle out. Then, oh shit, in this long, little channel, here comes a large Chris-Craft motorboat with a huge wake, but thank God it's slowing down, and the people aboard pass with a wave. Everyone tells me it will be hell on the lower Hudson, especially on weekends when the drunken maniacs emerge.

The paddling is not so tedious when I find a rhythm that works for me. If I fight the tedium and cannot enter a rhythm, I am lost. Sometimes random thoughts sabotage the rhythm, one thought leading illogically to another. I just realized, for example, that I have no name for my ship. Maybe I should call her "Lake Tear" to commemorate the birth of my journey. Now I am thinking how it's a drag to have to be at the Battery eight days from now. But I have no choice. I'm obligated to arrive at a certain hour (noon) on July 2, all for the Riverkeeper's publicity, for the photographers, the TV cameras. I hate it, being here and thinking about there. Too much thought takes away the freedom.

Two boys fishing yell, "Where you going?" I tell them. They say, "Really?"

It is a real river here, which feels nice. I'd rather be on a river than on a canal, even though this *is* the canal. Approaching Lock 5, I wonder if Ernie would be bored by the long, slow current.

On the opposite bank is a huge old tree. Three Huck Finns in cutoff jeans swing off a rope into the water below the tree. I drift listening to the delightful scream of one boy arcing way out and letting go the rope to land in the river. Another boy is too timid. His friends taunt him.

The water is chocolate brown, very much like the Amazon where the Rio Negro hits the Solimões at Manaus. The banks are bushy, and the trees lean out over the banks to get the sun. I hug the west shore for shade on this hot muggy, slow-dying day, one day before the summer solstice, the longest day of the year (good for long-distance paddling). Tomorrow is also Melissa's birthday. From the public phone at Lock 7, I sent flowers by credit card to arrive tomorrow.

Just before Lock 5, the dam comes right up to the channel, and the channel jogs to the right and gets jammed up against the west bank. Smitty's description was accurate—there is no warning here, only this long lip and the roar of falling water just beyond. A few buoys mark the route, but the river lulls you, and you have to be paying attention. If not, you could slide over that dam easily and crash on the rocks below.

Just before the lock, I get glimpses of a country road. Lining the river are a few colonial brick houses with crimson geraniums on back porches and canoes tipped over on the lawns that sweep down to the river's edge. Yet I haven't seen a single canoe *on* the water.

In the wild brush, in the abutments of old bridges, this portion of the river has the feel of the upper Hudson, the part Ernie and I paddled before the rapids. In fact, in the 150 miles I've traveled, I'm not sure I've passed one condo complex. The Hudson is surprisingly uncondominiumized.

"Come on," I say to my sluggishness, "Turn on the speed, Pete. Too much tourism and you'll never reach the big cities. Let's get this finished and have some caffeine and Stroganoff in the lock campground. Where the devil is it, anyway?"

The magic word *caffeine* instantly tightens the muscles in my arm. My right hand grabs the paddle so low it gets dunked in the water. Something swimming across the river heads straight for me. It looks like a snake. No, by God, it's a snapping turtle the size and color of a large cast-iron frying pan. It seems to be trailing a bunch of leaves on a branch. The snapper sees me and dives, but the leaves float free. Now it surfaces again to grab some air. Then down again. I wait for the resurfacing, but the leaves float free without the turtle. I pass on.

The Schuylerville lock appears, one of the oldest and most perfect specimens along the Barge Canal. Begun in 1915, Lock 5 was completed in 1917. Everything here is original. The incandescent lights, the hydro-generators, the powerhouse—all the hard surfaces are painted in the state colors, dark blue and yellow, everything according to regulations, no room for imagination, but beautiful really. Lock 5 and Lock 2 are the only locks in the whole state that still maintain the original hydro-generators. At most locks the powerhouses were torn down when the hydro-generators were taken out.

Smitty had said candidly, "We paint these locks every year, but I think it's make-work. You wouldn't paint your house every year. You wouldn't paint your lawn furniture every year. But we paint and maintain every single piece of equipment on these locks—so much I'd like to be the paint company who has the state contract. Christ, these locks got 150 layers on them already. All we ever do is paint them over and over."

But I think there's something old-world and respectful about their impeccable upkeep. In a land of shoddiness, in these river towns of abandoned mills and suffering economy, the locks are like a living museum. I pitch my tent, pull out my little stove, and start the nightly ritual of macaroni and coffee in the mosquito-attacking dusk. Tonight, a variation: Lipton's noodles and chicken sauce and Ramen Pride oriental noodles with shrimp.

The lock tender chats while a line of ants forms over the white roof of my pup tent. I ask how many boats came through today. He says, "You're the fourth pleasure craft today."

"Not much traffic, but I suppose it'll pick up in July, right?"

"Sure, but no one knows why we've had so few boats. Usually we have much more by now."

He's waiting for a sailboat coming up from Lock 4, fourteen miles downriver, but he's been waiting a long time. Perhaps the sailboat has ducked into one of the three marinas between the two locks for the night. Once he had a guy camp here who had been canoeing for two years all the way across America. The canoeist said he'd had a partner at first, but they started to fight, and he left his partner somewhere in Ohio. "We get all kinds," the lock man says. "They come, they camp, then we never hear from them again."

Hearing this, I vow to write Nichols, Alexis, Godfrey, and Smitty after my trip is over.

Schuylerville is the site of Burgoyne's October 17, 1777 surrender to General Gates, perhaps the event that decided the outcome of the Revolution. But this town, like the towns just south of here, is sadly neglected these days. Originally called Old Saratoga, Schuylerville was the central point on the new canal. The busiest street in town was Canal Street. Along the river was a big barn where a hundred mules were kept for towing the barges. During the boom of the canal in the 1820s, this region's potatoes were shipped by barge to New York City. Schuylerville was abuzz with freight forwarders, barge factories, merchants, insurers, boatmen, and teamsters. Between World War I and World War II, twelve factories in the area made window sashes and blinds and paper products out of pulpwood from the Adirondacks— cardboard boxes, toilet tissue, wallpaper. There was even a cotton mill in town.

Now the factories are defunct, the roofs caving in. An air of abandonment hangs over the hazy summer day like despair. Speaking about how the Reagan years of prosperity passed by so many of

America's small towns, Schuylerville resident James Howard Kunstler has written in *The New York Times Magazine,* "in Schuylerville, and in many of the old industrial towns up the Hudson River—Mechanicville, Fort Edward, Hudson Falls . . . it wasn't morning in America at all. It was more like 4 P.M. on the first day of winter."

Long before any hint of light, after a deep but too-short sleep, I am up carrying my canoe to the other end of the lock. I love early morning on a river trip. After coffee, I can approach the day from its belly side, and I've got a jump on the world.

I have no time for a visit to the little historic town of Schuylerville a mile from here, but I've already seen it from my car last month when I began to scout this section of river, and there's simply no time now to be a tourist of the Revolution. I want to reach Troy tonight, which is thirty miles away, making this my longest day of solo paddling. (Ernie and I covered roughly this same distance from Blue Ledge to the Glen.) Today I'm heading for a shower and a good meal. I don't know where, but somewhere in a big city.

I slide the canoe into the water and paddle in the darkness past a little boat basin.

Kunstler's point about Schuylerville is that until such small towns in America reestablish local economies, as in the old days, their communities will not flourish. Tourism doesn't work. As in Luzerne, people in cars only pass through Schuylerville, too. The few businesses here funnel the tourist money outside the community. Kunstler calls towns like Schuylerville and Luzerne, "colonies" and says: "I think we are entering an era when small towns will have no choice except to reinvent truly local economies using local assets. The Hudson is Schuylerville's prime asset. To me, a plausible future for the town is one in which people rediscover the river's value and harness its power to make something useful in a way that is not harmful and wasteful. And in the process, perhaps, rediscover their own value."

This is a vague but reasonable suggestion, yet Kunstler never gives concrete examples of what river towns like Schuylerville, Fort Edward, Hudson Falls, and Mechanicville can do to reinvent their local economies vis-à-vis the Hudson.

In the dawning mist, long, endless, sweeping bends float me past Bemis Heights, where Burgoyne's army engaged the Americans, where the Revolution's outcome "turned." The slaughter yard of the

Revolution is now farm country. "[It] is said that the fertility imparted to the soil by the blood and offal left there was visible in its effects upon the crops raised thereon." The 1990 barns look as hopeless and abandoned as the factories, their roofs leaning inward, tractors half in weeds.

An old tavern called Bemis, "famous for good wines and long pipes," once stood here. Lossing said the pleasant hamlet of Bemis Heights was "one of the numerous offsprings of the canal."

The day is long, and the heating of the earth is followed by the heating of the river, until the muggy day and hazy sunshine drive me right up to the western bank into the shade of the big old trees that weep over the water.

At "the head of long rapids," the village of Stillwater is about thirteen miles south of Schuylerville. Benson Lossing considered it "the most pleasing in situation and appearance of all the villages in the valley of the Upper Hudson."

Mechanicville, with its old buildings abandoned and half demolished alongshore, has a kind of archaeological beauty, those factories reflected in the still river. There is power in the veins of neglected history, a memory of Dickens and the dawning of the Industrial Revolution—memories of the free-polluting days when spewing smokestacks could not deter a nation's progress.

Mechanicville must be a hard place to live, however, especially for the parents of the idle young. In an April 19, 1990, *New York Times* article, I had read that although many towns in America had instituted curfews to control their youngsters, Mechanicville had recently established a curfew to punish *the parents of errant youths*. "The Mayor, dusting off a 1915 ordinance that seems to have never been enforced, is vowing to clamp down on any parent whose child is found out and about after 10 P.M. First-time violators will be fined $25, he said, but after that they risk going to jail."

I stop at a vacant cement pier, weeds shooting out of the cracks, just south of town. I tie up near a fifty-foot cabin cruiser. An elderly German woman hanging damp clothes on deck says to me, "My husband loves this. He's always wanted to travel around for a year by boat. But I don't know . . . I just don't know." The hot sun saps the life from her words. Her hair is unkempt. She moves about the boat sluggishly, lost on board her own ship.

Living aboard boats is a life apart. Her husband has broken a tooth and wandered up into town searching for a dentist. I ask her to watch my canoe so I too can wander up into the working-class neighborhood past sultry, dirty-faced kids hanging out of brick tenement factory housing. Some of the curfewed errant youths of this old factory town are smoking cigarettes outside a convenience store where I buy coffee and a copy of *USA Today*.

A tiny article in the sports pages today, Thursday, June 21, 1990, entitled "Author on Hudson River 'adventure'" begins jauntily, "To many, the Hudson River brings to mind a murky brown soup. But there is an effort on to show the river offers beauty and adventure. Author Peter K. Lourie will canoe the entire 315 miles. He started at the Lake of the Tears in the Adirondacks June 11 and plans to end in the Battery in Manhattan July 2. Wednesday he was near Troy, N.Y."

The journalist has Lake Tear of the Clouds wrong. "Lake of the Tears" sounds much sadder than its real name. The next part is pure PR from Cronin, my sponsor, "He and his sponsor, the Hudson Riverkeeping Fund [another mistake] want the journey to remind people—particularly those in New York City—how important a clean river is. The journey, promoters say [you'd think I was a prize fighter], will provide New Yorkers with a stronger connection to the environment outside of the city and help them gain a better understanding of why the Hudson should not be exploited."

I notice the German woman already has her copy of *USA Today*.

She takes my photograph as I shove off into the heat. Somewhere I come to the village of Half-Moon (though Hudson did not bring his ship this far).

At Lock 2, Lester Moll, son of a lock tender, stands high above me on the wall, and my canoe drops eighteen feet. He is a silhouette in the solstice sun. I cannot see Lester very well. The sun behind him blots out his face. He is not in a talkative mood. Reluctantly, he answers one of my questions. "The old days are gone. The river isn't the same. All we get now is barges of jet fuel."

I wonder where the jet fuel is headed, perhaps up Lake Champlain to Plattsburgh and the air force base there.

Finally I reach Waterford, a small industrial city that Lossing described more than a hundred years ago as "a very pleasant town, at the confluence of the Mohawk and Hudson river," with little more than 3,000 inhabitants. "Most of its streets are fringed with maple and elm." It was then "a young town, compared with Lansingburgh, its still more pleasant neighbour across the river."

The Champlain Canal meets the Erie Canal in Waterford. Here the Mohawk, the Hudson's largest tributary, flows through a network of islands to reach the Hudson. Some boys are skipping stones along the river where the two canals join. I come upon them suddenly, and they have to check their throws mid-arm so as not to hit me. I take their photograph, and they tell me they never swim here because it's just too dirty. "That's a shame," I say, "because I've seen kids swinging on ropes into the water all the way down from Newcomb."

The tallest boy points to the river. "We don't swim because of that." Dead fish float in the sudsy water, and I have to paddle through hundreds of bloated, smelly bodies.

I hug the shore because a strong south wind is picking up and driving the wide river into fierce whitecaps. When I pass the Erie Canal, I can see the first great lock as the canal heads west toward the Great Lakes.

The dead fish multiply near Cohoes and Watervliet, the floating white bellies everywhere. But I have no time to be sad. I paddle hard against a hard wind through sudsy chop, through bodies of dead fish flowing off my hull like soap bars in a bathtub.

Troy seems like the most polluted part of the river so far. Compare Lossing's observation: "The scenery about the mouth of the Mohawk, particularly in the vicinity of Cohoes Falls, is exceedingly picturesque." Benson Lossing and his wife took time to visit the falls, the spectacular ninety-foot drop where the Mohawk valley empties into the Hudson Valley. The energy harnessed from this cataract has run mills and factories for centuries. After witnessing the falls (invisible from the Hudson), Lossing planned—like me—to lodge the night in Troy.

Hugging the western shore, I reach Van Schaick's Marina on Van Schaick Island, where, exhausted, I ask the owner if he has any rooms, but his place is shut down for renovations. Greatly disappointed (by now I crave coffee in a china cup and will gladly relinquish my cowboy coffee and macaroni over a slow camp stove), I shove off into a swelling south wind. When I finally reach the other side, just south of the old village of Lansingburgh, my canoe seems to stand still in the whipping water no matter how fast I move my paddle. Here are my first real whitecaps, which bash me back if I take the slightest rest from paddling.

At last I paddle through the froth, the suds, the black and white water, and the fish bodies to my final canal lock. The dam that runs from the lock to the other shore is 1,200 feet long and was built by Henry Ford when he constructed a plant at the other end. Below the massive barrage, the Hudson turns tidal.

I paddle safely into the lee of the cement walls, when suddenly through a megaphone an angry voice is shouting at me, "Hold. Hold up over there. That canoe there, *what the hell* do you think you're doing? I have a boat in the lock. Pull over, pull over, god damn it."

I am confused. Is the voice directed at me? What have I done? I have come to expect more of Alexis's brand of courtesy—which has made this canal river such fine paddling—from all New York State lock tenders. But to arrive at Federal Lock 1, my final lock before the tides begin, to be screamed at—well, to put it mildly, I feel a riot of emotions. First, confusion; second, shame and embarrassment; and third, an anger so sharp I vividly imagine myself hopping out on the cement wall, running up to the lock house, and ramming that megaphone into the lock tender's choppers until his face bleeds.

The iron gates open. A twenty-five-foot pleasure boat runs past me, and soon the megaphone blares, "Okay. You in the canoe—proceed."

As I pull into the lock, a man in an official tan uniform walks up slowly to the lock wall. He's so fuming mad, he can't say much. "A canoe?" is all he says.

I have a great need to explain myself, and I take the soft approach. I tell him about my trip, about the kindness of the lock tenders at the state locks, who have always locked me through ("Didn't they tell you I was coming?" "No?"). In his silence I even explain that today is my wife's birthday, and that I really ought to get to a phone to give her a call.

I have noticed that when some people hear that you're married, everything is okay with them. After a few minutes, the federal lock tender, who is also married, does soften a bit. He even wants to help me to a motel, probably because he thinks I'll be safer off the river. "Okay," he says. "I'll lock you through, but be careful on the other side. The tides are strong. Stay to the left and go into the marina just down by the old city."

All regulation and superiorlike, he says, "Don't you have a fog horn? You really should have a fog horn, you know. That's regulations."

"Yes, sir. I'll try to get one tonight in Troy. Thank you."

Certainly, I have reached a river of regulations. Yet from Troy to Manhattan, a highly populated lower river, I will find in many ways the Hudson grows wilder, too, more raucous, even lawless. The lower Hudson River is one of the last wild places in a terrain of industry and commutation. Regulations on the lower river exist primarily on the roads and in the zoning laws of the towns and cities that surround and engulf this last piece of wilderness. The Hudson is like a straight arrow of watery freedom running its own law and timetables through the heart of the nation and leading finally to the sea.

A big boat waits just outside the lock doors to be locked up into the canals. I drop my final fourteen feet of the upper river. I've come safely to the tides of the Hudson, and I am glad to be free of canals now. I've traveled forty miles in two days.

Stretching out in front of me is a new freedom—tidal paddling on the largest freshwater estuary in the world. The freedom of saltwater ahead reaches out in front of me like a song. Gulls soar above the bridges that span the river between Watervliet and Troy. Gulls like the good omen of dolphins around the prow of a ship. I like to see them swirl above my little seaworthy canoe. They make me dream of the sea.

I dig the tide chart out of my Bills bag and realize from now on I better check it often. Right away, I can feel the strength of the sea and the moon pulling at my frail vessel. I paddle past Green Island a mile or so to the Marina just north of downtown historic Troy.

According to the New York State Engineers Survey of 1901, the elevation of Waterford at the junction of the Erie Canal is 15.2 feet above sea level. U.S. Lock 1 has a fourteen-foot drop, so the six-mile paddle from Troy to sister city Albany (at low tide) will be only 1.25 feet above the level of the Atlantic, yet I am still 151 miles away from true saltwater! So finally I've reached the level of my destination, yet am far from this destination still.

At the floating dock of Troy Town Dock & Marina, at near low tide, way below the level of the land, I am met by a pretty, blond college girl, who says a bouncy, happy "Hi there." Smiling Heather is dockmistress for the summer, and she calls the owner from her portable telephone.

An architect, a man about my age, upscale, upbeat, yuppy-ish, comes down from his office across the parking lot. He says, sure I can put my boat here. I can pay by the footage for storing my canoe in his basement. I shouldn't leave it out all night, either. It's a bad area, and the canoe could easily get stolen.

"So how long is it?" he asks as I fork over eighteen dollars.

"Eighteen and a half feet. You want the half-dollar?"

"Nah," he says smiling, "keep it. You'll need it."

I've arrived in the big city, all right. What I do not want this guy to know is that I'm so exhausted I would probably pay a hundred dollars to stop here. I don't want to paddle one more nautical inch today. I have a rendezvous with a shower and a phone call to my birthday wife. And somewhere I'd like to eat a fancy meal.

High on the wall of a nearby building, there is a sign that reads: "March 28, 1913: High Water." This was the same year the flooding Hudson wiped out so many bridges in Glens Falls and above. Logs from Mount Marcy were swept all the way to Troy.

I drop the canoe on his basement floor and walk my Bills bag across a highway. I feel like a bearded tugboatman pulling in for shore leave. The architect said there was a Super 8 motel just up the road. And for forty-two dollars I take a room and crash on a soft bed like a whaler in port with my TV dancing a loud blue light before me in a wonderful blur while I nap a dead man's nap.

PART THREE

The Tide

The Tides

MOHAWK RIVER

Schenectady
Cohoes
Troy
Albany Rensselaer
Castleton-on-Hudson
Coeymans
New Baltimore
Stuyvesant
Coxsackie
Athens
Catskill Hudson
Cementon Germantown
Saugerties Tivoli
Kingston Rhinebeck
Port Ewen
Hyde Park
Poughkeepsie
Wappingers Falls
New Hamburg
Newburgh Beacon

5   10   15
miles

3. From Troy to Beacon.

12

Canoeing the Tides

June 21. 8 P.M. All around me, laughter and Brahms and the sharp clink of wine glasses in the smoky air. The River Cafe in a converted warehouse along the Hudson is the best place to eat in downtown Troy. For the canoeist on a long haul, it's a refuge for drinking coffee with a tint of cinnamon, then three Saratoga waters with lemon twists, and still I cannot get rid of my paddler's thirst. After a thirty-mile, fourteen-hour paddle, I need no booze to give me this boozy feeling of pleasant dislocation. Having showered and wished Melissa a happy birthday, having then arranged to meet Jim Shaughnessy, the world's expert on the Delaware & Hudson Railroad, I am drunk on the pleasure of arrival.

It was here that Henry Hudson and his eighteen-man crew gave up their search for the Northwest water passage to China. Late in September in 1609, Hudson and his men turned around at this, their most northerly reach into a strange continent. The river would not take the eighty-four-foot, 122-ton *Half Moon* any farther north. The shallows began, the shores grew narrow, and the first European anabasis came to a disappointing halt.

The *Half Moon* anchored near Albany while a few of Hudson's men rowed their skiff the six miles to Troy (some say Waterford), where they found "but seven foot water, and unconstant soundings." Indians who gave the Europeans pelts and food near modern-day

Troy were fed liquor by the captain to see if "there was trecherie in them."

The *Half Moon* needed more than seven feet of water; my canoe requires only a few inches. I have seen the river that Henry Hudson could never travel, and now this city and the River Cafe mark the beginning of Hudson's river, the start of the famous lower river, the much-known, highly industrialized habitation of millions. From Troy to Manhattan is the river most people think of when they hear the word *Hudson.*

At seven-thirty, Jim Shaughnessy appears. He is a burly, gentle Irishman of about fifty or so, an engineering consultant and part-time teacher at the Rensselaer Polytechnic Institute. He looks slightly disheveled. His face is friendly. His great passion is railroads. I had called him months ago to see if he would meet me when I passed through Troy. I had been following the Delaware & Hudson tracks all the way from North Creek. Maybe he could give me a railroad perspective of this river.

Shaughnessy is curious about everything. He has a large appetite for ideas and details, and he wants to know all about my journey. "So," he says, "where did you start from today?"

"I left Lock 5 in Schuylerville very early."

"On the Champlain canal? Well, well, well, you're making some headway, but aren't you supposed to be camping on an island in a pup tent and roasting a hot dog?" Jim's bushy eyebrows dance with mirth.

"This is 1990. I'm not roughing it *all* the way," I say.

"Heh, I'm all for it," the Irishman says somewhat conspiratorially, as if I've been cheating maybe just a little. "I see no problem with your approach . . . but how did you come upon this idea of canoeing the Hudson in the first place?"

Shaughnessy wants to know *the real reason* I'm making the trip. He says, "What do you do for a living, *really?*" His eyebrows settle severely over his eyes, and he gazes intently at me, waiting for a straight answer. So I give him the long version—I tell him about my trips to South America and to Africa in my carefree, bachelor days; and then marriage and settling down and a baby; and now, on a whim, a desire for adventure close to home.

"How's your wife look at all this?" Shaughnessy's smile cannot hide his amazement.

"Right now she's busy with a Shakespeare Festival. I wonder if she even misses me."

"Beautiful. Couldn't work out better, eh?" I order him a glass of wine.

Shaughnessy attributes his fascination with the Delaware & Hudson Railroad to an uncle who used to work with the company and who took him for train rides when he was a boy. "It was just contagious," says the train enthusiast.

He's studied the canals, too, because "the railroad *grew up* with the canal. The D & H Railroad was originally the D & H Canal Company, the oldest continually operated transportation company in America." He says, "The D & H has existed since 1823. In the 1930s they owned steamboat lines and lime quarries. The company was a multinational before the term was invented!" Although in 1990 the D & H is in Chapter 11 and may not exist much longer, it has not yet dissolved. Shaughnessy speaks about the company as if it had the longevity of a Tibetan monk.

"Both the canal and the railroad opened up the North Country," he says. "They brought Adirondack lumber overland to city markets. Downtown Troy has changed since the old train yards disappeared. I'll give you a tour after dinner if you have time."

One Samuel Wilson of Troy, who was concerned with army beef supply during the War of 1812, is said to have been the original "Uncle Sam." These days, Troy is famous for Freihofers Bakery, and for America's first engineering college, the Polytechnic Institute, and for Emma Willard School for girls, one of a dying breed. Shaughnessy says Troy used to be a city of shirts and ironworks. It was once the detachable shirt-collar capital of the East. He remembers also the big iron industry in the south of the city, where iron came from mines like the one at Tahawus. Troy iron companies were the first to manufacture the machinery that made horseshoes during the Civil War, he says. "In fact, one local company worked on the iron plates of the Monitor!"

Known originally as Ferry Hood, Troy grew rapidly in the early days. Town lots were laid out in the summer of 1787. Two years later residents met in Albany to resolve that "in future it should be called and known by the name of Troy" and that it "may not be too sanguine to expect, at no very distant period, to see Troy as famous for her trade and navigation as many of our first towns."

Incorporated into a city in 1816, Troy was settled by enterprising New Englanders, who "perceived the advantages of their location at the head of the tide-water and sloop navigation." By 1860, it boasted 50,000 residents.

In October 1825, Governor De Witt Clinton arrived after a ten-day trip from Buffalo on the newly opened Erie Canal with a flask of water from Lake Erie, which he dropped into the Hudson. This was the famous "wedding of the waters" ceremony, the mixing of Great Lake water with Atlantic seawater flowing up the 154 miles of Hudson tides.

With canal completion, Troy replaced Albany as the head of navigation on the Hudson. Troy was the ideal spot for freight to change from boats to railroad cars, but eight years after the Champlain Canal was finished in 1833, the Troy to Saratoga railroad began to compete for freight. The state, which had promoted the canal system, was reluctant to grant permission for the railroads that might steal freight business from the newly opened canal. In the end, however, the train to Saratoga was successful in obtaining a charter to build a bridge over the river here in 1834 (it has since become a highway bridge).

"The most difficult section to build from Troy to Waterford," writes Shaughnessy in his book *Delaware and Hudson*, "containing four bridges including the large one over the Hudson at Troy, was opened October 6, 1835, and the cars that rolled over the bridge at Troy that day were the first ever to cross the Hudson. The trains were pulled by horses through the Troy streets from the depot at 10 First Street to the bridge and across to Green Island where the locomotive was hooked on."

"So now you could come up from New York by steamboat to Troy and then board the train for Saratoga, which was very popular in those days. When the Whitehall section was completed, you could travel all the way from New York to Montreal by steamship and rail."

Shaughnessy politely orders another glass of red wine.

"I saw dead fish near Waterford," I say hesitantly, not wanting to sound too critical of his portion of the river. "What's going on around here?"

"After the war, the pollution increased. Since the mid-sixties, however, I've seen it go back down. Maybe part of what you saw was the natural cycle of spawning and dying smelt, suckers and whitefish."

True, but judging from the filthy suds in the river at the meeting of the two canals, and knowing the Mohawk River's reputation for pollution, I cannot help believing this must be the most polluted part of the entire 315-mile Hudson.

Downstairs we pass the owner of the River Cafe, whose face is red from cooking over flames. Shaughnessy says, "This guy has just canoed from Lake Tear of the Clouds."

"Oh really. I tell you," says the chef-owner, "sure is beautiful country up there. Harsh enough, too, to keep all the assholes out. But the blackflies are *murder.*"

We climb into a plush Ford Crown Victoria, vintage 1980s, and drive to Monument Square a few blocks away. Troy is a city in transition. Like so many river towns, with its heyday long past, Troy is having a hard time making a comeback. A big hotel has recently been sandblasted and converted into apartments and offices, but much of the building remains vacant. Urban redevelopment, Shaughnessy says, is like dropping a pebble in the water. The first to be refurbished are the buildings at the center, then buildings are redone further away, and the fixing up moves outward in concentric rings.

As we walk through the streets of this partly redeveloped city, Shaughnessy points here and there trying to re-create the old days of boom-town Troy. "Up here," Shaughnessy lifts his arm, "was the *Troy Citizens Night Line,* a steamboat competitor of the *Hudson River Day Line.* You could book a stateroom for the night and wake up in New York. This is where they docked. Those buildings over there were commercial buildings related to the river trade around the 1860s. Cargo was loaded right here."

Shaughnessy's excitement is infectious. His pointing finger and lifted arm are like paintbrushes as he colors the old city canvas once again. I can almost hear the bustle of the river days as the scene grows vivid before me. I know, however, that nostalgia tends to cleanse the past. This must have been a busy, dirty, grubby industrial city in its prime.

"The original D & H branch from Troy to Saratoga, in fact, had its station right there where that building stands, see it? They used to bring the train cars down this very street *by horse*. The citizens didn't like locomotives coming into town because it scared their horses."

Urban Renewal was the state program in the '60s that led to so much tearing down of old buildings along the Hudson. Up and down the river, you hear good and bad things about Urban Renewal, which was essentially a demolition program. The idea was to demolish buildings that were beyond repair, many of which were also historically important.

"Urban Renewal was an attempt to modernize things," says Shaughnessy. "The automobile created the problem. In an old city like Troy, all the businesses had concentrated in one little area, but public transportation was bad. There was no parking. So when the cars came, they closed the center down. Suburbia thrived. Historic buildings were torn down. The inner cities along the Hudson died by strangulation. The concept behind Urban Renewal was to create open space and invigorate downtowns, but it had the opposite effect. True, we can't keep places that aren't viable, but some buildings of true architectural value must survive at all costs. It's always a compromise."

Shaughnessy is a good amateur photographer, so I ask him what I might photograph on the river tomorrow.

"Maybe you can find some old icehouses left—if they exist. There were a lot of icehouses in the old days. Great chunks of ice were cut from the river in winter and stored until the river was navigable when the ice went out. Then these huge blocks of ice were barged down to the city. I can remember barges with windmills on them which helped pump out the water from the melting ice as they went. After the war, the icehouses were turned into mushroom houses. My dad used to take us by boat to the icehouses just below Castleton. I remember rows of dark buildings, growing mushrooms in there. Those icehouses ran along the river from Albany south."

A man who loves railroads naturally loves nineteenth-century industry of all kinds. "Don't forget the brickworks along the Hudson," he tells me. "Hudson River bricks were shipped to New York City.

The old skyscrapers of New York are built from Hudson River bricks."

We walk out to the new City Hall building right on the river, where a Disney version of a paddleboat is about to sail with a party aboard. It is all lit up and loud with cheering passengers. American flags are draped around the boat. There's a slight Bourbon Street, New Orleans, feeling about old Troy these days, a real attempt by the tourist bureau to capitalize on the past. Glorification of what has come before us is a way of making the drab present seem more colorful, I suppose. Celebrating history is another way of throwing a big party.

Shaughnessy and I lean on the railing, gazing out at the party boat that runs dinner cruises down to Albany and back. In the bright lights from the boat, Shaughnessy's eyes appear damp. "*Sure* we're looking at *a fake boat*," the friendly Irishman says, "but the river *has come back*."

I hear triumph in Shaughnessy's voice. "It's come back as recreation. There was a time, not long ago, when you'd come down here and the river smelled awful. Maybe today it's not pristine like the earliest days. But I'll tell you, it's a hell of an improvement from the way it was."

Cheers and screams rise into the belly of the hot night as the mock paddle wheeler draws away into the dark tide of the river. A fanfare of trumpets and banjos fills the balmy air.

"This kind of thing promotes the river. Maybe no one on that boat knows what you and I know about the river, but the fact of the matter is they're here and they're enjoying it."

"Well, it's getting late, Jim. I've got an early tide to catch. Perhaps we'll meet again," I say.

All night my arms lie limp from so much paddling. No matter what position I take, the nerves in both arms get pinched by the heaviness of my inert flesh. I'm too tired to dream of tomorrow, of my journey on the "drowned river," the 154 miles of Hudson estuary.

June 22. I wake up in a fit of sunlight, the day already hot. I hike a block to McDonalds for an Egg McMuffin and coffee. A bum is putting his cigarette out in the glare of the street. I hold the door for another bum, who thinks this is great. In a flourish of mock chivalry, he enters with a bow, then holds the door for me, too.

Clusters of unshaven men reek of alcohol, and sip coffee. The polite manager is perhaps thirty or so, and he too looks a little unshaven.

The Hudson River is only a block away, so I ask, "What do you think of the Hudson River?" It's a question to which I expect no answer, like casting a lure into a deep sea.

The manager's eyes drop to the floor. Slowly, deeply, he speaks, "I can't talk about it."

He has put my food into a bag before he continues, "I grew up here. But I don't go down to the river no more. I don't even fish down there no more." He and his best friend were drinking in a rowboat five years ago, when a Coast Guard cutter came along and swamped them. His best friend drowned.

"I tried to help him." The manager looks at the counter, his eyes lifeless, "but I had enough trouble saving my own life." His whole face pleads for sympathy. "We were drunk. Neither of us could swim."

"I'm sorry for asking. Are you okay now?"

"Sure, but I don't talk about it no more. There's a lot of suicides off Congress Street Bridge. There's dying all around the river. I don't like the Hudson no more."

A grey-bearded drunk steps up to the cash register. The manager says, "Hey, Ted," and the old drunk pours pennies onto the counter.

"See you later," I say.

The morbid story disturbs me. I am keenly aware that the big water, the big ships, the sea wind, and the tides with their strong currents lie ahead of me. John Cronin warned me before I left that the river is most dangerous when the wind blows one way and the tide drives the water the other way. He said to be careful and always watch the other boats to see what the tide and current are doing to them. I know one thing: at least I will not be drunk out there. And I will pull ashore if the water gets too rough.

Dockmistress Heather is unfortunately not at work this early in the morning. I'd like to see her smile before I go, but the basement of the architect's building is unlocked, and I lift my canoe from the cement floor. It seems heavier today. As I carry the Odyssey to the river, I wonder when I'll begin to feel the good fear, the fear of adventure and the thrill of getting on the river once again. I'm waiting for that rush of love for the Hudson that I've felt on some recent days.

I will be following the *Half Moon*'s 1609 retreat to the sea, and the smell of the sea is unmistakable. The gulls lift and soar in the briny breeze. The great salt Poseidon beckons, and it is fitting that Lansingburgh was Herman Melville's home when he quit the sea and began to write. In 1844, seven years before *Moby Dick* was published, Melville came back to write romances at his family's house in Lansingburgh, now part of Troy, ten miles up the Hudson River from Albany.

Today, the porch of Melville's home is falling off. Paint chips lie about the house. The backyard is completely overgrown. The year 1991 marks the centennial of his death, and the local historical society is making plans for restoration of the house. Only part of the first floor is now used as a museum. The rest of the house is divided into apartments, which help pay the historical society's bills. One of these apartments includes the very room where Melville wrote his first book, its window looking down on a riverside park, which was a shipyard in Melville's day.

Melville may even have gleaned some of his sea stories from sailors living along the Hudson. After he left Troy he moved to Pittsfield, Massachusetts, and then to New York City, where for nineteen years he was a district inspector of customs. In his later years he lacked an audience. His disappointment and obscurity at the end of his life are reflected a hundred years later in the disrepair of his family home along the great river at the head of canal navigation.

On the back cover of my tide book, a chart displays the distances in nautical miles between all major ports from Albany down to the Battery and Melville's beloved sea. In the next ten days I'll pass Castleton, Hudson, Catskill, Saugerties, Kingston, Poughkeepsie, Beacon, Cold Spring, Peekskill, Haverstraw, Nyack, Yonkers, and Englewood Cliffs before I finally reach New York City's Battery Park. From Albany to the Battery will be 125.4 *nautical* miles, and there are only 71.9 nautical miles to go from Albany to my home in Beacon. This doesn't sound like much.

Merriam Webster's Collegiate Dictionary says a nautical mile is "any of various units of distance used for sea and air navigation based on the length of a minute of arc of a great circle of the earth and differing because the earth is not a perfect sphere" (whatever that means) and "an international unit equal to 6076.115 feet . . . used officially in the U.S. since July 1, 1959." A nautical mile is 796.115 feet longer than a land mile. Multiplying the 71.9 nautical miles from Albany to Beacon by the 796.115 feet per nautical mile extra I'll have to paddle, I come up with a total of about 57,240 feet, which is an extra 10.84 landlubber miles. About 83 land miles then remain until I eat a home-cooked meal. But these are 83 miles of river that Ernie thought might be harder to paddle than the rapids.

To understand what paddling a tiny canoe on the lower Hudson is all about, I will relate what my nautical chart says about tides. In *Hudson River Tide and Current Data*, distributed by Sea Explorer Ship 168, an arm of the Boy Scouts of America, I find the following:

> A northbound current is a "flood" current (F), and a southbound current is an "ebb" current (E). The "slack" is the time between flood and ebb when the current pauses before reversing direction. A typical cycle will begin with a "slack before flood" (SBF), when the current has zero velocity and then starts flowing north. It will pick up speed until the time of "maximum flood" (MF) is reached, whereupon the northbound current starts to lose speed, reaching zero velocity again at "slack before ebb" (SBE) time, when it turns south. The southbound current will speed-up until "maximum ebb" (ME) is reached, whereupon it will start to slow down, coming to a stop at SBF.

As a canoeist heading south, I am of course mainly interested in the ebb tide. But each tide is more complicated than a simple flowing of water in one direction. Each tide is affected by myriad forces. The momentum in the river during any one tide builds up so inexorably that it takes a long time to reverse this momentum. It actually takes one and one-half hours for the full volume of the river to change course, even after the tide has long changed. This lingering effect is strongest mid-channel. Low tide, for instance, can be at noon but the slack between the tides might not come until two o'clock.

My tide booklet goes on to explain that when the moon is full or new, the tidal range for that day will be greater than on a day when the moon is near its quarter. Also, tide and current predictions for any given day can be off as much as thirty to ninety minutes. "The effects of several days of abnormally high or low barometric pressure, or several days of continual north or south winds, or a period of heavy rain—producing great discharges from the Hudson's tributaries" can change the tables drastically. Also, warns the Sea Explorer's booklet, "tide and current times are given for mid-channel points in the Hudson. The times of current events along the river's banks DO NOT correspond with the time of the events in mid-channel, and *local knowledge should be applied*" (italics mine).

In the winter from my house in Beacon, I have watched ice moving alongshore in a southerly direction while the ice in the center of the river is moving north. Apparently the current starts to reverse alongshore first while the main current is still moving the other way in the center of the river.

All of this tide stuff seems very confusing. My chart tells me approximately when the river will go slack and when it will reach maximum ebb (my ticket to ride downriver on a watery conveyor belt). I will have to depend on these projected times. But the same document tells me I cannot rely on these figures, either. One thing is for sure—I don't think I'll be in the middle of the channel if I can help it. That's where the currents are the strongest and where the big boats might knock me down.

7:31 A.M. A late start. Darn, I should have left earlier. The wind is coming up from the south. Just as Ernie said: "When you're in a canoe the wind's always against you."

Today I'm feeling as sluggish as the air looks. It's going to be a humid, hazy day, too. At 8:42 the river will reach maximum ebb (ME), after which point, the water will begin to slow its course to the sea, and the tidal drop—the level of the water where it hits the land—will gradually ease until it reaches the slack before the flood (SBF).

The tidal drop around Troy is roughly five feet, and I'm told the currents are worse in the spring, when they can reach five knots from a swelling river fed by snow melting in the mountains up north.

I pack all my gear just in front of the center seat. The architect comes down to the water to say good-bye. He has a mug of coffee in his hand. "Good luck," he says. "Stay close to shore."

I point my canoe into the water. Just down from the floating dock, I paddle quietly past the abandoned party boat lashed to its cement pier. I am sitting on my life vest to keep my tailbones from getting sore even though I probably should be wearing the vest. When I stop paddling, the canoe glides on the tide. *This* is the way to travel.

To my right, the six lanes of Route 787 that link Troy to Albany come into view. The highway is so jammed with cars, I hardly hear the swoosh of my paddle. My morning sluggishness vanishes on the river, and I feel renewed by the powerful peace of water. I am the only boat on the river, and the big water soon muffles the din of commutation. Even as the cars clog the bridges and everywhere the air is filled with the distant hum of people out to make a living, I feel protected in my canoe. Car-commuters stuck in traffic cannot touch me.

Just past Troy, a line of thick vegetation alongshore blots all evidence of industry. In the shade of the bushes along the east bank, it is even cool. Then I pass a thirty-foot cement wall and a sewage treatment center. A fin sticks out of the water; I wonder if it's a shark. Sharks have been known to swim up the Hudson from the sea. Reports of dolphins coming upriver last year made big news. Jim Rod, an Audubon biologist from Constitution Marsh in Cold Spring, told me that the bottlenose dolphin is the one species that often swims up into fresh water. There is at least one record of a dolphin swimming 160 miles up the Mississippi River. Apparently dolphins can survive for several weeks in freshwater; not so for sharks. He said that when a shark swims up the Hudson, it's a sick shark and it will die. But the fin in the water turns out to be only the metal lip of a water intake pipe.

I wonder if the water is salty today. The salt line during a drought has been known to run far upriver but never as far as Troy. The Hudson salt line shifts with the seasons and the rains. Much of the year, this shifting line cuts across the wide Newburgh-Beacon bay, sixty miles north of the Battery. I wonder where it is today or whether one can say it is any one place and not another.

I paddle around an old steel girder just below the surface of the water, and move out into the channel to avoid scraping my hull. Cement buttresses under the surface are reminders of former times, industry gone under. I wonder how many old bridges and docks and man-made structures have gone down in the lower Hudson. Each generation constructs its own bridges, its own monuments. And then these monuments are destroyed. But new generations love to rebuild. Shaughnessy's analogy of a stone tossed in a pond, the concentric rings moving out into the suburbs, and then another stone tossed into the center, and a rejuvenation, a rebuilding of the old city, is a good one.

Looking at so many crumbling piers along the overgrown shore, I see human folly. We think we can endure; our cement structures, cement forever. But only the water will remain. Time easily ravages cement, stone, and steel, but it cannot cut so deeply into the Hudson. How many decayed factories I have spotted on shore, the weeds working the cracks in the cement. But the river is renewed. The river is flexible.

As Bob Boyle has noted, Henry James found the Hudson a "perpetually interesting river." James, who might have agreed with my reasons for making this journey, said that "a decent respect for the Hudson would confine us to use of the boat." He is right. There's no other way to come to grips with this leviathan of watery paradox, especially the lower river. Getting out on the water is the only answer.

Riding the tide is like receiving a free passage to the sea. Although maximum ebb is gentle this far north in June, perhaps only a knot or two close to shore, any help is great, and I welcome the lunar assistance. Two mallard ducks swim near shore. At the River Cafe last night, mallard was featured on the menu.

A speedboat passes. I will wave at every boat, friend, or foe, simply as good policy. Motorboats can run me down; I have to respect them. The wake of this powerboat is good evidence. It shakes me up. I spin the canoe around so the bow takes the wave head-on. I brace just as I braced my paddle in the rapids. When the waves pass, I continue. I am the tortoise; they, the hares. A tortoise must defer to a hare.

Across the river, approaching Albany I notice a bike path between the highway and the water. A biker has stopped to gaze at me. He waves. I wave back. The slack before the flood is coming soon, so I better get somewhere quickly before the current changes.

A police boat cruises by. I wonder if he will stop me for not using my life vest. . . . At low tide gazing up at the wet rocks where the river has been, the wet roots of trees look naked and surprised. Time, privacy, solitude, and space—these are the qualities I crave in the 1990s. When the world becomes one huge cellular phone and fax-modem, satellite, and electric car, I will come down to the river to be renewed. Will push my canoe into the tides. Will greedily gulp this lawless river to quench a thirst for freedom.

My canoe, however, has unfortunately filled with junk. Over the past days, I've managed to collect too much "stuff," much more than I took with me on the hike to Lake Tear, when economy was everything. Now that I don't have to portage anymore, my boat has taken on extra food, spare water bottles, candy I don't need, all those topographic maps I picked up at Lock 7. I've got to get rid of this junk soon, or I'll swamp. I can just see trying to pull out at the Battery in front of the cameras: "Man Encumbered by Possessions," "Man Canoes the Hudson But Is Unable to Get Out of His Boat onto Dry Land," Or "Canoeist and His Precious Acquisitions Drift Out to Sea."

A bright red tug in the channel pulls a blue barge, empty and high up out of the water, and I think about what Nichols and Godfrey have told me, how the powerful tug motor can easily cut through opposing tides. A few weeks before my trip began, I went into White's Marina in the little village of New Hamburg, just north of my home in Beacon. I was searching for river charts. Old, white-haired Mr. White stood behind the counter, quite deaf but good-natured. I had to shout so he could hear me. I told him I planned to canoe the river, and he said, "No one worries about the currents anymore. It's all powerboats on the river now. You don't see any canoes out there. No one wants to work *that* hard."

But I'm not really working so hard anymore. Paddling has become a routine, a habit. I lift, swivel, and pull this wonderful instrument of momentum, my paddle-through the changing tide. My hips are loose. So many miles of paddling have worked the stiffness of fear out of me. Everything has changed since Perry Ehlers the day before Ernie and I left for Lake Tear. Thinking back, I do miss Ernie and the upper river, but this river of cities and tugs holds its own perils and fascinations.

Here is Albany, for example, suddenly sprouting up out of the

28. Racing the big boats on the lower river.
Courtesy Pat Shafer.

trees on the far west bank, first the two tallest buildings, then more
buildings blossoming out of the lush chartreuse into the hazy sky. The
city appears like a mirage of bleached concrete and albino steel.

In the water I find Styrofoam cups, a rubber glove, a condom
filled with air. There are no boys' ropes around here. No one would
swim in this messy river at the edge of the big city. Bob Boyle often
says, "The river is cleaner, but it sure isn't healthy yet." I wonder why
we find it so easy to pollute a river. Perhaps it is because all our junk
is swept away with the current to someone else's river—out of sight
like Winchell's spring debris piled at the edge of his island, waiting
for the tide and the currents to carry off the gook.

Yet there are multitudes of fish in this river. One jumps for a bug
as I pass by the old Delaware & Hudson office buildings, now used
by the state university. Downtown Albany, capital of New York State,
doesn't seem so threatening from a boat on the Hudson.

I canoe beneath a bridge. High overhead the bridge-repairing jackhammers numb the air. I spot a tiny marina there on the east bank just south of downtown. I paddle hard to reach a bevy of moored boats. A mallard and seven tiny panicking ducklings skim the shore. The river is big; the marina is small and safe. I will wait out the tide and talk a little.

13

Albany

Halyards clank in the breeze. White is the predominant color of the yachts jostling at their moorings. The fuel pumps on the dock look like petrified trolls. Green garden hoses run here and there, snaking around the electricity hookups for pleasure boats.

A sign above the door of the dockmaster's house reads, "Transients: restroom, showers, telephone." A soda machine delivers an old-fashioned cream soda and a ginger ale to this thirsty canoeist. I stuff a sandwich and potato chips from a nearby deli down my gullet.

One of the other transients is Captain Evans. The captain is perhaps forty-two, and trim. Underneath a golf visor, his ponytail and two shiny earrings make him part Gypsy, part ex-hippy. He is tan, his voice slightly haughty, as if long ago he might have been a preppy.

I first noticed Evans polishing cleats aboard his fifty-two-foot motor sailer. When he came up to the pay phone to make a call, we greeted one another, but now he seems a little uneasy about answering questions. Like one of Joseph Conrad's wounded expatriates, Evans must have some bizarre story of his own, but I'm not sure I have the time to extract it from him.

"I was made captain of this boat three weeks ago," his voice is quiet, deep, shy. The phone rings; it's his boss. He hangs up and tells me he has to pick up some clients for the weekend. He'll go south in the winter, probably Antigua.

"Seems like a nice job," I say.

"If I wasn't doing this, I might have to get a *real* job," the transient captain says. "I had one of *those* once." He smiles sardonically.

"You've been at this for a long time, I guess."

"Been sailing professionally for eighteen years, in the Caribbean, Mediterranean, South America, Pacific, Europe . . . "

"So tell me about the Hudson, from a captain's point of view."

"The Hudson is probably the most beautiful river on the planet," he says giving emphasis to "beautiful" and "planet."

"Twenty years ago you could smell it before you saw it. But it's now clean enough that the bass and sturgeon have started to come back. You can fish in it, swim in it, use it for whatever purpose you wish. The only danger is navigating at night. There's a lot of logs out there, especially in the north section, from here down to Catskill. They float just at the surface and you never see them until you're hit. Closer to New York City you find railroad ties that kids throw in the river, and telephone poles and Jimmy Hoffa . . . "

He laughs, but I have wondered more than once if I might see a dead body in these waters, especially around New York City. I know one thing: this captain has made a superficial observation about the Hudson's fish. As Bob Boyle once explained to me, the Hudson estuary from the Troy dam down to the sea is the only major estuary on the East Coast of the United States that still *retains* all of its original fish species. The river has always been productive. Even when the Hudson was the most polluted, the striped bass and the sturgeon never vanished from these waters.

"Logs are the worst. At night, the first intimation of a log is when the log takes your propeller off or when it stoves in your planking."

"Has that happened to you?"

"Uyup. Twice here in the north."

Evans's use of "north" is fresh evidence for my belief that millions of people living in the lower Hudson Valley think the Hudson begins at the capital and runs south.

"So I guess you don't sail at night anymore?"

"Nope." He shakes his ponytail.

"The Hudson is an *extremely* deep river. The controlling depth of the Hudson is thirty-four feet from New York City to Albany. The Army Corps of Engineers guarantees that depth mid-channel. But unlike a lot of rivers, the Hudson carries deep water right up to its edges almost everywhere you are. Some of the little bays shoal up, but the rest of it is deep water.

"Another danger is other boats: *99.9* percent of people who have boats on the Hudson River know absolutely *fuck-all* about what they are doing."

Evans's bitterness is volcanic. The captain erupts at the injustice. Other motorboaters are his enemy, and make his job difficult when it should be easy.

"Unfortunately anyone can buy a boat, and there is no requirement *what-so-ever* that you know how to run it. If you can figure out that the pointy end goes first, that's all you have to do to drive a boat on the Hudson.

"People are dumb, stupid, ignorant, inconsiderate, and dangerous. And there is *a lot* of drinking on this river. Boats will do eighty miles an hour, zipping in and out, paying *no attention* to *anyone else*, having *no regard* whatsoever for the rules of the road. They know *none* of the proper signals, nothing. So when I'm out there," he says, gazing at the flat light on the midday Hudson, "I keep a good lookout. And so should you, especially in a canoe. When you're out on the water, you're in a hostile environment to the human condition. Any vessel becomes dangerous if the captain doesn't know *fuck-all*."

Evans says he doesn't drink, but I would guess he used to drink. He looks like a man who partied for decades. I ask, "Where did you get your training?"

"Just being on a boat. As captain, my responsibility runs twenty-four hours a day. When clients are aboard I'm responsible for their lives and for the safety of the vessel. And when no one is aboard, I can work fourteen hours a day, seven days a week, just on upkeep alone. If you figure the hourly wage, the pay comes to about 80 cents an hour. But, as I say, if I wasn't doing this, I'd have to get a *real job*." His smile is smug.

Compared to him, I'm an interloper. A mere weekend boater.

As if to verify what the captain has just been telling me, a cabin cruiser speeds up to the marina and rams the dock so hard it is cast back into the tide and must use power again to come ashore. Captain Evans shakes his head in disgust.

"Are you the kind of captain who knows when the anchor is slipping even when you're asleep?" I ask.

"Pretty much. Every boat has its own symphony of sound, and

once you grow accustomed to it, that sound disappears into the background. But any time there's a new noise, no matter how slight," he says snapping his fingers, "instantly I wake up and set out to identify it, good or bad. Then I go back to bed or I'm up all night pumping the bilge."

Evans's boat has everything: autopilot, radar. Alexis Nadeau would love this boat. Captain Evans calls the master bedroom "a pleasure palace." It is plush and air-conditioned. The galley has a washer and drier and a microwave.

"There's no law on this river," says the captain, confirming my opinion of an hour ago. "Rensselaer County went out and bought a few of these fancy twenty-six-foot runabouts, but they just sit here. Albany county has a few sheriff's boats. Albany police has a Boston Whaler. They send out a couple of guys from the motorcycle squad, one guy who's been there fifty years. They too know absolutely *fuck-all* about anything maritime."

Evans again wags his ponytail. In spite of his disgust, he is a handsome man. I imagine more than a few ladies in ports around the globe have pined for—or dreaded—his return.

Before I shove off, a young journalist from the *Albany Times-Union* asks about my journey. His photographer drives up and slams on his breaks. Blond and confident, in his early thirties, the photographer is a maverick of the lens. He shoots me and my canoe, paddle in hand, bandana and all, sunglasses dangling from my neck, with the tall Corning Building across the river behind me.

When I come ashore he asks, "You saw the boat show across the river, did you not?"

"I did not."

"That's why I'm late. Check it out. It's the First Annual Albany Wood Boat Festival. You'll fit right in," he says and hops in his car.

A few miles of backtracking won't hurt, I guess.

Paddling against the new ebb tide in the raw heat of the late afternoon is a solid reminder of how stupid I was to think I could do my trip in the opposite direction. Maybe I will just camp the night in Corning Park between highway 787 and the river, adjacent to the old city.

Today is ponytail day. I paddle up to a man with a dark ponytail, rigging one of his own, handmade sailboats, which is a replica of a dory with a dark green hull and varnished gunwales. He's about to launch it on the river while two self-conscious reporters videotape him for a local cable TV station.

Dan is an affable hippy, about thirty years old. He is quite proud of his boat, which he says he designed from the original, and which took him 225 hours to construct. He's got patterns, he says, to sell the public.

His girlfriend, with smooth dark skin and long black hair, explains how their company, North River Boatworks, which has been in the business for ten years, came up with the idea for the First Annual Albany Wood Boat Fest.

"We were sittin' around one day in the shop at coffee time," says Dan's girlfriend, "and we said, 'You know, we really should have a boat show ourselves.' So North River Boats just *did* it.

"If you want to camp here for the night, you're welcome. A bunch of us are going to do it."

Okay, but first I plan to hike down that street over there and under the highway into downtown Albany for a good meal. Then I will come back, set up my tent, talk some, sleep some, and leave on the early tide before anyone is up.

Strolling through Albany during rush hour with my camera bag and yellow-nylon paddling pants, I feel like a geek. Here, I come across the perfect restaurant, just what I was looking for. Jack's is a North Country version of Jim Gallagher's New York City Steak House, a bit fancy for these duds, but I have money in my pocket, and the manager admits me to a table, which just happens to be in the back corner.

I wonder what I've gotten myself into—to step out of a rocky canoe into this room full of snow-white, pressed tablecloths, gleaming cutlery and waiters, all older men, many from Eastern Europe. This feels strange and wonderful. Certainly, Jack's is one of Albany's established institutions.

I am eyeballed. I order coffee and a big steak. When my waiter comes back, I apologize for lookin; so hillbilly-ish. "You see, I'm making a canoe trip down the Hudson." I pull out the article from *USA Today*.

"Do you mind if I show my boss?" he says politely.

The manager (could this be Jack himself?) comes over to shake my hand. My waiter, smiling, brings me a free Mud Pie at the end of the meal.

Back at the Wood Boat Fest, I pitch my tent near a childish-looking man and a sultry-faced, dark-skinned woman who are sitting in picnic chairs, drinking beer and eating something from a bag. The loud whine of the highway makes us shout to one another.

I have never met someone so enthusiastic about boats before. I think his name is Tom. He left his computers at the office in Connecticut and has brought his first handmade wood boat to the festival.

We chat deep into the dropping dusk, drinking coffee and beer, when suddenly the ghost of a ship passes before us on the river, its phantom white sail luffing, its tiny outboard engine flapping against the tide. It is a vision from "The Rime of the Ancient Mariner." Three ghostly skiffs trail behind like frightened ducklings.

"Is that a Chinese junk?" someone screams.

Another cry goes up: "O my God, is this for real!"

A strange figure of a man with a black sailor's cap stands at the helm as the boat passes Corning Park, then circles like some restless soul in search of peace. Up and down the river it goes. The other boat builders are silenced by the sight. An old man with a thick white beard stands beside his sleek, elegant, wooden kayak, gazing out at the dark river, dumbfounded by the restless ghost ship on the Hudson.

I wonder what the ghost captain is doing over there, when finally the junk moves in close to the far shore. The engine dies. The captain seems to be anchoring. Now he is fooling with one of his skiffs.

Long after we think we have only dreamed the junk, the night deepens, and there is finally talk about hitting the hay. Suddenly the junk captain is walking out of the blackness from the nearby boathouse. He is about to stroll right past us. Tom hails him in his friendly way: "Hey, you, are you from that strange ship over there? Come have a beer with us."

His name is Steve, and I can tell right off that he is proud to be from "that strange ship over there." Steve is shy. He is stocky and short, with dark flowing hair and a silver barrette holding his ponytail in place. He is wearing clogs. He sits down in the grass with us.

He will talk about his boat but not much about himself, although speaking about one is like speaking about the other.

He says the boat is from Hong Kong. Typical questions people ask, he says, are "How did I get it here?" "How old is it?" and "Did I sail it across the Pacific Ocean myself?"

"Well, it's twenty-six years old, but the design hasn't changed in the last two thousand years. I didn't sail the boat across the ocean. It came here aboard another ship. I've always loved the way junks look," says Steve, who looks ghostly even close up, "and when this one came up for sale on Lake Huron (I saw the ad in *Wooden Boats*), I bought it." He's had it for two and one-half years, he says, and now he lives on it.

How does a junk handle in the Hudson?

"Great, but I don't sail. I motor," Steve says. "The sails are in bad shape. My sails are twenty-five years old, and they've been sitting out in the weather all that time."

When Steve finishes talking about his junk, the night is late. He laughs politely at something Tom says, then disappears. Vanishes really, just as he had arrived.

A few minutes later we can barely distinguish a vague object piercing the black river just below where we have gathered along the shore. Steve is rowing home to his junk. He said he'd be heading south to Saugerties in a few days, and if we ran into one another he would show me the ship.

All night I have bad dreams and toss in my tent. Then at about 2 A.M. I hear threatening voices: inner-city, angry boys' voices gathering around the park somewhere very close to me. These are not dream voices. One tough voice says to another tough voice, "Joe, let's get out of here. Just leave the damn tent alone. Put that pipe down!" Another says, "Over here." A herd of feet stomp through the park. Those voices are imprinted like branding irons on my heart for the fear they have instilled. What makes these voices so scary is their unpredictability. And a mischief maker holding a pipe over a nylon tent.

The highway whine never lets up. In a paralysis of groggy half-sleep, I feel so vulnerable lying in this little tent with all the other defenseless wooden-boat people in their tents, too. At the edge of a massive river, I know if I can just drag my body up, and make a dash for the safety of the dark water, I can survive even in the city.

Instead I lie here praying for dawn, and fortunately the kids run past us all.

Without any more sleep, when first light comes at four, I rise to make coffee. I squat on my haunches and look around in the morning mist. I feel like an australopithecine come down to the edge of Old-uvai Lake for a morning drink.

In a predawn hint of light, I haul my ship to the godly river. The silhouette of Steve's junk across the way is punctuated by a pale, solitary warning light hanging in the spectral halyards.

14

The Catskill Hudson

5 A.M. Saturday, June 23. I scan the shore for John Cronin. No one in sight. I don't see how he's going to find me today. The river has grown too wide.

Literature for the Riverkeeper Fund describes John Cronin as "the eyes, ears and independent voice of the public on matters concerning the estuary. From his headquarters in Garrison, New York, the Riverkeeper patrols the Hudson, gathering evidence for the prosecution of polluters and other environmental lawbreakers." The idea for a Hudson riverkeeper first came to Bob Boyle when he read the biography of William James Lunn, the riverkeeper of the Houghton Club on the Test in England, a famous trout stream. Boyle writes:

> In my mind's eye, I imagine the job to be somewhat like an expanded version of the role played by the late William James Lunn. . . . For almost fifty years, Lunn worked on the river, restocking it with aquatic insects, cutting weed, hatching trout. There is a marvelous photograph of him, elderly and bewhiskered, tweezers in hand, sorting out insects. . . . So, I like to imagine, will appear the river keeper of the Hudson in future years, a no-nonsense naturalist, with the idiosyncrasies, migrations, and workings of the Hudson engrained in his mind. We need someone like this on the Hudson and on every major river in the country.

Today I hope to make a rendezvous with John and his photographer, Pat Shafer, somewhere below Albany, but John's vagueness on the phone yesterday makes me doubt we'll connect. He said, "Oh, don't worry, Pete. We'll find you."

I first saw John in action during an ash-dump hearing in Fishkill, New York, near my home. The state was looking for a site to dump ash from the Poughkeepsie Resource Recovery incinerator, and it was investigating a few sites around the edge of the Hudson River. Speaker after speaker got up to object. The firehouse hall was electrified by the strained voices of outraged citizens.

Then it was John's turn. He got up, neatly dressed in a tie and coat, his blond hair wavy thick, and his voice soft at first. He had the slightly pudgy face of leftover boyhood, but he was tall and impressive and confident.

He said, "I can't *believe* the state is even *contemplating* any dump within runoff distance of the river." He shook his head in disbelief. The pitch of his voice rose with its volume.

"But if you should *ever* decide this is where the dump has to go, right next to an important wetlands area along the Hudson, then . . . " His voice, building power, was also gaining in depth. "Then you will be the subject of perhaps *the biggest environmental lawsuit ever filed in this country.*"

When he finished, the hall shook with standing, clapping, joyful citizens. John had turned the tide, and sounded convincing enough for me to leave the firehouse in good spirits. I felt the river was in good hands if we had John Cronin as its steward.

Later I wanted to help the ongoing cleanup of the river, so I met John at his Garrison office and said I would like to give something back to the Hudson, pay homage to the river god, as my friend Scott Overdorf put it.

John said he might be able to get some press out of my trip. He wanted to know if I wouldn't mind carrying a jar of water from the Adirondacks all the way to the Battery and then dumping it into the harbor while the cameras clicked away. "It's a poetic idea," he said. "All people should be riverkeepers."

I said, "John, I don't really see myself as a bearer of water. I'm no De Witt Clinton."

He seemed slightly offended that I didn't like his idea, but we agreed to hold a press conference when I arrived in Manhattan, and he promised to visit me a few times along the way. He said he was particularly looking forward to seeing me on the river between Albany and Kingston. "That's one of the most mysterious and unknown parts on the whole river," he said with enthusiasm.

Vainly I keep scanning the horizon for John and Pat. Seven miles below Albany in the dawning light, I approach the forgotten river town of Castleton on the east bank. On the opposite shore, just up from Castleton, flows what Lossing called "the romantic Norman's-Kill (the Indian *Tawasentha*, or Place of many Dead)." On an island at the mouth of the Norman's Kill—a noted place of encampment and trade for the Iroquois—the Dutch built their first fort on the Hudson in 1614. The island was named Castle, from which the town later got its name.

Out here are islands that only local boys know well. This is a region of secret caves and legends, of ghosts on creeks that feed the river. I paddle quietly past the Moordener Kill Creek, which Melissa's friend Jim Britt used to explore as a kid growing up in Castleton. "A haunted creek," said Jim. "Moordener Kill means murderous creek. It's a wild stream where an Indian on horseback is said to have dragged a settler through the creek bed."

Jim Britt went to college with Melissa. On one of his visits to our house in Beacon, when I told him I was about to canoe the river, he was excited and amazed. He said, "A canoe in the shipping channel around New York City? I don't believe it." He said he would never have thought of canoeing the lower river.

Jim and I talked for hours. He had many profound memories of the river from childhood. In fact, he was so enthusiastic about the river again, I almost talked him into making the journey with me. Jim grew up thinking of the river as a place of commerce. River towns were connected to each other by daily trade. But around 1966, he remembers, the river became too dirty to swim in. The filth was trumpeted, and the river became a source of shame. Already depressed, Castleton sank into despair.

Jim said, "Around 1971, Pete Seeger docked his new sloop, the *Clearwater*, in Castleton and pronounced it the deadest town on the deadest river in the world. And you know what? The townsfolk got behind Seeger. They agreed.

"When I went off to college, I just stopped thinking about the Hudson. But of course it was in my blood. It's *still* in my blood."

Jim recalled the brick industry of the region. "Our clay gave birth to the greatest city in the world," Jim said. "Bricks are beautiful. They're symbols of a time when people married the river and we all lived by the rhythms of the water. People woke and slept and thought about the river. But the industry faded. All we can think about now is how dirty the water has become."

"What is the best thing you can say about the Hudson today, Jim?" I asked.

Jim did not hesitate. "That you can swim in it again."

New York State recently classified the river from Castleton to the New Jersey line, around Dobbs Ferry, as swimmable. Contamination by sewage has been the main reason for not jumping into the Hudson. But thanks to the watchful eyes of environmentalists, sewage treatment plants are working better these days, and most towns are not discharging raw sewage into the river the way they used to.

Jim thought about swimming in the Hudson for a moment, as if he were reliving a boyhood swing into the river from a rope tied to a big tree alongshore. Then he said, "I don't know how you get people interested in the Hudson again. It might take a long time. Rivers have always been ambiguous in the American mind. They've never been all pleasure. There's hard work on rivers."

Jim looked at me wistfully, "None of us who grew up on the Hudson can *actually see* the river anymore. Maybe we need a new look at the Hudson. Give us a new look, Pete, from a canoe."

I climb out at the Castleton marina. I pull my gear and boat up onto the dock. Three Canadian yawls are preparing to continue their journey upriver. I walk across the railroad tracks. A sign says, "Caution: High Speed Trains." On the railing of a sagging porch not ten feet from the track is a line of crimson geraniums. I walk the main street that parallels the river. A few stores are open, but many appear bankrupt. Sitting in a chair outside his run-down little shop, a heavy Greek-looking man scowls at me. I buy coffee and a candy bar at

Stewart's. Three young men are buying beer. I think of Jim's graduating from the little high school here, then his escape to college.

I, too, have a desire to escape Castleton. Something in the atmosphere feels like flypaper, so I follow the tide, with long stretches of undeveloped land on either side of me now, and coves and a few houses set back from the river on hillsides. As I paddle, I wonder what this river was like when Native Americans still roamed its shores. Lossing says "the Mohegans . . . extended their villages along the eastern bank of the stream, as high as Lansingburgh, and their hunting grounds occupied the entire counties of Columbia and Rensselaer."

Huge Schodack Island splits the river into two channels. Bob Boyle says *Schodack* is an Indian word meaning "'place of fire,' because this island in the Hudson was the traditional Mahican capital and site of the council fire." In 1664, says Boyle, the warlike "Mohawks forced the Mahicans to move their council fire from Schodack Island in the river to what is now Stockbridge, Massachusetts. A few Mahicans lingered on in the Hudson Valley, but they disappeared around the early 1800s."

I hug the western shore of Schodack. Across the river are the hamlets of Coeymans and New Baltimore, each village with its own marina, a scattering of boats at anchor.

8 A.M. The tide will turn in four hours. Soon I will look for a hamlet as a refuge to wait out the flood tide, but after I pass New Baltimore, there is none in sight. So I'll just keep paddling along this uninterrupted verdure. Except . . . look there. Along that wide beach, a big old tire is sticking out of the sand.

In spite of the tire, this stretch of river seems a mystery, full of strange sandbars, islands, and coves. Now I pass the site of the famous, hidden sandbar, called Overslagh by the Dutch (here no longer because of dredging). Many ships ran aground. It was not unusual to find fifty sailing vessels stuck on the Overslagh at low tide, and as Wallace Bruce has written in *The Hudson: Three Centuries of History, Romance and Invention*, "the amount of profanity uttered by the vexed sailors was sufficient to demoralise the whole district."

I wonder if it was the Overslagh that Robert Juet, mate and chronicler of Hudson's historic journey, was describing in his record of the *Half Moon* the first day after the ship turned around and headed downriver. On September 23, 1609, fair weather saw the *Half Moon* come to a "shoald that had two channels . . . and had little wind, whereby the tide layed us upon it. So, there wee sate on ground the space of an houre till the floud came. Then we had a little gale of wind at the West. So wee got our ship into deepe water, and rode all night very well."

The next day, it happened again: "the winde at the North-west, wee weighed, and went downe the River seven or eight leagues; and at halfe ebbe wee came on ground on a banke of Oze in the middle of the River, and sate there till the floud. Then wee went on Land, and gathered good store of Chest-nuts."

I pass big houses, estates with great green lawns sweeping down the hills to the shore line. Olympic-sized pools overlook the Hudson. On wide patios, Adirondack chairs face west. No longer are these the cheap, wire chairs of the North Country. I've come to the river of expensive, plush, well-made weekend chairs, on which corporate executives retire with evening cocktails.

Paddling is very hard against this south wind. I keep praying in vain for a northwesterly wind, like the one Henry Hudson had when he beat it to the sea.

My affection for the silent beauty of my canoe grows thin when suddenly—boooooo boooooo sounds the foghorn of a container boat, an ocean-going vessel looking more like a freighter as it rounds the hook before a cove.

The leviathan fills up the river like a rodent in an anaconda. *London Spirit* must be making ten knots against the tide. In the view-finder of my camera, I can see the captain and the pilot looking at me through binoculars from the pilot house. I wave my paddle high in the air. They wave back, then vanish into an air-conditioned cabin.

Cove after blue cove recedes into the distance before me; a blue-green haze of coves outlines my future. Perhaps it is better not to see the future. If the river were more intricate and had less straight distance and more obstacles to mar the view, perhaps I could delude myself into thinking today's goal is closer than it really is.

11:30 A.M. The tide is almost all the way out. Long, wide mudflats lie exposed along the shore. A deer bounds into the bushes, my first deer since the Adirondacks. I really should stop for lunch and get off the water during this slack before the flood tide, but I keep paddling.

Too late. The whole river betrays me and starts to push me backward. If I look at the water of the opposing tide, it seems I'm going very fast. I'll dare the flood awhile. I dig my blade deep down and yank the full five feet of gunwale toward me. But the result is nothing. Why won't I get off the river? This is stupid. I'm actually moving in the opposite direction from the way I'm paddling, but still I refuse to pull over. Maybe it's sun delirium.

Here's a strange sight. In the middle of nowhere, with no road in view, a picnic table rests on a mudflat in a marsh. Set back in the reeds, a blue plastic tarp is stretched above a table and chairs. Perhaps it's a hideout for hunters or truant kids. Nearby are open areas for bonfires, then more chairs by the shore. And then a whole row of old truck seats with the stuffing half falling out of torn vinyl.

A fierce feeling of doom strikes me in this silent heat. I feel like fainting. Just under the surface of all the bucolic scenery lurks something ominous. Perhaps this is nothing more than my expectation of drama, of a secret crime unfolding, of someone's life unraveling by the water. As if at any moment there might ring out a gunshot, or a cry for help.

I'd get off the river but I'm on the wrong shore, and now I have missed my chance to cross over to that hamlet there. Across the flooding tide, where I want to be, is the town of Coxsackie. Two American flags flap in a gentle breeze over a small gazebo.

For a while I use my paddle to pole off the mudflats, but the tide is too strong to buck, so I pull ashore, defeated beneath an abandoned brick smokestack shooting out of the weeds like the ruin I once saw of a Portuguese colonial fort in the jungles of Brazil.

1 P.M. No drinking water left. Bad planning, Pete. I'm stuck here now with a parched throat. I cannot cook any coffee or macaroni, either. Water everywhere, but I refuse to drink from the river. Becalmed and frustrated. It's no one else's fault but my own. I vow to plan better from now on, that's all. I'll never let myself get caught out like this again, with no drinking water, no people to talk to, nothing to do but read or lie here in a summer daze, until the moon gives a reverse message to the river at my feet.

Three weekend powerboats in rapid succession cruise upriver, wave after wave launching toward my canoe. I guess I'm not thinking clearly because I'm resting on the sandy edge of the water feeling sorry for myself, when, DAMN, I should have known by now that it's always better to be in deep water where I can brace with my paddle or to be out of water altogether, but never half in, half out. The action of the waves hitting shore sends the canoe over, all my gear tumbling into water. Everything soaked.

I curse the powerboats. Not even 300-foot container boats make waves like some power cruisers, which are too heavy and too poorly designed to plane properly.

Across the river in front of the village gazebo, three figures move along the river shore. Yes, I can just make them out. A little girl is walking with her parents, one hand held by her father, the other by her mother. They are swinging her. I can almost hear her glee. I cannot stop tears rushing to my eyes. I'm lonely, depressed, hot, tired, hungry, and just about at the lowest point of my trip. The question that comes back over and over is, "Why the hell am I here and not at home with *my* family?"

Waiting for the tide to turn, with no food and no water, feels like an eternity. Four hours later, the Hudson is still flooding, but the flood is winding down into the slack before the ebb. I challenge the ebb to come early today and begin to paddle in the weakening flood tide. In the village across the river, water never tasted so good.

It is beginning to rain. I cover my camera. It starts to pour. The wind picks up, the raindrops so thick they sting. Now I'm running with a gale. I'm going for shore. I'm caught in the middle of the river because I had to paddle around a point. I'm in a big bay heading due east paddling as hard as I can, praying for shore. But the clouds settle, sheets of rain block all vision, and I cannot see where I'm going. STEADY, PETE, STEADY. The rain is filling up the canoe fast. This canoe is like a bucket. *Steady.* Gallons are sloshing at my feet. *Steady.* It's a typhoon, a tropical squall.

But I've reached shore. I'm safe. I lug the rain-filled Odyssey onto the marsh sand. So much adrenaline running inside me, I pull the loaded boat right out of the water with one arm. A crack of thunder. I dash up the marsh to the bank, and find a tree. I crouch below the tree. The river disappears behind gray sheets of rain.

"Give me back the river!" I shout into the storm.

Dark puffs of cloud run along the hills like smoke after cannon fire. Thunder and lightning will not stop.

I'll make coffee under the tree. I dash the hundred yards back to my ship to grab my mess kit. Lightning like incoming missiles. Running over the sand through the reeds, I feel like a ten-year-old boy; I shout, "U.S. MARINES. Yeah!"

The canoe is half-full. I try to pull it farther up on the beach, but it's too heavy now. I'll have to bail later. Lightning, thunder. I run back to the tree.

I set up a tarp over myself and drink cowboy coffee. Nowhere to go, nowhere to be, content and sheltered.

The storm ceases as abruptly as it began.

Twenty yards behind me, a train whistles past. I hadn't seen the tracks in the bushes, and it's like being outflanked by the enemy.

The wide marsh takes on a tawny light as the sky clears and the lower clouds fade into the upper air. Pink wisps of mist flee high above. The air cools rapidly, washing clear and so clean.

The water goes flat; whitecaps become a distant memory. I bail and tip my boat, then I am away again, drenched and happy, my blood racing from three cups of caffeine.

5 P.M. The river below Castleton has to be the most beautiful section of the lower river. I wonder where John Cronin is anyway. Maybe it was not today that we'd planned to meet on the river.

The sun breaks out of clouds. My wet clothes dry quickly. A plane circles overhead then dives low for a good look. I wave, but the aircraft banks away and disappears.

With the early start out of Albany, the eight-hour paddle, then the long hot wait for the right tide, and the prospect of another eight-hour paddle on my second ebb, this is beginning to feel like a long day in Job's desert. I've gone through storm, whitecaps, hail-like rain, and now such a flat, flat river and a sky so hazy hot, my canoe heats up like a tin can in a salt flat.

In a small park I am lying limp on a picnic bench resting when I spot two shirtless men paddling toward me in a canoe. John sits in the bow, Pat Shafer in the stern. Together they look like a couple of weekend canoeists. Their accumulated weight seems too much for that light canoe. Their strokes are not in unison. They have little control of their craft, and I wonder if this is why they haven't found me until now.

When they hit the beach, we talk, then together we paddle. Talking after so much hard lonely work is not easy, but after a while I get the swing of it. A couple of ski sleds race by us. A Chris-Craft slows for us, but in slowing down, loses its plane, and sends toward us a tsunami.

John says, "You're doing a great job, Pete."

I appreciate his encouragement. "Somebody's got to do it," I say, knowing full well, no one *has* to make this trip.

We paddle across the river to Shafer's car and say good-bye. I wish I were going with them in air-conditioning, downriver along the highway toward home.

A few hours later I pass a man and his son on a pier in the village of Athens directly across from Hudson, New York, which I've decided to bypass in favor of the longer run to the town of Catskill. Behind the man is a restaurant that smells of fried food. The man yells, "How come you're not doing the J-stroke?"

Since Ernie left me, I still paddle three strokes per side to get maximum push with minimum effort. It's not beautiful, but it works.

"Where you going?" says the J-stroke expert.

"Manhattan," I say.

"When do you hope to be there?"

"July 2." Good God, I realize, that's only eight days from now.

He pats his son on the head. "You'll never make it."

"Thanks." I push on.

Along the shore at Hudson, I spot the river's first condominium complex. Some friends of mine think the Hudson is wall-to-wall development, north to south. But it's still a lush river. I also pass my first lighthouse. At the end of a large island called Middle Ground Flats, the Athens Light sits empty, noble, confident, almost in the center of the river. The lighthouse brick is an orange fire in the setting sun, solitary and desolate in a darkening river scene. I tip my baseball cap at the Light as if it were an old man deserving respect, and I pull along the flats before moving out into the main channel between red and green shipping buoys. Here the current gives me an extra boost while I keep a nervous eye out for tugs and barges.

When a tug comes up on my rear, cutting at least fifteen knots to my three, I stay well out of his way. With so many "pleasure craft" in the river this Saturday evening, I wonder how he can navigate at all. Godfrey and Nichols would be shaking their heads today.

Above the right shore over the shoulder of the Rip Van Winkle Bridge, a long line of purple shapes rises into the sky—the misty silhouette of the distant Catskill Mountains, which Native Americans aptly called "Mountains of the Sky." Indeed they seem part of the sky, not at all attached to the planet.

As the tide begins to turn against me, I reach the village jetty at Catskill. I come around its long arm and duck into the first marina I see. The dockmaster at the Riverview Marina will allow me to camp tonight on the gravel between two sailboats on blocks.

Marinas are campgrounds by the water. People share bathrooms, Coke machines, telephones, and showers. I brush my teeth in the bathroom, and I'm in my tent early.

5 A.M. Sunday morning, June 24. Awakened by a maniac pulling into the marina with a bass boat trailing behind his Blazer. He maneuvers the trailer with difficulty into a parking spot just behind my tent. In the bathroom he is loud and hungover, perhaps still drunk. He's throwing water on his red face. His eyes are puffy. "I haven't slept in three days," he booms. "Going to be a bass tournament today. I'm going to get breakfast in town. Want to go?"

"Sure, why not." There is no diner close to the marina, and no way for me to get to town unless I hitch a ride. Besides, what else do you say to a big friendly bear of a guy with tattoos on his arms, a blustery face, and sleepless bloodshot eyes? Catskill, he says, is the bass capital of the world. In the month of June, Catskill will hold no fewer than twelve bass tournaments.

We hop into his Blazer, slam the doors, and plow out of the marina parking lot nearly denting a few parked cars. We accelerate past the trucks and trailers of other bass fisherman lining up for the contest that begins at six.

He says his name is Tiner. He's a corrections officer during the week and a bass fisherman on weekends. His recklessness reminds me of the American helicopter pilots and oil rig workers I met in Rio de Janeiro for a night on the town. He says, "There's a twenty-four-hour diner somewhere up here. There it is." And he whacks the brakes, his trailer wheels ramming potholes.

Tiner flirts with our middle-aged waitress at the counter in that tough, bossy way that some women adore. The waitress pours two coffees. The wild bass man says, "That's not decaf is it? No? Good. I was going to say, decaf is a little like pissing on your sister. I need a big glass of ice water, too, doll, okay? And give me two egg sandwiches with sausage to go, and one for my partner, too."

He tosses his money on the counter with royal disregard for cash. There are other bass fishermen in the diner. He and his partner drive up and down the East Coast for these weekend bass tournaments. "Hell, I enjoy competition. I'm a competitive kind of person. But competition fishing takes a lot of time. Most fishermen leave home on Friday after work. They pre-fish on Saturday. That's practice fishing, or whatever you want to call it. They do the contest on Sunday and get back home late Sunday night."

"But what about your family?" I want to know.

"Hell, I'm getting divorced."

We take our egg sandwiches and coffee into the Blazer.

"You know," Tiner says, "I used to drive a truck past the Colorado River and think about a trip like yours. I always wanted to take a canoe from the headwaters of the Colorado all the way to Baja."

"Baja? You never tried it, eh?"

"Nah, never had the money. And there'd be too many portages. If you lived, you'd be lucky."

"So tell me about bass fishing on the Hudson."

"We put our boat in here, and we'll fish thirty miles downriver. If we don't get anything, we'll go thirty miles north. You can cover a lot of ground in a bass boat. We'll cover a hundred miles today. At least.

"One guy from Albany has a boat that does eighty miles an hour. He'll go straight to Albany. He'll be there in a half hour, and he'll fish areas he knows are good for bass. You'll have guys today going all the way down to the Tappan Zee Bridge to fish, too."

"Really? Down to Tarrytown?"

"Over an hour down and an hour running back, which'll cut their fishing time down to about six hours."

If this is true, and if I had a bass boat, I could be home in less than an hour.

Today's contest is a semi-pro tournament with a hundred boats, a relatively small contest. But these fishermen are serious. Two weeks ago, Tiner and his partner lost a $3,000 engine in the middle of a tournament. They pulled into a marina where the old engine came off, and a new one was installed in just two hours. Tiner and his buddy zoomed away without paying a penny. They kept fishing, too. They had no checks, no credit cards. The marina owner just said, "Don't worry about it. Send me a check on Monday."

"Boat people are honest," Tiner says. "All your gear is right there so anyone can take it, but they don't."

When we find the marina, it is almost six. A man with a megaphone stands on a floating dock. Two hundred fishermen sit in bass boats of all shapes and colors. I see only three boys and one woman out there, who is dressed like the men. Most everyone wears a baseball hat. Many of the fishermen have mustaches. Young and old, the men sit poised in their water chariots ready to zoom off to all parts of the river. Some of these fishermen will even lock upriver into the Champlain Canal. Some will go down as far as the George Washington Bridge and be back in eight hours.

Their boats are streamlined, sinister-looking creatures of the water. Big letters, names like *Bass Tracker,* run along the sides of boats. The huge outboards weigh the sterns down close to the river. Each boat has an electric motor somewhere near the bow. Fold-up fishing seats sticking up into the air make the bass boats seem like counter-intelligence surveillance machines—water versions of high-altitude espionage airplanes. A couple of the fishermen even wear motorcycle helmets in case they turn over on the river while going seventy-five miles per hour.

The national anthem is played from a small tape recorder into a megaphone while the men stand in their boats, hats off, hands across their chests.

The guy with the megaphone says, "Okay, ready, boats Number One and Two." Four men raise their hands. "Good luck." A fog horn blasts against the soft morning sky. Two boats race out into the river into the sunlight. High overhead, a jet trails an exhaust streamer. "Ready Number Three and Four?" Hands in the air. Blast. And off the next two boats go, one downriver, one upriver. Tiner is out there somewhere, but I don't see him and his partner.

After twenty minutes, all hundred boats have vanished, and the

29. Bass fishermen in Catskill.

port resumes its early Sunday silence. The boats will not be back until 2 P.M. The guy running the contest says to me, "I ain't fished since I started this seven years ago."

I am only an hour's drive from my home, but I feel as if I'm still 3,000 miles up a swamp. It's too early to call home, so I check my tide chart for Catskill, June 24, 1990. The slack before the ebb was at 5:32 A.M. Maximum ebb will be at 8:49 A.M. The slack before the flood is at 12:35 P.M. So I will be able to paddle until about 1 P.M. I'll have lunch in Saugerties (about ten miles away) and wait for another good ebb tide, then get back on the conveyor belt of the river.

I walk over to my canoe, drop it into the water, and paddle quietly out of the harbor with my sandwich. The wind is exceptionally strong today while I follow the weedy shore. Bass boats race along the river. There is a frenetic quality in such fishing. Try one lure, try another, okay, let's get moving. The big engines fume into the white-caps. Then just as suddenly, from eighty miles per hour, the boats shush to a dead stop. New lures are tossed into yet another cove, another set of reeds. Okay, that's enough. No fish here. Let's go. Like race-car drivers, the fishermen turn their baseball hats around in the seventy-five-mile-per-hour wind.

Meanwhile, I am still just a river tortoise. I keep dipping my blade into the river of mountains. I may be slow, but I'll be damned if I don't get home to Beacon soon.

15

Catskill to Poughkeepsie

Saugerties, Rondout, Kingston, and Poughkeepsie—these are my next river towns, requiring my greatest physical struggle against the wind, a constant battle with arm-exhaustion and despair on endless water.

On a beautiful brisk morning out of Catskill Creek, I run along the west shore under a distant blessing from the fuzzy-blue Mountains of the Sky. My strongest wind to date snaps out of the perfect day, a day with unlimited sight, the air clear and inspiring. The river grows oceanlike, its bays widening under so many seagulls.

The great estates line up on the eastern shore with their rolling grass lawns, while cows contently graze in pastured slopes to the west. Some bass trackers roll and bob in the waves over the reeds. Other more restless boats skim the shore, racing for fish, the spray behind them like rooster tails.

I follow the shore for safety but have to move into deeper water in order to cut off long distances between big bays and tidal flats. Empty duck blinds on shore wait patiently for other sportsmen in a different season. The wind from the east gathers the river into whitecaps before I have a chance to cross to the lee shore. This is a classic case of what Cronin said I should watch out for. The tide forces the river one way while the wind drives it another, and sometimes the wakes of the bass boats drive the water in a third direction. The river turns choppy. My canoe pulls and pushes, slaps and snaps in every direction.

The fish are jumping, making a mockery of the fishermen who race elsewhere. Just below Catskill is the town of Cementon. The topographic quadrant for this area is also called Cementon. Alongshore are the quarries and piers where the rock is loaded onto barges. At one point, very early out of Catskill, I paddle way out into the river to circumvent the biggest pier I've ever seen. I paddle into the whitecaps, frightened of tipping over so far from shore. When I reach land again, I ride the whitewater that forms along stone pilings where the ebb turns the river to froth. I whoop for joy and brace my paddle against the water behind me.

A lone chair sits among the reeds above a marsh just below another cement quarry, which hums away even though it is Sunday. Here in yet another Hudson River chair a man or woman, boy or girl, comes perhaps to witness the sunrise, or to fish and think, or simply to feel the rhythms of the water.

After Cementon, in the white hyphens of the cresting waves, I think only of my destination. I want to reach a particular shoal, a lighthouse, and a creek called Esopus.

I pass a naked woman sunbathing around her pool. She is lying on her stomach reading a novel and cannot hear my soft paddling in the rough water. Her husband reads the *New York Times* on a lawn chair.

Farther along, an old wood barge rots where the waves slam the shore. The brush here is a deep, dense green.

Finally, the Saugerties Light is just ahead across a bay. But the wind is a challenge. I worry I won't be able to reach the solid structure, that beautiful white brick ablaze in the bright day, my beacon.

Two hours it takes to paddle perhaps 600 yards with the waves directly off my bow. Maybe it is all an illusion; perhaps I'm not really moving at all. It's hard to tell, there are many setbacks, but I find if I tack, just as sailboats tack upwind, I can make a little headway. The key is to maintain forward movement at all times.

Noon. I round the lighthouse and canoe up the Esopus Creek past a Coast Guard cutter, to a beautiful 150-year-old brick building, a marina run by an old Saugerties river man, who is sitting on his porch. Mr. Lynch is drinking Pabst Blue Ribbon. His eyes are a leached green.

"You can leave your canoe here, if you want," says the old man. "This country's going downhill," he adds. "Here's one of the greatest rivers in America, and there's no business on it."

Mr. Lynch remembers when the river was all business, and people understood the river. "Not today. These boaters don't even understand the tides. It's not like the old steamboat captains who docked here from Pier 44 in Manhattan. No siree." Lynch takes a swig of beer. He is the owner of the only genuine remaining Saugerties freight and passenger terminal. His family's business used to be called the Saugerties-New York Steamboat Company. The name is written in faded letters on the brick.

"I been here when Saugerties was Saugerties. The paper mills are gone. The big steamers are gone. The stone dock is gone. The gashouse is gone. The big brickyard is gone. The big stone barges are gone. They used to bring the stone here from the quarries, then take it down to the city. I miss the stonecutters. They did good work.

"My father's business was ice-cutting," Mr. Lynch says defiantly, while I sit on his porch recovering from the morning's battle with whitecaps. "The ice industry had thousands of men in it. Just like the brickyards, thousands of men. 'Come on,' they'd yell, 'the canal is going to shut.' It'd be ten below zero. They had to keep the canal open so they could start around seven in the morning to get the ice out onto the river."

There is something in Mr. Lynch's green eyes, so youthful, that dances when he talks. Perhaps nostalgia has the power to kindle the passion deep inside him.

Remembering Shaughnessy's love for icehouses, I ask, "Are there any icehouses left?"

"I think they're all gone," he says, his eyes dancing with a touch more pain. "Oh, they were tough men," Mr. Lynch continues when his beer runs out. "The river was hard work, and they'd be out there all day long. Maybe they carried a little sandwich in their pocket, maybe not.

"A cake of ice was twenty-two by thirty-two, and it weighed twenty-three pounds to the inch, so no one could fool you. All you

30. Lynch's Marina in Saugerties.

had to do was measure twelve inches, twelve times so and so. It was a great day when the river broke up and the barges could budge. They'd take the ice out of the houses and down to New York. We had real freezes up here. Down toward Poughkeepsie, the channel might stay open a lot longer."

Mr. Lynch's eyes grow even a lighter green from staring at the flat light of the midday harbor. "They didn't use no sawdust, neither. They used *saw hay* about two feet deep, and they put the ice cubes on that. The biggest icehouse was twenty-eight rooms and a thousand feet long. It had six elevators. That was just downriver from here."

"When did the ice business stop on the Hudson?"

"Around 1900 it started to go down, but we had icehouses all around these parts. Yup, I remember when you didn't just bypass Saugerties. In those days, there was no radar, you know. The old captains knew the river. No one knows the river no more. Most of these people here," he casts an arthritic hand into the air, indicating all the yachts at his own dock as well as the boats across the creek, "most of these people wouldn't know what to do in a storm. None of them knows how to row a boat. Hell, I used to row across the river *all the time* when I was a kid. A dollar a head, I'd get to take people over to Tivoli. One morning at five o'clock I put two big Italians and a kid and all their suitcases in my rowboat. There was a bit of a breeze. When I got out, the tide was running down—it can run six miles an hour here, you know—and a southeast wind was blowing. They grabbed both sides of that boat and they never talked to me. They got out at the Tivoli docks and never said good-bye. I don't think they picked any berries that day."

What Mr. Lynch misses most about the old days, however, are the big wooden docks no one builds anymore. "They're too expensive today," he says. "And no one wants to work hard anymore."

When I tell him I've been working pretty hard to canoe this river, he warns me, "Stay on the flats. Some of the tugs have no heart at all, and the motorboaters will run you right over. They think they're in a race. So watch out, and remember, if you tip over, take your shoes off. If you get your shoes off, you'll be okay, son."

I promise to keep my shoelaces loose from now on, just in case.

Rested now, having to wait out the flood tide, I hike up a steep hill behind the harbor and down along the creek and up the main street to a quiet cafe. Saugerties, like Catskill, is a town on the mend, but a town never quite mended, it seems. A persistent feeling of poverty hangs over Hudson River towns like Saugerties, although less here than, say, Hudson or Athens. It is a kind of perennial sadness.

I order coffee and call an old girlfriend who lives in town with her husband and two children. She is home and says she'll be right over. When I spot her bright blue eyes and blond hair at the door, I feel a dangerous heart-warmth flowering in my chest. Being in the presence of a woman friend, after all that wide glare of river, is like starting a fire in an old wooden church somewhere on the outskirts of an abandoned town.

We talk not as much about my trip as we do about marriage and happiness. We talk about the hardships and the wonder of raising children. But the tide is turning, so I pay the bill, and she drives me to the marina. When she drives away, the emptiness rushes in. Perhaps I've been on the river too long, and so much water has disguised important feelings. Maybe loneliness lies dormant when there is such a huge job to be done. But if I stop on dry land or give in to my hunger for companionship, I may never get under way again.

4:30 P.M. It is particularly hard to push on, but I hitch a ride on the day's second ebb tide with only nine nautical miles to Kingston. As I pull away from the dock, Mr. Lynch says, "Be sure to visit our lighthouse, it's a beaut, but we haven't had a lighthouse keeper for thirty years. My brother-in-law was raised in that lighthouse. He could swim the river back and forth all day long."

The lighthouse is only a few minutes away. The local architect in charge of the restoration, a heavyset man with a big beard, shows me around. This lighthouse was last occupied in 1954, at which time, he says, the light was automated and "they chased the family away."

As we walk about the spacious building, the architect says, "Here's the cistern where the family collected rainwater. Here's the kitchen." An elaborate scaffolding inside and outside the tower shows how much work is going into the restoration of the old Light. The scaffolding itself has been specially designed to fit around the tall tower.

We step into the lantern room at the very top. The whitecapped river looks like a silent movie through the glass panels that sweep in a 360-degree panorama. Before the lights became electric, they were kerosene. I can almost smell the kerosene.

A forty-five-foot tour boat called the *Sea Explorer* motors to the dock. When the tourists step into the lighthouse, the captain, a powerful-looking man about my age wearing sunglasses, with a three-day growth on his chin and with a serious-looking downturn in his mustache, says his name is Captain John Cutten. He grew up on the river in Hyde Park next to the Vanderbilt Estate.

In a deep, raspy voice he says, "When I grew up, I always hung out on boats." One day Cutten gave up his job as the manager of an automobile dealership and got back to his first love. He bought and restored the *Sea Explorer*, an air-sea rescue boat built by the navy in 1944. This is his first season running sunset tours from the Rondout to

31. The Saugerties Light.

the Saugerties Light. He says it is tough to make a living this way, although I can tell by his energy he has a lot plans for the future.

Cutten says he loves everything about the Hudson River. But especially he loves the legends of the river. "You want legends? How about pirates on the Hudson? That ought to grab you. I've been interested ever since I was a kid. Heck, I'm still a kid when it comes to the legend of Captain William Kidd."

"Pirates? Captain Kidd *on the Hudson*?"

Legends about pirate loot were popular in the old days, he says, and he himself has heard some of the old-timers speak about buried silver and Kidd's gold. In fact, Cutten has come to believe (and he believes this with conviction) that the Hudson Valley millionaires made some of their money from nefarious dealings with men like Captain Kidd. "My suspicion," says Cutten, who stands at the helm in the *Sea Explorer* wheelhouse sipping a Coke, "is that rich families settled here in the valley because they themselves were hiding out. Maybe they had something they didn't want people to know about, eh? Did you ever think about that? Three hundred years later, they're the new gentry. Look at the Morgans, the Astors, the Vanderbilts.

32. Captain John Cutten aboard the *Sea Explorer.*

They were merchants. And who did they trade with? *Pirates.* Back in the late 1600s, men like Robert Livingston were running ships to the pirate island of Madagascar to trade with buccaneers. Sure they were.

"In 1696 Captain Kidd, the biggest pirate of all, was hired by Robert Livingston to captain a ship called the *Adventure Galley* and to fight pirates and steal their loot. Kidd got most of his crew from up this way because Livingston had an estate up here.

"When Kidd couldn't find any pirates on the high seas, he turned pirate himself and raided the commercial ships he was supposed to protect. Legend says his biggest prize was an Arabic ship called the *Quedah Merchant,* richly laden. They say he came up the Hudson with his treasure, but was soon after tried and hung for piracy.

"I've heard stories all up and down this river that Kidd or his crew brought treasure back to the Hudson before Kidd was hanged.

He was sailing north in the Highlands (the crew was on their way home), when a violent storm hit around Peekskill. The ship sank at Kidd's Point, which is now called Jones Point on Dunderberg Mountain. They say that on calm days you can still see the spars of the sunken ship in the water off the point. Kidd took the treasure up into the hills and looked for a big tree to mark the spot. But before he buried the loot, he slit the throat of his mastiff, a 200-pound guard dog, and then buried the dead dog's body over the treasure in a pit under the tree."

"Why did he do that?"

"He knew that when a dog is buried over a treasure like that, any treasure hunter who comes looking for the gold will be haunted by the ghost of the dog that will rise up out of the grave and *never* leave the treasure hunter alone."

"Do you believe that?"

Cutten is not smiling. "Who knows? Perhaps the Livingston wealth came from Kidd? Hey, who's to say? I'll tell you one thing, I'd sure like to do some digging on the Livingston Manor over in Germantown. Want to do that with me sometime?"

Cutten is smiling, but he's serious. I say, "Sure."

He continues: "Maybe it was Kidd's treasure that helped Livingston back Fulton's steam engine. Did you ever think about that? Livingston was granted a quarter of a million acres from the king of England, right across the river there." Cutten points through the windshield of the *Sea Explorer*. "What kind of treasure do you think he might have kept on his land, eh? Isn't it a possibility he stashed some buried Inca or Mayan gold from the pirates?"

"Anything's possible, I guess." I'm a sucker for treasure stories, too. I feel like setting out on a treasure hunt right away, but Cutten's passengers are stepping onto the *Sea Explorer* for the ride back to Kingston. Cutten says we should meet up in the Rondout, where he keeps his boat, and talk some more.

"How about dinner?" I say, wondering if I sound too eager. Here is one of the best stories I've heard on the Hudson so far, and I have to hear more.

I pull away from the lighthouse into the wild river about twenty minutes before Cutten passes me. The *Sea Explorer* splits the waves like an ice cutter. The flumes of mist around its bow hit the air and are blown back across his deck.

The long ride to Kingston with the waves from weekend boat traffic and the high winds makes me dizzy. I ride the top of a wave, then drop into its trough only to be hurdled again upward, then smashed back and forth from crest to crest.

High overhead another bridge spans the Hudson, and I wish to God I could grab ahold of it.

6:35 P.M. I smell barbecued chicken. Voices shout high above on a hill. I hug the shore past a family graveyard behind a house probably handed down for generations. The waves let up very little; the tide is stronger than I've ever seen it. I race a tug to the Kingston lighthouse and around the long jetty and up Rondout Creek, but not before real panic has set in because the tug almost runs me down. What began as a game ends in near disaster. Men stand in the pilot house waving fists and cursing.

The tide, which has been working for me on the river, is now very much against me on the Rondout. When the tide ebbs, it ebbs from every tributary, every bay, every little creek. The water seeps out of mudflat nooks and crannies, each gallon adding to the mid-channel rush to the sea. I paddle hard up the Rondout only as far as the Hudson River Maritime Center museum. Cutten's boat is moored conveniently in front of an Italian restaurant.

Rondout is a town that has seen busier days. Like Saugerties, the Rondout is struggling with its rebirth. Boatyards and restaurants try desperately to draw attention to this once-great Hudson River port. But the general depression of river towns is like the maximum tide for a canoe, a little too strong to buck.

Above and behind the Rondout is the city of Kingston, which was for a short while the state capital during the Revolution. The Rondout remains separate from the town of Kingston.

In the nineteenth century, you came to the port to work, but it sure wasn't a place to live. The river was where you made your living. There were chicken-rendering factories. There was blood in the water and huge piles of coal and stone and barges everywhere you looked—not a place to bring children. There were whorehouses and bars.

Before meeting Cutten, I drop into the Hudson River Maritime Center and ask the director of education, Allynne Lang, about the old steamboat and tug captains. I tell her I'd like to interview any captains living in the area, as Godfrey had suggested when I was at Lock 7. Allynne, who is quite professorial, says, "You're just a little too late. They're all dead."

Soon after Henry Hudson's trip to Albany, the Dutch East India Company built a trading post here at the Rondout and called it Esopus. After 1660 it was renamed Rondout, from the Dutch *reduyt* for "redoubt" or "fort." In the beginning there was only a little dock on the river, and it was not until the time of the Erie Canal, when two brothers decided to bring coal from Pennsylvania to tide water, that Rondout came into its own. Begun in 1825, the Delaware and Hudson Canal, 108 miles with 108 locks, was built by Vermont Yankees and Dutch and Irish immigrants. The canal helped carry coal from Honesdale, Pennsylvania, to the Hudson River on narrow barge boats. The coal was reloaded at the Rondout onto wider Hudson barges for the trip to New York City. In addition to coal, Blue Stone from the Catskills and cement from the hills of nearby Rosendale were all shipped out of the Rondout. Bricks and ice, too.

Today there is little evidence of the old barges, which have sunk or been towed away. Allynne shows me old photographs of icehouses and ice barges, coal-loading operations, and big scruffy boatyards. The Rondout was a "rough and ready" place, she says.

In 1990 it still feels pretty rough and ready. Perhaps the feeling comes from my acquaintance with Captain John Cutten, that renegade historian and fellow pirate addict. He's waiting for me on the terrace of the restaurant under a high bridge. Trucks and cars shake the suspension above us like thunder.

Cutten must think I'm a little strange. After one whole meal, I order a second main course and eat it just as voraciously. He says, "A little bit hungry, huh?"

Cutten advises me to watch the shore closely, especially on weekends. He says, "I don't want to ruin your day, but yesterday I found kids shooting high-powered rifles from shore. I reported the incident to the police. One or two bullets could end your trip pretty fast."

Cutten, too, thinks the river is a lawless country. That is what he loves about the Hudson.

"Hey," he interjects, "Want a paddling partner?" Cutten says his wife can pick him up in Poughkeepsie, "if we *get* that far."

I don't have the energy to go any farther today, but I would like to paddle the river at night. It would be an adventure. Also, I haven't paddled with anyone since Ernie left me on that other, northern Hudson. I could use some company.

"Okay, Captain." Tonight I'll camp here, then explore Kingston and the Rondout during the day while Cutten does his tours. Then we can leave in the late afternoon on the second ebb tomorrow.

6 P.M. June 25. The western sky blazing a Catskill sunset. The water dead flat. We paddle through weeds. Cutten repeats over and over how he should do this more often. "There's nothing like a canoe. Jesus. I haven't done shit like this since I was a kid. Rowing is *fun.*"

"You mean *paddling,*" I correct him. "You *paddle* a canoe. And *row* a boat."

"Okay. Paddling, then. Whatever. I need more of this."

Cutten has had a few beers at dinner, and he takes a couple with him in the canoe. He is relaxed, but his 200 pounds and unfamiliarity with a forty-seven-pound Kevlar canoe make him an awkward companion. We're a little tippy going over the mudflats. Then he settles down, and we cruise well together. When we each pour it on, we can make six or seven knots, he figures, with maximum ebb approaching.

I notice once again the hard edge I first detected in Cutten's anger toward the wealthy merchants of the Hudson. Cutten spots two men fishing from a pier.

He says, "You see such a difference in the classes of people down here. Those fishermen are fishing because they *have* to eat. They don't care about PCBs. At the same time you'll see a $75,000 pleasure boat cruise out into the river, a boat rich people will use only five times a year. They'll run up and down the river burning fuel like there's no tomorrow."

Out of the creek a mile or two down on the western shore, an ugly set of condos rises like a beehive in a swath of cut vegetation. In the next town, Port Ewen, we stop to visit Frank Parslow, a commercial fisherman with whom Cutten has worked in the past. Cutten says, "Frank is seventy-three years old. He's amazing. He still sets thousand-foot drift nets. He works like two guys our age. He says shad fishing keeps him young."

We pull up to Parslow's dock, his red house high above the river with an American flag beside it. Parslow is mending nets on his dock, which is exactly fifty-five steep steps below his house. A homemade sign on the dock reads, "SHAD." On separate boards, signs read, "Boned," "Smoked," and "Roe."

Parslow is a ruddy-looking old salt with forty-four years of shad fishing behind him. He says, "I fish as a side-line. My real job was lab technician at Hercules Incorporated. We were responsible for some of the devices used in the moon landing."

"So how did you get into fishing?" I ask.

"I got into it by mistake," he tells us. Parslow had gone to buy a boat that belonged to a shad fishermen who died, but the family would not sell the boat to him unless he took all the nets and other equipment with it. "I've been fishing ever since," Parslow smiles.

"My wife's after me to stop. I work twelve hours a day. I'm always out in the cold. It's so cold out there the tears come down your cheeks, so windy sometimes the tears just fly off your face."

Parslow is tying shad nets for next spring. He says, "My attraction to the river is a sort of a *phobia*. You start fishing and you don't want to give it up. It gets you out on the river. I just love the river. Fishing gets you out in all sorts of weather, hot sun, rain, wind, snow. But you see that net there? I got some big money in that net, and I'll probably never see any profit come out of that net."

Parslow is happy in spite of spending more on fishing than he takes in from the fish.

He says, "A lot of strange things happen out there, too." He recalls a time he was fishing with his son and a friend when the wind capsized his boat. "We had a bow roller, and we took on some water. We started going under. I didn't notice it at first, we had so much gear in the boat, but I was driving the outboard motor deeper into the river. It was like a power dive in a submarine.

"You'd be surprised how long an outboard motor will run underneath the water. She just sank and kept running, driving deeper and deeper. The three of us managed to hold onto the boat. Then the other guy started to holler. I'd been out with him so many times, I never knew he couldn't swim!"

33. Fisherman Frank Parslow.

Parslow told him to hang on to the boat. "It's not going to sink, just hang on!" But the guy kept crawling up on the boat, and Parslow started to get scared.

"We had our boots on. We always buy our boots one size too large, so if we go under water, we just kick twice, and they're off. All three of us kicked our boots. Then I noticed my son trying to rescue a box he'd had in the boat."

Parslow screamed, "What the hell are you doing? Leave the box." But Parslow's son said he had a six-pack of beer in there.

Somehow this idea of rescuing a six-pack was the best thing that happened to Parslow that day in the water, and now the fisherman is all smiles recalling the near disaster. "Hell, I was worried about a man's life, and my son was worried about a six-pack of beer! So that settled me right down. I said to myself, 'If he ain't worried, then why the hell do I have to worry?' Everyone was rescued.

"My boy, he likes his beer," Parslow jokes.

Parslow describes the old days on the river. "Back in the 1960s the water was so bad you put an oar in the Hudson and you couldn't see the tip of your blade. The shad were scarce, but then the shad came back to their spawning grounds in the mid-sixties when the river started to get cleaner.

"Nowadays without all the pollution and the river clearer, the shad can see my old nets. It seems the fish have a sort of reverse gear that makes them just back up and go around. The water got so clear, I had to buy more expensive, less visible nets. But the price of shad is down. If I can't get the price I want, I think I'll get out of fishing. Maybe go to Florida."

It was Frank Parslow in 1983 who first alerted the Hudson River Fisherman's Association about the Exxon tankers discharging seawater and then taking on fresh Hudson water for the long trek back to Aruba. The water was used in refining operations and was offered for sale on the Caribbean island.

"I got a kick out of watching those boats discharge water and take it in. They had fire drills on board. Some of the crews spoke nothing but Chinese. Some spoke Spanish. It was a regular circus out there."

John Cronin had just become the Riverkeeper and, alerted by Parslow, he confronted the Exxon tankers in his new boat, the *Riverkeeper*. This led to the threat of a lawsuit against Exxon, which was settled out of court and which left the Hudson River Fisherman's Association half a million dollars and a future as a force against polluters of the Hudson.

Parslow stays away from the river on weekends. "It's crazy out there. I leave the boat and go for a drive Saturdays and Sundays."

Cutten and I have some miles to travel before we sleep, so we leave the happy fisherman on his dock working on his tackle, his wife probably waiting for him in front of the TV, fifty-five steps above.

The canoe frightens a big fish over the mudflat, perhaps a sturgeon. Hudson River fishermen call the Atlantic sturgeon the "monster fish." These creatures can live for forty years. They have five rows of armored plates on their bodies, and their mouths are like vacuum cleaner hoses that extend below the snout. Caught commercially between May and July from Haverstraw Bay to Catskill, these leviathans can run fourteen feet long and weigh as much as 800 pounds. Cutten says they look "thoroughly prehistoric, and if you try to land one, they can easily tip your boat over."

In *The Hudson: Three Centuries of History, Romance and Invention,*

Wallace Bruce calls the sturgeon "a pig, without the pig's obstinacy. He spends much of the time rooting and feeding in the mud at the bottom, and encounters the net, coarse and strong, when he goes abroad. He strikes, and is presently hopelessly entangled, when he comes to the top and is pulled into the boat, like a great sleepy sucker." Yet, says Bruce, for so dull a fish, the sturgeon has been known to leap completely out of water and into a passing boat "to the alarm and consternation of the inmates."

The great estates continue to run along the ridge on the eastern shore. Now we're in perhaps the wealthiest stretch of the Hudson. Cutten is a good guide through this alleyway of mansions. Having grown up, as he puts it, "across the Hyde Park railroad tracks," and having spent his youth on the river, Cutten can fill me in on the gossip of the rich and famous. First he points to Edith Wharton's old home, then to a Spanish-looking hacienda with a wide manicured lawn dropping to the river. "That one's owned by Billy Joel, although he probably doesn't want anyone to know that. You can't blame a person for wanting his privacy." Cutten points also to the Dinsmore Estate, now occupied, he says, by the publisher of *Penthouse Magazine*.

We pass a little shack near the shore. Cutten's voice grows strained. "Now that's the way it *used to be* along the river—*before* all the mansions."

When talk turns to the mysteries of the Hudson, I get excited. Cutten speaks about an old map with "Indian caves" marked on it around Indian Rock, a spit of land just above the village of Esopus. He also talks about the American naturalist John Burroughs, who chose to live humbly in this region of mansions.

"Black Creek, just down from Indian Rock is where Burroughs built his log house and named it Slabsides, for it was made from the slabs from logs." Burroughs knew the Hudson countryside as well as Thoreau knew Walden Pond, but he chose to live up a swampy creek rather than along the side of the river. The naturalist's own explanation was that he would rather see glimpses of the river through the trees than view the wide river all at once all day long. Burroughs wrote naturalist's tracts at Slabsides, which still stands on Black Creek and remains today much as it was when he died in 1921.

Then there is Cruger's Island. Cutten says over his shoulder, "According to one Indian legend, no person has ever died on Cruger's

Island. They say Colonel Cruger built a replica of a Mayan temple on his island in order to store his collection of Central American statues. I've never seen it." Cutten and I decide to explore Cruger's Island someday.

Cutten is equally fascinated by the religious orders that line the escarpment along the western shore, which some call Monastery Alley. Across from Norrie State Park, first comes the Mother of Perpetual Help Monastery, followed by the gargantuan Mount Saint Alphonsus Seminary, Sacred Heart Church, Marist Preparatory School, Marist Brothers Seminary, Ascension Church, Holy Cross Monastery, Santa María Novitiate, Saint Gabriel's School, and finally. the Mother Cabrina School, which is directly across from the F. D. Roosevelt Home and Historic Landmark.

Some say the western shore is haunted by apparitions. Driving down Route 9W along the escarpment, people have seen visions of flaming saints, they say. More people have crashed on this road than any in the state; that is what Cutten heard anyway. "But," Cutten says with a wicked laugh, "I'd attribute it more to liquor than revelation."

A family of swans glides against the shore, white necks like pale question marks in the deep dusk. They swim past more duck blinds, a sight Cutten thinks will soon disappear from the river because so many people moving up from the city "don't like to hear shooting when they sip their cocktails."

Cutten himself knows all about guns. He says his father taught him to shoot and to respect a gun. He has a license and often carries a pistol. Perhaps he is carrying one tonight.

When we cross the river, Cutten points to the silhouette of big mountains to the south. "There's where you're headed—the Hudson Highlands." We pause letting the tide carry the canoe, when a fish jumps high into the air and comes crashing down like a log dropped from a bridge. "Whoooo. What the hell was that?"

"Probably a carp."

We pass Esopus Island, "Shirley Loves Tom" written on the rocks. Blue herons stand alongshore, and cormorants float nearby. Kunz mentioned the island as a good stopover. I was planning to camp here for the night, but the strong tide drives us quickly past it.

Cutten says, "Supposedly there was a Jesuit missionary who was martyred on Esopus Island, killed by the Indians back in the 1600s.

That's what a Marist brother told me, anyway." He looks at the illuminated watch on his wrist. "Jesus, we're making better time than I expected. We've only been rowing for an hour."

"Paddling . . . You *paddle* a canoe and *row* a boat."

"Right. Paddling, whatever. I sure didn't think we'd be this far along. I once swam across the river here eight times when I was a kid. On the eighth time an ocean ship came up on me doing nine knots. It came right up onto me and I closed my eyes and to this day I don't know why it didn't kill me. But I got out alive."

We dip under a railway bridge, ducking our heads, and lean into a turn. We come sloshing into Elbow Creek and the little harbor of Hyde Park-on-the-Hudson, where John grew up.

"This is Hyde Park? Home of the Vanderbilt mansion?"

"Hyde Park-on-the-Hudson. Like I said, it's the other side of the tracks from Hyde Park proper. I used to keep my boat here." Cutten tells me he bought his first car from the Vanderbilt's chauffeur.

On a night river, everything seems unfamiliar. I've been to Hyde Park many times, and I've probably driven right to this spot, but the darker it gets out here, the more foreign the land becomes from a river perspective. It's as if, for this night journey, I have been studying the wrong maps.

When we pass the little beach where Eleanor Roosevelt used to take her kids swimming (the Roosevelt home hidden from view by a bluff), the land goes completely dark. The only light anywhere is a lingering evanescence in the charcoal sky over the broad river.

We cut off a big bay and head out into deep water with no running lights. We scan over our shoulders nervously for any tug or container boat that might suddenly appear.

Cutten says cryptically, "There's a hole in the riverbed here at Crum Elbow that goes down 190 feet. It's the second deepest spot on the river."

"What's the deepest?"

"World's End at West Point is over 200 feet deep."

This journey is not at all like canoeing the lakes and streams of upper Ontario at canoe camp. This is more like canoeing the middle of the ocean at midnight, with ancient fish, 800-pound dinosaurs, dwelling below us in the eternal night of the bottomless Hudson.

The moon tops the trees, and I remember what Kunz said to me in New Hampshire. His trips down the Hudson taught him to love the cycles of the moon, he said. When he followed the night tide, sometimes it would rain hard; then suddenly the rain would stop and everything would clear out on the river, and the moon would emerge bright from dissolving mists.

Without my glasses, I can make out only a blur of lights along-shore that mark the beginning of Poughkeepsie. Thank goodness Cutten knows the river so well from his childhood. He is my Huck Finn. He leads us safely over the deep holes and past the Culinary Institute of America (alias CIA) and past some Marist College students shooting off fireworks on a point high above the water. They do not notice two ghostly paddlers pulling into shore just below them. If we were the enemy, we could sneak right up to them and capture all fifty drunken revelers at gunpoint.

When we pull the canoe up on the floating dock in the big marina at the Brass Anchor, Cutten looks at his watch again.

"Jesus Christ. We rowed fifteen miles in two hours and forty-five minutes! No one's going to believe it."

Cutten drinks a second beer at the Brass Anchor while we wait for his wife to pick him up. It is sad to see him drive off an hour later. But now I know where he keeps his boat, and I will return someday to the Rondout to explore those Mayan ruins on Cruger's Island or the Indian caves near Black Creek.

For now, on a small patch of flat land in the bushes on the point near the restaurant, I pitch my tent in the river darkness and lie here listening to the distant party music, remembering what Kunz had said about rivers, how you can just drag your boat up into the bushes, stake out an area, and sleep anywhere you want. Tonight I feel invisible. Beside the calmest Hudson water I have ever seen, I sleep in a no man's land and dream of home.

16

Home

5 A.M. June 26. In the early morning mist, grotesquely pink from the Poughkeepsie incinerator, I spot a figure stirring on the deck of a single-masted ship moored at the Hudson Psychiatric Hospital landing. The bearded sailor raises his torso from a sleeping bag on deck, rubs his eyes with his knuckles, and flashes me the peace sign as I stroke by the 106-foot sloop *Clearwater*.

When Pete Seeger and some partners first had the idea for a boat that would sail up and down the river, educating school children to the ecology of the Hudson and bringing environmental focus to a polluted river, many thought the Hudson was beyond repair. A 1966 *New York Times* headline read "Life Abandoning Polluted Hudson." Government reports referred to the river as an "open sewer." In 1969, the same year that Bob Boyle published his seminal work, *Hudson River: A Natural and Unnatural History*, the Clearwater began its mission. Or in Seeger's words, the sloop was launched to "clean up this polluted stream and make it the way it was on the river a hundred years ago."

For more than twenty years now the sloop has been a prime symbol of a river on the mend. Other environmental groups have been born in the meantime, and the river, if not healthy yet, is far cleaner than it was. Hundreds of thousands of school children have worked and sailed on the sloop and understand the ecology of the river better now than anyone did in Jim Britt's and my generation.

281

A lone rowing scull skims beneath the Poughkeepsie bridge just off the Marist College boathouse. The sculler raises his fist into the air and shouts over the quiet water, "Wenonah. Right on, Wenonah!" and immediately goes back to rowing, but is already well past me when he grabs his oars again.

Near the condominiums at the base of the Poughkeepsie bridge, a man is collecting cans from trash barrels. A woman is out walking her dogs in the riverside park.

The air over the river has never seemed as polluted as it is south of Poughkeepsie. To witness such pollution while at the same time to hear the commuter trains running from Poughkeepsie past my house in Beacon to the Big Apple makes for depressing paddling. The train rumbles along the shore like a mechanical mockery to my tortoise journey. I watch the 5:45 zoom past; followed by the 6:06. Now I'm only two stops on the railroad from my home, but . . . water water everywhere and not a drop to drink . . . it's a paddler's eternity away from home still.

At New Hamburg the 7:09 comes to a stop, then quickly chugs downriver. I glide past White's Marina, where I bought my charts months ago. I hope old man White is looking out here today. I want him to see me in a canoe.

Just behind the river village of New Hamburg, a hundred years ago, in a cluster of houses now called Hughsonville, a woman named Talmadge had three dreams about the ghost of Captain Kidd, each dream identical. A tall man was burying treasure at the base of an old oak tree. She said she saw the gold coins that were being handled by the pirate. Her sons Mat and Jim went out on the third night by the light of the moon to look for the treasure. The lady fretted and urged them not to speak once they got to the oak tree.

The grove where the oak stood was black, even though moonlight shone everywhere beyond the trees. One son began to dig, and when he tired, he passed the shovel to his brother. Suddenly Kidd's ghost appeared by the tree. It was exactly the ten-foot man described in their mother's dream. The ghost lifted his great ghostly arm and gestured for the interlopers to leave the grove immediately.

Mat and Jim fled for home and later told their story in a local pub, but they were laughed at. The next day they returned to find their tools exactly where they had dropped them, but the pit had been filled in, and the ground was absolutely level, as if the earth had never been touched.

7:45 A.M. "Halaloooyahh," I shout, for now I see the thin pencil line of the Newburgh-Beacon Bridge with silver trucks heading east and west along Interstate 84. Across the river the Danskammer coal-fired Central Hudson energy plant adds oil-smelling ash into the fetid sky. The black smoke mushrooms from the stack into the upper wind, joining the overall haze from other stacks in Rockland, Westchester, Orange, and Dutchess counties. The lower river could be categorized as the river of spewing smokestacks.

The Algonquins danced ceremonial dances on the Danskammer point, and the great Jova Brick Works operated here for a century. Just south of New Hamburg, the controversial Chelsea Substation is prepared to pump a hundred million gallons per day of Hudson River water to Manhattan in-case of drought. Cronin and the Riverkeeper's lawyer, Robert F. Kennedy Jr., have fought this operation for years, complaining that New York City has no right to alter the ecosystem of the river by stealing water from the Hudson unless they do a better job conserving the water they waste every day. (The city itself estimates it loses 240 million gallons a day to leaks, water running in vacant buildings, open fire hydrants, and illegal connections.)

Already the morning is firing up to eighty degrees, a typical summer ozone morning. A freight train on the opposite shore adds decibel pollution to the smog. A tug hums deeply as it strains to push three loaded barges against the tide in the deep channel.

Six swans land very close to the canoe, swooping low over the surface of the Hudson. Their wings make the noise of "whoooo-whoooowhooooo" before they come to rest.

Distances on the open river are deceptive. I have been able to see the bridge and my destination for hours, but have not reached it, which is a form of torture only canoeists can know. Suddenly the wind rises out of the south. Perhaps I should have headed into the riskier shipping channel to catch a faster current, but instead I have chosen caution close to the eastern shore. The whitecaps multiply and transform the river into an exercise in violent frustration.

Finally, I pass the massive concrete pilings of the Newburgh-Beacon Bridge and scoot into Beacon harbor. Looking at a nearby hill, I recognize the spires of the Dutch Reformed church, which is visible from my house. Mount Beacon rises in a sick blue haze behind this little industrial city that was once the hat capital of the nation.

This is my hometown, but it feels like somewhere else.

In the quiet of the Beacon harbor, not twenty yards from the Beacon Sloop Club boat ramp, one of the four bolts securing my solo seat to the gunwales snaps, sending me to the floor of the canoe. I have to paddle these last few yards home on my knees, and I touch the dock just as the 9:36 Hudson Line pulls into the Beacon station.

I drag my Odyssey up the boat ramp and turn it over, leaving my Bills bag underneath. I watch the commuters bunch up around the sliding doors of the train cars. Each car has a name: one is called *Scenic Hudson,* another is *Tear of the Clouds.*

I grab my two paddles and walk up the hilly street toward home. No one knows I'm coming at ten this morning. Melissa thinks it will be later in the day. I want to surprise her. I sneak up to the house and open the front door like a thief. When I step into the front hall, I can hear a silver voice in the parlor. Around the corner Suzanna is babbling in her old-fashioned wood playpen.

The delicacy of the moment frightens me. I have been away a huge portion of my daughter's life, only to return with a black beard looking like someone else's father.

I place my paddles softly on the floor. I take a deep breath and step around the corner. At first she doesn't notice me. Then she looks up. Her face does something I have never seen a human face do before. Her face contorts with a riot of emotion, fifteen different feelings digging at her flesh at the same time. If she could speak, that face might shout, "Dad! You're home!" "Where the hell have you been?" "I missed you so much." "I'll kill you for leaving me for so long." So many conflicting emotions all bunched up and stored these past few weeks—longing, anger, love, abandonment, and maybe even hatred. Unable to cope with this much feeling, suddenly she drops her head, unwilling to look at me anymore.

Still she cannot smile.

She looks up. She looks down, then she does not look up again. I wait for a sign that it's okay. This is the longest moment of my life.

With her head still down, she raises one arm slowly into the air.

However ambiguous, it is indeed the signal I need. So I reach down and lift an eighteen-pound, one-year-old girl to my chest.

Impossible to describe exactly how it feels to paddle a hot river for two and a half weeks, to come home out of the glare with arms like steel, to lean over a playpen, to reach down and lift up a one-year-old, eighteen-pound girl.

She wraps tiny white arms around my neck, her hands tapping my shoulders ever so lightly. She drops her limp head into my neck, then quickly tilts her head to see if I'm still here. But no smiles yet. There is no room for smiling in her pained happy heart.

She can manage only one word, the best word in the English language. Softly, seriously, whispering close to my ear, she says, "Dadadada."

When I pull her from my chest, I know my journey is almost done. I say again, "It's okay. Dada's home." She taps me one more time ever so lightly; then she wriggles and is down on the floor scurrying, laughing, pretending nothing is afoot. It's just another child's day of toys, books, laundry . . .

Melissa is out in the yard hanging clothes. She enters with an empty basket. "Oh," she says, "You're always early." Holding her is the best feeling I've felt in weeks. I will not describe what chemical reaction occurs when marital affection is poured into the mad scientist's beaker of long, hot, river absence. I will only say that a great river like the Hudson softens a paddler's soul with wild gratitude for having a wonderful home and family to come home to.

June 27 and 28. Some details to attend to: family, being a dad, and meeting with John Cronin. I also have to kill an extra day because I'm ahead of schedule. Reporters, radio interviewers, TV cameras will not be at the Battery until Monday, July 2, noon. As much as I love being home for a few days, even the beds and the walls seem unfamiliar. I feel awkward not being on the river to finish my trip. I am neither traveling, nor truly home, neither here nor there. These few days pass in a kind of dreamy limbo, and I keep thinking about the sixty miles that remain.

When I take walks down by the river, I sense its proximity to the sea. In Beacon, the Hudson bargains with the ocean, which sends

34. Home at last on the Beacon Sloop Club dock.

gulls and long whiffs of salt air inland on the drowned river. I never realized how close Beacon is to the ocean. Perhaps it is necessary to make the long journey out from Lake Tear, out of the interior of the state, down from the mountains, to know just how maritime are these lower Hudson cities along the riverbank. No wonder pirates sailed upriver to hide their loot in the Highlands. The last sixty miles of river feel like a long chunk of the sea.

One morning I drive down to John Cronin's Garrison office, eight miles from my house, to discuss what he sees as my mission, the mission I will want to convey to the press. CNN is going to place a camera crew on the George Washington Bridge as I pass under it a few days from now, and perhaps Mayor David Dinkins will come down to the Battery to deliver a speech about New York City's environmental policies.

Last night there was a message on the Riverkeeper's answering machine. Some attorney in Albany, responding to the recent article in the *Albany Times-Union*, thinks I am a fraud, that I could not have canoed the upper river.

Right away I find myself constructing a defense. I've never maintained that I made this journey all alone, or that it hasn't been done before by other people in other fashions. But as far as I know, I will be the first to carry up to Tear then take a canoe all the way down the Hudson.

The Riverkeeper's offices are a seven-room farmhouse on an estate in the rolling hills above Garrison Landing. John sits with his hands entwined on top of his bushy hair. When I sit down, he leans forward, picks up a pencil, and begins to twirl it in both hands. He looks tired, his eyes sunken, his voice hoarse.

"So you made it this far," he says. "You're doing a great job."

When Cronin first started his job as Riverkeeper, he wondered how any one person could be a "riverkeeper." His tiny wood boat was dwarfed against the metal hull of the Exxon tanker that had been stealing Hudson River water. The result of that confrontation was so successful, Cronin's celebrity was instantaneous, his mission defined.

As we talk this morning in late June, I notice that Cronin describes my journey in his own terms, "Peter, you have traveled through many Hudsons—the pristine, the PCB-laden, the civilized. And now you are heading into the most polluted river of all. Connecting the pieces of the river is very important. The point I'd like to see you make in the media is that *my river today is your river tomorrow*. If people understand this connection between the different pieces of the river, maybe they'll respect and care for it."

It is easy to let Cronin talk. I sit back and listen as he articulates the environmentalists' position. "The river's great diversity is threatened by people who want to develop the shoreline. People are building now on rock and land that twenty years ago they would have laughed at as a place to build. I say, let's keep the river the way it is. We don't need residential development along the river. Huge developments are being planned at this very moment, and the Hudson could lose all its beauty."

As Cronin talks and twirls his pencil, taking a call or two during our conversation, I am thinking how truly beautiful I've found the river to be. This has come as a surprise. Before I left, I was afraid I would find "the Rhine of America," which is how many people describe the Hudson. But the Hudson is far cleaner than the Rhine.

Development along its shores could be slowed by the new Greenway, too. In his 1989 State of the State address, Governor Mario Cuomo suggested that Albany be linked to New York City by a Greenway, a trail of green all the way from Albany to Manhattan. Various environmental and local civic groups have since banded together to implement such a plan. It is a loose coalition and a vague concept unified around the idea that each river community will be in charge of developing and maintaining such a "greenway." At the very least, developers will be facing more red tape.

When Cronin speaks of New York City, he looks frustrated and angry. "The city takes freshwater out of the Hudson, but it dumps its waste there, too. My interest in your trip is to show that the river is *a living river*. From Lake Tear to the Sea. The Hudson's past is alive, it isn't lost. But if we let the whole river go the way of New York Harbor, God forbid!"

The telephone rings. John answers. It happens to be the lawyer from Albany. When he hangs up, John says, "Don't worry, Peter. He's a scout leader who always wanted to canoe the whole river by sections. But he just never thought anyone could really do it. He wants to know how you got around those dams."

PART FOUR

River of Mountains to the Sea

4. From Beacon to the Battery.

17

The Hudson Highlands

5:30 A.M. June 29. I wake long before Suzanna and Melissa, to drag my gear to the river. I walk down the hill with my neighbor, a lawyer for a pharmaceutical company in the city. He is headed for the train; I am heading for the canoe. He wears a dark suit in contrast to my yellow nylon pants, bright as bananas. He says, "Good Luck" and joins the other sleepy commuters lining the platform.

I slip my Odyssey into the calm slack before the ebb tide at the Beacon Sloop Club dock and wait a few minutes for the photographer from the *Poughkeepsie Journal* who is supposed to meet me here, but I guess he has decided to sleep in. So I'll just shove off under this hazy sun coming up over the train platform.

Former waterfront activity is suggested by the rotting ferry-slip posts. Ferries ran frequently between Beacon and Newburgh until 1962. When Interstate 84's Newburgh-Beacon Bridge was built, the ferries steamed downriver, never to return.

Beacon is not what it used to be. With 14,000 residents, it is a typical small river city in suspension, waiting for that revival that never comes. As in Troy, much of Beacon's waterfront was destroyed during the state's Urban Renewal Plan. The old hotel on the water and the great Tompkins hat factory, the row houses, and many of the Victorian homes like ours were demolished. Prefabricated town-houses have taken their place.

Formerly called Fishkill Landing, or Fishkill-on-Hudson, and connected in its heyday of industry by electric tram to the nearby manufacturing village of Mattewan, Beacon was once famous for its incline railway, which ran from the base of the mountain to a brightly lit casino atop Mount Beacon. From the river now, as I pull away from shore, I can see the dark scar of the old tracks rising straight up the mountain behind the town. Burned and abandoned, the incline railway cars have been smashed and strewn in the weeds.

During the Revolution, signal fires built high above the river gave warning of the approaching enemy. If the first beacon pyre atop Storm King Mountain was set ablaze, then signal fires on Mount Beacon were lit, and so on up the river.

In a nearby parking lot, a light-blue station wagon with Alabama plates is filled with junk, including a number of bamboo fishing poles. This might be a scene from the deep south. Two black men with poles sit on their patio chairs out on the jetty. Three black boys about seven, nine, and eleven are swimming off the floating dock. I paddle right up to them. One says, "Mister, is that a canoe?"

Holding his hands across his naked chest, he stands on a piling, bewildered. All three giggle and jump into the water at once. The day will be very hot and hazy. Like dolphins, they swim back and forth under my canoe as I paddle out of the harbor.

After two full days of shore leave, my arms are stiff; my whole body is like cardboard. I have repaired my solo seat with a new bolt, and finally I've taken out the yoke, so I can move my legs freely. I have also switched permanently to my beautiful wood Mitchell paddle. For the remainder of the trip, I'll keep the epoxy whitewater paddle strapped to my hull for a spare.

This early in the morning, fish are splashing all about my canoe as if crazed by the heat. Below the Beacon docks is the now-abandoned Nabisco box factory. Laura Haight, in an article for the Clearwater's newsletter, has written about her involvement in trying to save the Hudson's waterfront properties: "I see the battles we won and those that we lost. For me, the hardest is seeing the land unbroken yet condemned—Piermont, Yonkers, Hastings, Beacon, and elsewhere—future riverfront homes for the few, lost to the rest of us. . . . Or maybe not forever. The ruins of old factories give me hope. Ivy tearing brick from brick, sumac seeking out cracks in the cement, expanding them, grasses creeping over parking lots."

She sees hope in the powerful destruction of weeds. But I see nothing but despair in the old river factories on shore, the hopelessness of industry that works the river too hard only to depart, leaving behind weed-grown shells. The real hope of the river—for me anyway—exists out here on the water itself, away from land, free of the factories, free of the discontent of pavement. As I pull far out into the river, I feel the power of the ebb. The freedom returns. I swivel my canoe in a complete circle or skim like a water spider down the glass of the early morning tide. I am happy again.

I gaze back at the city I've come to live in and say the name "Beacon." It sounds so metallic and industrial, so unlike the names of the wild northern Hudson in its early stages. Gone are the forgiving names of rocks and streams, of Feldspar, Opalescent, North Creek, and North River. Dominating the river now are Dutch names, settlement names like Yonkers, Peekskill, Fishkill, and Hoboken. And harsh-sounding names like Saugerties, Beacon, and Verplank—names hardened by tugboats and dredging, by Dutch and English conquests, names no longer harmonious and lovely to roll around in the imagination of forests.

In 1783, across the river from Beacon in Newburgh, notice of the cessation of hostilities was proclaimed to Washington's disgruntled army, and a celebration of cannon fire shook the sky. "The mountain sides resounded and echoed like tremendous peals of thunder, and the flashing from thousands of fire-arms, in the darkness of the evening, was like unto vivid flashes of lightning from the clouds," wrote the rhapsodic Wallace Bruce in *The Hudson*.

Here, too, in Newburgh Bay is the summer and early fall residence of the salt wedge (which resides in spring and winter down by Haverstraw and the Tappan Zee). This ambiguous border of salt- and freshwater commingling moves up and down the river with changes in weather, seasons, and tides. Robert Boyle sees the presence of saltwater on the Hudson as an ecological mystery: "Whatever the complexities of the salt line, marine fishes and other creatures from the Atlantic use it to work their way upriver to places where they are not supposed to be found. For instance, sea anemones . . . live on the bottom of the Hudson near the George Washington Bridge."

As a writer for *Sports Illustrated*, as a longtime fisherman and resident of the Highlands, and as the man who inspired much of today's environmental action along the Hudson, Boyle is a good guide for a canoeist paddling on the sunken river with its gulls swirling over-head and swans in coves and cormorants in the wetland marshes. Boyle fills *The Hudson River: A Natural and Unnatural History* with information about the estuary and the marine life that invades this sunken river.

Perhaps Beacon's greatest asset is that it stands at the gates of the Hudson Highlands. For now I can see the outline of famous Storm King and Breakneck Mountains just ahead on either side of the river. The next thirteen miles of the journey's remaining 53.5 nautical miles will take me through a drama of mountains that plunge fjordlike into a narrowing Hudson gorge (the other and more famous gorge). In fact, so much has been said about the Hudson Highlands that if it were not for the wonderful wackiness of scale and proportion of these "endless hills," as the Delaware Indians called them, I might pass without comment. Over-painted, much-eulogized, yet somehow misunderstood, the Highlands are indeed spectacular.

With each paddle stroke southward, the tide feels even more like an ocean magnet. The river grows massive, and the population multi-plies. Ever since I came to tidal water 154 miles from Manhattan, I have marveled at the idea of tides on the river. I am mystified, for example, that the tidal drop that was nearly 5 feet at Troy is only 2.5 feet at West Point. I wonder how a tide can be stronger when the tidal drop is so much less. It makes no sense.

Proportion in the Highlands is completely out of whack, too. Six-teen-hundred-foot rock faces plummet into a narrow span of deep water (the deepest stretch on the whole Hudson, close to 200 feet near West Point). When a monstrous container boat from the north passes into the Highlands in front of me, the hull is dwarfed by these "mountains," which are not really mountains but which only seem like mountains in comparison to everything else around here.

To add to my increasing feeling of dislocation, Bannerman's castle appears on tiny Pollepel Island ahead, its brick facade fiery orange at daybreak. A Scotsman, Frances Bannerman made a fortune at the age of fourteen after the Civil War by collecting Confederate and Union weapons, saddles, and all kinds of discarded military equipment, which he then sold for a huge profit to governments and armies over-seas. When his munitions business on lower Broadway in Manhattan could no longer accommodate an increasing inventory, he bought Pollepel Island and built the castle as an arsenal. Barges would deliver and take away goods to all parts of the world.

Beginning in 1900, Frank Bannerman worked on the castle until he died in 1918. He never used an architect, the son of Bannerman's gardener told me in Beacon. He built everything according to his whims. One day he would say, "Well, how about putting a turret there," or "I think today we'll build an Explosives Room." As a result, the castle was never too sturdy. After years of fires and deterioration, now the walls look as if they might come tumbling down in a strong wind. The whole place has a bombed-out quality. New York State has condemned the island to keep people from getting hurt, although there is evidence everywhere that motorboaters visit any chance they get. Old rubble, scraps of metal, and haunting-thick brush make it impossible to follow the brick path that runs around the castle.

When Bannerman died, his wife stayed on. In 1920 she was asleep in her house on the hill above the arsenal when 200 pounds of gunpowder and shells blew the castle tower into the river. Chunks of castle landed like burning meteorites in the middle of the shipping channel. Another fire ripped through the castle in 1969 just after the island was completely abandoned and taken over by the state. The cause of the second fire was never discovered.

An intricate network of turrets along the castle walls creates the effect of burlesque. Some say the island is haunted by the ghost of a tug captain who was forced by Bannerman himself to sink his ship to be used as the foundation for a rampart. Archaeological remains of Native American encampments can be found on the nearby mainland but not on the island itself, which leads some to speculate that Native Americans never slept on Pollepel Island. Perhaps they too thought it haunted.

Remains of the old rampart that once surrounded the island sit in shallow water like submerged ruins, and I paddle through an arch and back out into the river. Many years ago, before Bannerman's time, the state had planned to purchase the island in order to erect a statue of Henry Hudson, but the statue was never built. Someday soon, however, it seems inevitable that the state will bulldoze the rest of the crumbling castle.

Paddling between Storm King and Breakneck, like Scylla and Charybdis on opposite banks, is an eerie experience—like having to

35. Under the rampart of Bannerman's Arsenal.
Courtesy Pat Shafer.

make a mad dash past the shoulders of two giants about to clash. Both "mountains" have been blasted and cut back by humans. The rocky face of Storm King was chipped away by railroad men in the nineteenth century. *Harper's Weekly* ran a 1881 print showing "Negroes" hanging from ropes over the cliff to chip the rock. It was treacherous work, and many died. Across the way, a large quarry on Breakneck Mountain supplied sandstone for the Brooklyn Bridge.

Looking south, well beyond the castle, below another castle high on the east bank with its turret puncturing the grey sky, I see a freighter begin its ninety-degree swing to the left around Constitution Island and through World's End, past West Point on the right. I wonder how a ship perhaps 300 feet long can pass through a channel so tricky and narrow. Even as I think the boat cannot possibly fit between the island and the point—especially if another boat should be coming the other way—as if by magic the ship vanishes behind

36. Through the Endless Mountains—the Hudson Highlands.
Courtesy Pat Shafer.

Constitution Island. I do not hear a crash of metal against rock, and I assume the ship has fared well.

This was not the case with ships long ago. World's End was named during the age of clippers and Hudson River sloops. Without motors, sailing craft had a devilish time trying to buck the tides, the winds, and the currents. Bad enough that a sailboat must make a loop like this. Worse that the winds are so contrary in this Highland canyon. No wonder the fortress at West Point was built here—if an enemy ship foundered in the tricky current and winds, it would be cut to pieces by cannon fire.

9:30 A.M. The day very hot. Cronin, his fourteen-year-old daughter Sasha, the photographer Pat Shafer, and Pat's seven-year-old son Joffrey have all joined me now. Pat takes photos from the *Riverkeeper,* as I race past West Point. Joffrey hops in the canoe with a bulky orange life jacket and my other paddle, much too long for him.

Joffrey, blond, smiling, and terribly excited to be in a canoe, shouts, "I love to canoe because you don't have to stop at gas stations." Joffrey dips the big paddle into the water but forgets to pull it backward. The paddle drifts in the river, a stroke known as "lily-dipping."

"Also, a canoe is quiet," says the joyful, articulate boy. "We can paddle as long as we are alive. We can rest, and resting is our fuel," he says. But he likes the quiet best, he says, and I agree with him.

"Also," exclaims the little philosopher of canoes, "when a barge comes, we have to get out of the way and hurry up before the waves get us."

"Keep paddling," I yell in jest, and Joffrey actually takes a stroke or two.

"Do you hear that thunder?" asks Joffrey who has turned completely around and is now facing me from the bow and paddling the wrong way.

I hear distant thunder all right, but not the thunder of summer storms or of Hudson's crew bowling in the mountains but, rather, the lesser thunder of cadets firing rifles near West Point.

Even in a slow canoe, the swift current through the Highlands makes these thirteen miles pass so quickly. For it is not even noon yet, and we have already come to the Bear Mountain Bridge. High up over the bridge on the eastern shore is a large lump of mountain called Anthony's Nose. Washington Irving wrote that a man named Anthony had just washed his face and was gazing into the calm water admiring his reflection, when a ray from the sun bounced off his shiny nose and shot a sizzling beam into the water where it killed a sturgeon.

Across from Anthony's Nose is Iona Island, winter home to a handful of bald eagles. Eagles live on fish, and the fish were so polluted with DDT that eagle sitings on the Hudson and in the contiguous 48 states declined drastically through the 1950s and '60s. Recently, however, they have been easier to spot around Iona Island.

Just past Iona is a portion of narrow river called the Race Horse, so-named because the channel shoots a huge volume of water through the last of the Highlands with a vengeance. Fishermen have shortened the name to "the race."

Directly across from the city of Peekskill at the very end of the "endless hills," I hug the western shore to pass Jones Point. The river heads southwest, and I can cut off a big bay here. The mountain

37. John Cronin and the *Riverkeeper* in Haverstraw Bay.
Courtesy Pat Shafer.

above the point is the Dunderberg, a place much dreaded by Dutch mariners, according to Irving, because the hill was inhabited by imps and goblins wearing sugar-loaf hats and short doublets, tumbling "head over heels in the rack and mist." These imps hated captains of ships who "failed to do them reverence, and brought down frightful squalls on such craft as failed to drop the peaks of their mainsails to the goblin who presided over this shadowy republic," says Wallace Bruce. Apparently the old burghers of New York, before making the dangerous trip to Albany by boat, and thinking of the Dunderberg, would update their wills.

What interests me most about Jones Point, however, is that it is sometimes called Kidd's Point. Here Captain Kidd and his crew foundered in a great storm off the Dunderberg. I look over the gunwale for signs of a shimmering mast or spars from Kidd's ship, but today, unfortunately, the river is anything but calm.

I like to dream of the days of pirates on the Hudson. At the mouth of this great river in the late seventeenth century, New York harbor was a pirate's haven. New York City was home to thousands of buccaneers, and the Albany Records of 1696 claim, "pirates in great numbers infest the Hudson River at its mouth and waylay vessels on their way to Albany, speeding out from covers and from behind islands and again returning to the rocky shores, or ascending the mountains along the river to conceal their plunder."

The Scotsman William Kidd had been a buccaneer at sea for some forty years before he settled down in 1691 with a New York woman of means and reputation. For the next five years, records show, he lived with his wife and two daughters in a house along the East River of Manhattan. As far as we know, he was happy. To his name he added the epithet "Gentleman," for by now he was a well-respected man in the city.

In 1695, on a trip to London, Kidd was approached by his friend Robert Livingston of the Hudson Valley Livingstons, who, along with a group of English Lords, including the newly appointed governor of New York, and with the tacit support of King William III, coerced Kidd to go to sea again, this time to capture pirates and their loot. The plan was to make a profit by plundering the plunderers and simultaneously to rid the seas of the buccaneers who were so damaging to sea commerce. Kidd was promised 15 percent of the pirates' booty. The King would receive a tenth, and the project's politically powerful backers would take the rest. Never mind that this "booty" had rightful owners before it had been stolen by pirates. Kidd's mission was a form of legal piracy under the guise of a public good deed.

Kissing his two daughters and wife good-bye, Kidd sailed out of New York Harbor in September 1696 and headed for the Red Sea, the Indian Ocean, and the pirate island of Madagascar. His new vessel, the *Adventure Galley,* was equipped as a fighting machine. His crew (many from the mid-Hudson area, Captain John Cutten told me) were described by the former governor of New York as "men of desperate fortunes and necessities, in expectation of getting vast treasure."

By the time the *Adventure Galley* reached the Indian Ocean half a year later, Kidd had not caught one pirate ship, and many in his crew wanted Kidd to turn to piracy. Faced with a possible mutiny, Kidd later claimed at his trial, he had had no choice but to comply with their wishes to begin raiding commercial vessels. Precisely what happened at sea, how Kidd was transformed from legal pirate to illegal buccaneer, is unclear. Nevertheless, Kidd started to plunder not pirate ships but the legitimate trade vessels he had sworn not to harm.

Once again he was a pirate. Sent on so ambiguous a mission, tempted by the very premise of his goal, Kidd had crossed the rather vague line between privateering and pirating. When Kidd was tried in 1701, his backers, their political reputations in jeopardy, denied their involvement. Kidd became a scapegoat for an undertaking gone awry. His former supporters watched silently as Kidd was convicted.

The first time they tried to hang him, the rope broke, and he had to be strung up again. As a grisly example to any would-be pirates sailing in and out of the Thames, Kidd was painted with tar, wrapped in chains, and strung up in London's port where he remained for a long time—some claim years—while the gulls plucked his eyes and his flesh rotted. The tides washed away his bones.

Legend in Kidd's case has magnified his villainy. Over the years the Kidd story has grown in stature. Fact blooms into fiction. His escapades in the Indian Ocean seem almost mystical now. Fears and superstitions were generated by newspapers at the time of his trial. Yet historians say he was simply a foolish man who made poor decisions but who was no cutthroat, as he is often portrayed. Myths about Kidd abound even today. In whatever port he anchored or might have anchored, there is talk of buried treasure. From Martha's Vineyard to Gardiner's Island, up the Hudson and down the eastern seaboard, in a thousand places, treasure seekers have dug for Kidd's gold bars, gold dust, silver plate, rubies, fine silks, and doubloons. In a few places, such as Gardiner's Island, treasure has actually been found.

Irving, Stevenson, Poe, and Cooper were likewise inspired by the story of Kidd. Kidd legends, I have found, run up and down the Hudson River like secret gossip. Some say that before he gave himself up in Boston, he or his crew or both sailed up the Hudson to Dunderberg Mountain near Peekskill and burned his ship, and the treasure went down with it to the bottom of the Hudson. Others say he sailed as far north up the river as Coeymans or Albany, where he stashed his loot, hoping to return when he could be cleared of the charges against him.

Another legend says the desperate Kidd, pursued by the authorities up the Hudson River, may have burned his ship below World's End, then stolen his treasure away by rowboat to the mouth of Indian Brook near the Highlands village of Cold Spring. When he decided where to bury his doubloons on the brook, he slit the throat of his dog and buried him on top of the gold so the canine ghost would watch over the loot forever. Cutten had first told me the story, but I heard variations along the river.

Months after my trip, in the tiny Foundry Museum library in Cold Spring, I was leafing through old newspapers when I came across an editorial in *The Putnam County Recorder* from 1880 that told of a local farmer who became rich overnight. Some thought he had found Kidd's gold. In the same paper I read that a man by the name of Philip Vantwist was digging around the mouth of Indian Brook, when his shovel made a loud "chink" sound of metal against metal. Suddenly, a phantom vessel with big white sails raced noiselessly across the smooth waters of the Hudson and struck its proud bow at his very feet. Vantwist knew the man standing in the bow could be none other than Captain Kidd himself.

Vantwist turned to run and forgot forever the location of the gold.

About the same time as Vantwist's encounter with Kidd's ghost, the pirate's mastiff was spotted just below Indian Brook Falls. The 1880 newspaper reported: "The dog's haunts are around the bridge that spans the chasm, just below the falls, sometimes being seen on one side of the bridge, sometimes on the other. . . . A Carriage load was returning to Garrison one evening about ten o'clock with six persons in it and just as they were approaching the spot where the mighty mastiff strides, one of the company jokingly remarked, 'Now let us look for the dog.'" No sooner were the words out than a giant dog appeared alongside the carriage, its bristles upright, menacing, and terrible. Pulling a revolver from his pocket, the driver fired six bullets into its hide, but the dog did not move.

Late morning, but it feels like late afternoon. Pollution getting bad. It is a sad commentary on our times that across from magical Kidd's Point and goblin-infested Dunderberg Mountain, south of the city of Peekskill, a Resource Recovery plant (love that euphemism for incinerator) is now spewing burned garbage high into the air, spreading a sickly rose mist over the Highlands. Just south of the incinerator, something even more disturbing meets the canoeist's eye, and no other river scene on my journey has prepared me for this. The nuclear reactors at Indian Point, decades old, stand alongshore like space-age relics, two huge grey domes on either side of a red-and-white striped phallic needle that punctures the polluted sky—a twentieth-century exclamation mark declaring the old river dead.

18

Big Bays and Big Water

Through the narrow gates of the Hudson Highlands I enter the river of the big bays, first Peekskill Bay, then Haverstraw Bay, Croton Bay, and Tappan Zee Bay. These are not the small lifeless pools that lie between the power dams of the upper Hudson. These are the populated Atlantic coastal bays of the estuary—big water, Ernie's nightmare.

Shafer wants to get a photograph of a canoe in front of a nuclear reactor, so I have to paddle across the first big bay. Approaching the Indian Point nuclear reactors in a canoe is a terrifying prospect. The water grows turbulent, and there is a deafening roar at the plant, a loud hum extending way out on the water as I paddle closer.

The forklifts stop. Workmen in hard hats stare, if not at me, then at Cronin's boat with the bold *Riverkeeper* across its hull. Cronin has been suing Indian Point for years to get them to stop discharging hot water and killing the fish. I try waving. None of them in their hard hats waves back. In a frozen gesture of hatred, the men stand like angry statues. They keep watching us. We do not belong here.

We are only a hundred yards away from the plant itself. The water beneath us is boiling because millions of gallons of river water are being sucked into the reactors, and then discharged. The hot roiling water rocks this little Odyssey. Cronin says the heat of the water is greatly altering the ecosystem.

As with the International Paper dam in Corinth, and all the other dams on the upper Hudson, so too this huge power plant uses the Hudson for its own purposes, then, its reactors cooled, shoots the water back into the river, and the water is never the same again.

The wind picks up. I'm afraid I might tip over. It's getting really rough out here, and I don't like those guys staring at us.

"I think we better get going," I say.

Pat, looking into his lens, says, "Go in for a closer shot, Peter."

"I don't think so, Pat." I refuse in favor of caution. Guards are running out of the plant with walkie-talkies, and John says with a smile of defiance, "If we get close enough, they'll chase us away." I think they must hate Cronin and all environmentalists, whom they view as job wreckers.

Pat is disappointed. He would like me to get so close those men could spit on me. But the water is too rough now, and the wind comes barreling upriver from Haverstraw, so I point the canoe away from the plant. Pat takes the helm of the *Riverkeeper* when John steps into the Odyssey to canoe with me from Indian Point to a marina in Haverstraw. He is not a light man, and we are quite unsteady at first.

John and I battle whitecaps across Peekskill Bay. Heavy industry, smokestacks, and factories line the big bay for miles. The Great River of Mountains is gripped in a new kind of industrial fury—something modern and ugly. From Indian Point to Battery Park, the river and its people hunger for electricity and potable water, but they seem to forget about the air they breathe.

I desperately do not want to turn turtle having come this far. I try to relax but can't. Coming out of Peekskill Bay, Cronin paddles obliviously, and I settle deeper into the canoe for better balance. The bow hits the waves broadside. We take on water as we come into Haverstraw Bay, the widest part of the Hudson at three miles from shore to shore.

I aim the canoe for those white mounds of gypsum and the Grassy Point marina at just the other side of the gypsum-crushing plant. John likes to keep his boat at Grassy Point because the marina is protected and safe, and he can be on board the *Riverkeeper* within half an hour of leaving his office in Garrison.

At the western top of Haverstraw Bay, we pull into the lee of Grassy Point at noon. The tide I caught in Beacon has yet to change.

John climbs back into his boat and docks in his slip. Together we pull my canoe up onto the deck of the *Riverkeeper.* I throw a chain around a thwart and lock it to a railing.

It feels odd to walk away from my Odyssey like this. I cast a look backward at the indecent view, the long, tan sliver of a canoe draped over the stern of John's boat. Hope no one steals it tonight. Wouldn't that be a fitting "civilized" end to a trip begun in the hemlock and spruce trees.

6:30 A.M. Saturday, June 30. Thinking about another weekend of hazardous paddling, I rise early in Haverstraw to take my canoe off the stern of the *Riverkeeper* and to wait for my friend Scott Overdorf.

Haverstraw used to be the home of the biggest brickyards along the Hudson in the heyday of bricks. Now bricks are a vanished industry. Last year I came here to meet a descendant of one of the great Hudson River brickyard families, Daniel deNoyelles, who had gone to work in his family brickyard in 1919. When I met him, he inscribed my copy of his book, *Within These Gates,* this way:

> The Industry of brickmaking, almost as old as civilization itself, was an art (see the Bible, Exodus Chapter 5) that flourished in the Hudson River Valley for well over a century [1815–1942] as generations of hardworking men, many newly arrived immigrants from Europe, dug the rich blue-grey clay from the vast pits, molded it into billions of soft brick, laid them in the drying yards to develop firmness, set them into the kilns, which fired and burned them to a hardness, useful finally to erect much of the great metropolis to our south, Greater New York, and to build attractive, durable cities and villages on the riverbanks and inland too. But we were blessed with a coincidence of Nature! Up and down the Valley were probably the greatest deposits of quality clay, a residue of melting glaciers of the last Ice Age, a deep navigable river to freight brick to the largest market for building materials, and an ever-burgeoning New York City. But vanish it did in the mid-20th century as times and people changed; newcomers with new ideas changed the valley in shape and lifestyles.

In his shaky handwriting, the words of my inscription hold an ancient sadness, too. An industry that had seemed so permanent to the brickmakers of Haverstraw, blessed with such good clay, is now long forgotten. Like the bricks of Babylon, the bricks of the Hudson that built New York City are no longer an architect's material of choice. Yet brick is natural, fireproof, durable, and still inspires that same love of geology that miners feel about what they mine—a kind of loyalty to the earth.

There is an everlasting, almost spiritual quality in the little red blocks.

Around 1815 the brick industry exploded when the cities began to build in earnest (New York required over a billion bricks a year). As deNoyelles puts it, families "lived with the news of the brick markets in their ears. Wives often helped their husbands in brickyard tasks."

Haverstraw was the center of the Hudson's brick production, employing as many as 2,400 workers. By 1883 there were no less than forty-one brickyards in the Haverstraw area. In a single year, 300 million bricks were shipped to New York City from Haverstraw Bay. One advantage for the brick industry in Haverstraw was that the river did not freeze over here as often as it did farther north, so the shipping channels could be kept open during the winter, and brickmaking was not a seasonal industry.

In the 1920s, European brick came into the American market. With World War I, glass, aluminum, and veneer facades "all spelled the end of brick demand and production." The Great Depression and World War II brought the Haverstraw brick boom to an end. But the famous blue clay is still abundant along the river. If brick ever comes back into vogue, there is enough Hudson River clay around to make many more cities like New York.

Even the remains of the old brick industry in Haverstraw are scarce now: water-filled clay pits, unrecognizable and decaying docks, ruined boiler houses here and there in the tall marshy grass along shore.

7 A.M. Scott Overdorf arrives. I haven't seen him since we met at the Donohue house in North River two weeks ago. A tall, intensely quiet man in love with whitewater, Scott grew up on the Hudson in Poughkeepsie. When I met him at the Masters School last year, he quickly heard about my upcoming trip, and we cemented a friendship over

lunches talking about the river, "his" river. He helped greatly with my planning for this journey, and he wanted to paddle with me part way, but has not had any time until now.

Scott also has dreamed of canoeing the entire Hudson, but unlike the rest of the dreamers, Scott will accomplish it someday, I'm sure.

Scott and I hike the canoe over to a fisherman's shanty on a small beach at Grassy Point. This is one of the few remaining fishermen's shanties on the river. Last night's hard rain has filled the big holes in the muddy road. In one puddle a live crab, fallen out of a fisherman's bucket, is stranded.

Tim DeGroat, a fourth-generation commercial fisherman, offers us coffee when we step into his one-room shanty, which he and his friends have built, he says, "stick-by-stick." DeGroat is a foreman in the gypsum plant in Haverstraw, where Sheetrock is made from Nova Scotia gypsum. Fishing is DeGroat's avocation because "no one can make a living at fishing anymore." If DeGroat had a choice, though—if the fish weren't so polluted—he would be out fishing commercially just as his father and grandfather used to do.

DeGroat is a kind man with thick blond hair and a blond mustache. He is stocky and perhaps in his late forties but still quite youthful. He sits with two friends at a poker table, all wearing high rubber boots. A potbellied iron stove stands in the corner with nine pairs of rubber gloves hanging over it. Everything in the shanty is practical—benches and chairs, rain gear on pegs, and lots of bright windows through which to watch the river closely. Covering the walls are charts and pictures of fishermen beside fish, some larger than the men. The floor is linoleum, and an old air conditioner sits in one window. The atmosphere is definitely that of a men's club. In the winter the fishermen come just to meet and chat.

DeGroat and his friends are going crabbing for Jersey Blue Claws. They used to fish all winter long for perch, sturgeon, and striped bass, but with all the new rules about fishing, they are not allowed to put a net in the water for bass, or "they'll lock us up."

"This is the best area on the river as far as your fishing goes," DeGroat explains. "Here you got shallow water. The fish don't have to fight the currents, and this is where your grasses grow, your eel grass and your other grasses."

We step outside onto the dock. Nets and boats and fishing tackle

38. Tim DeGroat and friends at one of the last fishing shanties on the Hudson.

lie everywhere. There are picnic tables and grills, too. DeGroat says he collected the picnic tables from the river "in the spring drift." Every spring DeGroat brings one or two back to the shanty. "Kids have beer parties and throw 'em into the river. I find 'em and bring 'em back where they're needed."

"My sons say I'm crazy. But I just love being out on the river. Like this morning. Look how beautiful it is today." The river is a wide platinum sheen in the early morning mist with Croton Point across the bay in the faded distance.

"But it can get pretty nasty out on the river," says DeGroat. "This spring we earned every shad we caught. The water was rough. It's the time of year when the water's dirty with rain and wind. Then the river cleanses itself, you know. . . ." He seems to be reliving shad season as he speaks.

"Storms scare the crab, and they move with the salt line. We got saltwater here, but after a big rainstorm, the runoff pushes the salt line down to Nyack. This time of year I have to go to Nyack to catch crab because of the big storms we've been getting."

The entire time the fishermen talk to us, they keep looking at us as if we are a little stupid, until one of them says, "Where do you fellows live, anyway?" And I reply, "Beacon."

"You mean you live on the river and you don't know nothing about it?" DeGroat's friends are shaking their heads a little smugly, but DeGroat comes to the rescue. "Well, there are plenty of people right here in Haverstraw who live on the river and don't know nothing about it, neither. They don't even know it's here. It's a shame."

Before we launch the Odyssey, I ask DeGroat about the pleasure boats out there on weekends. He says, "Let me tell you something. We'll go out and fish this morning, but this afternoon, when the boats get thick, you wouldn't catch *us* out on the river. These people don't even wake up until nine or ten. Then they fire up their engines and hit the river until dark. It's *dangerous*. I call them 'weekend warriors.' Those boats have no respect. They know we're hauling nets, but they don't slow down for us."

Scott and I also hope to be off the river by noon. It's fifteen miles to Dobbs Ferry, and we're leaving early enough, we think. But I am thankful when we actually get into the Odyssey and start paddling. Something DeGroat has said keeps running over in my mind. "No, you don't see canoes on the river. It's not a river for canoeing, you know."

Harper's Weekly ran a print on October 5, 1889, called "A barge party on the Hudson by moonlight." The scene was drawn from the Tappan Zee Bay. A long rowing boat moves through moonlight with about twenty people aboard, men and women, two abreast, and six oars on either side. This is the heyday of the rowing clubs. A captain stands in the stern facing forward with his hands on rudder lines. A flag in the bow flies the letters NRA, the Nyack Rowing Association. The text reads, "These rowing parties are a keen delight to the lady friends of the members of each association. So far the clubs have not yielded to the spirit of the age to admit lady members."

I suppose the "lady friends" aboard that "barge" are the wives of NRA members. Their faces seem so serious and not at all amused. I wonder what it was like to be a member of the Nyack Rowing Association. The *Harper's* print makes it look somewhat tame. Yet I have learned that nothing on the Hudson is *tame*. Perhaps that is why no one on the barge is even smiling. Maybe they expect a night squall. The fishermen said it wasn't a river for canoeing. And the "barge" didn't look so stable either. As far as I can tell, the rowing barge is nothing but an elongated canoe.

Scott and I plan to run down by the Tappan Zee Bridge, mid-channel, to catch the swifter current, and then paddle a few more miles on the east shore to Dobbs Ferry before the tide changes. The river sure looks like a canoeing river to me.

8:25 A.M. A perfect paddling calm as we begin. And we make good time. First we head down the western shore, around Hook Mountain, across from Croton Point. We can now see the Tappan Zee Bridge in the mist ahead of us and the beginning of the Palisade cliffs in the west, although just below Haverstraw there are only a few outcroppings of this volcanic escarpment that does not begin in earnest until after the bridge.

Scott is the most relaxed paddling partner I've had since Ernie left me in Luzerne. He is unusually talkative after this morning's visit with the fishermen. On the surface, Scott is a deliberate man. He is tall and not at all he-manish looking, but he has a strength and steadiness both in his paddling and in his personality that are like rock. All last year at school I was struck by his silent good humor, but today his love of the river percolates. "There's so much to learn about the river," he says with great admiration.

He is surprised to find the fishermen in tune with environmentalists, but it makes sense because their livelihood depends on the health of the river, much the same way the rafting companies in the Hudson River Gorge depend on a clean wilderness.

"Did you notice, Pete," Scott says as he digs his paddle into the river, "when the fishermen talked about the decline of fishing on the river, they didn't really relate it to pollution. It seems they still believe in the spring *cleansing* they talk about."

I agree it was a beautiful image, the spring runoff from the mountains cleansing the Hudson, the upper river purifying the lower.

"But I never think of the Hudson as clean this close to the city. Do you?"

"No way," Scott says.

10:15 A.M. Something is taking hold of the river and changing it everywhere. I know why the rowing "barge" was boating at night under moonlight. Even Kunz had said his groups liked to paddle at night because the wind died at dusk and didn't start up until late morning. Late morning wind.

I kick myself for not getting away earlier. As Scott and I have been talking, we've hardly noticed the wind pick up, the chop grow choppier. Gentle waves have turned imperceptibly into nasty white-caps, and the weather in the Tappan Zee by ten-thirty this morning is the roughest I've witnessed on the Hudson.

"Here comes the wind," says Scott. "Boy, this canoe feels every little movement, doesn't it?"

The north wind unexpectedly swings around to the southwest.

"Maybe I should have kept the Grumman."

"Nah. You'd still be in Albany. By the way, Pete," Scott adds, "I've been wanting to tell you. You've come a long way since we canoed the rapids on the Ten Mile last spring. You really look like you know what you're doing."

The compliment and the feeling of accomplishment are quickly buried under a wave of fear of rough water. I realize I've never tipped the Odyssey over in deep water before. I'm not even sure, especially with all my gear lashed to the thwarts, that I can right it again if we go over.

As if to demonstrate exactly what the fishermen meant, the wind gusts. How Scott stays so calm in the bow is both a mystery and an inspiration. No amount of dipping and gyrating seems to deter his steady spirit. There's something implacable, almost inhuman, about the way he approaches the increasing chop in the great Tappan Zee Bay a mile from shore, here in the middle of the shipping lane.

We notice DeGroat's fishing boat way over by the Nyack shore and know we should be hugging the shore, too. By the time we reach the center of the three-mile-long bridge, the waves are monolithic, approaching from the southwest, hitting us broadside and knocking us out of control. It is not so much the size of the waves but rather the distance between the crests. If that distance grows really short, and especially if it diminishes to less than the length of the Odyssey, we can be in big trouble. There will be no way to ride the sides of waves. We'll be caught in a maelstrom.

What makes our situation worse is that we're now running *with* those short waves. If we could face the chop head-on, there would come a steadying effect, but running with the waves, we roll in weird ways and cannot anticipate them. One wave drives our bow upward; another is already driving our stern down, trying to swamp us any way it can.

The canoe lurches and turns when I stop paddling even for a second. I crouch as low on the floor of the canoe as I can get. All the training I've had with Ernie—all that loosening of the hips and riding the canoe in a relaxed fashion, all the confidence of a week in the Adirondack headwaters and nearly two weeks alone on flat water—goes to hell. My body stiffens, and I fight with a novice's rigor mortis.

Perhaps it all comes down to expectations. I simply have not expected rough weather this close to the end of my trip, though why not, I don't really know. I never thought there was a possibility of turning turtle in the quiet, early morning platinum at Haverstraw.

Scott paddles steadily, and still he doesn't look scared. Maybe he is, I don't know. The waves begin to dangerously cross the ebb current. We try running due west toward the Tarrytown lighthouse and the big General Motors plant there, when suddenly a motorboat the size of a house streaks out of the marina heading straight for us.

Scott says, "He's not going to give us much room, is he?"

"Typical bullshit."

Perhaps the bozo can't see us through the haze of his hangover. It is already 11 A.M. We've got to get off the river. I'm sure the fishermen are off by now. But the big boat keeps coming. Maybe he cannot see us in the whitecaps, our sleek form lost in the hyphens of white spume.

At the very last minute, with perhaps 150 feet until collision, he swerves as if his girlfriend has just now come on deck with coffee and screamed or slapped the big guy conscious.

"You want to turn into that wake?" asks Scott with such nonchalance.

"Absolutely," I yell as we roll on the mammoth wake, adding surfer insanity to the crazy chop from the bridge pilings and the contrary wind and the current. It is a deadly confusion of waves, but the Odyssey is holding up.

We ride waves as if on a surfboard, then roll backward when we lose the crest, our bow shooting to the sky. The stern gunwale touches water, then the bow gunwale. We seesaw our way along in silence and hard work.

Another problem, I think, is that the tide has turned earlier than I expected. Rain on the upper river has changed the nature of the ebb. DeGroat mentioned this back in Haverstraw, and Scott says, after we are out of danger, "Pete, you're reading what *should* be happening to the Hudson, what your booklet says. But the fishermen, they look at the river and tell what *is* happening. It must take a long time to read the Tappan Zee."

At the bridge, utterly fatigued, we eddy out behind one of the pilings. Scott says, "Here, eat this," and he passes me a banana. After near panic in rough water, a banana calms the nerves as would a pacifier. We each eat one.

Scott and I make our way toward land in the lee of the pilings and follow the eastern shore past Sleepy Hollow, Lyndhurst, and Ir- vington to Dobbs Ferry, where a photographer from a local paper has arranged to meet us. An old man with a dog on the beach says it's illegal to land our boats in Dobbs Ferry, he just thought we should know. "Why is that?" we ask. "Because the town doesn't have a boat ramp," he says shrugging his shoulders. He can see we've had a rough time of it. "You mean, we can't even take our canoe out of the water if there's no ramp?" "Nope," he says, "not officially," as he shakes his head at the laws of the land.

"Well, that's civilization for you," says even-tempered Scott. We gladly break this stupid law. Scott jumps out. The photographer hops into the bow of the canoe and faces me with his long lens as I try to keep the canoe from turning over in the waves from the west. I say, "So, where's the reporter?" The young photographer says, "I guess there's no reporter. You just get a photo."

We will sleep the night at the Masters School, in Scott and Patty's apartment. After hiking up the hill, Scott drives down and throws the canoe on his boat rack.

July 1. Another calm early morning ebb. Scott and I paddle the few miles to Englewood Marina just north of the George Washington Bridge—my last stop on the river before I reach the sea.

From Dobbs Ferry we shoot across the shipping channel and take our time along the western shore, the side of the river that seems unspoiled still. Towering above this little sliver of a canoe, the great 500-foot Palisade cliffs rise vertically out of the Hudson. Often perceived as one long volcanic face running from Haverstraw to Staten Island, the Palisades are mostly viewed from the opposite shore, and rarely from the water directly below them.

Scott and I let the canoe drift as we look north and discover the cliffs are really a series of abutments, rocky points jutting into the river. Beneath them are strips of grassy beach and huge wedges of dark volcanic talus fallen from high above.

Scott and I wince at the industry across the river on the eastern shore.

Scott says, "Well, *there* it is, Pete."

The smudge of Manhattan comes as a shock. Rectangles of brick and steel shoot skyward through the thin pencil line of the George Washington Bridge. A wall of mountains made of brick, glass, and steel. These are the final peaks on the Great River of the Mountains.

My canoe has come into the heart of the metropolitan region that holds as many people as half the population of Canada, and yet from the river the metropolis is dead silent. I don't even hear its hum, as if we might have sneaked up on the monster unawares. Perhaps it could be a dream vision, except for the nine pleasure craft plowing upriver now like a convoy of tractor trailers. They cut the river to pieces, and I'm glad we are being sensible and hugging the shore under the Palisades.

"Look, I see the World Trade Center way down there, see it?"

When we pull into a slip in the Englewood Marina, teen-age boys hang around the docks looking city-tough. Tough stances, tough faces, cynical smiles, cigarettes, and insolent mouths. They have the hardened look of subway survival.

A weekend warrior approaches the gas pumps. We hear his wife screaming through her nose, "Honey, we're going to crash." And she is absolutely right. The $70,000 motorboat crushes the dock, bounces back, then circles in again, still too fast. "Honey, we're going to hit again." Again she's right. But someone manages to catch their ropes this time, and somehow the boat comes to an uneasy rest before refueling.

Scott calls a friend from school, who drives over the bridge to pick him up. Before Scott drives away, he shakes my hand and says he's sorry he can't be there tomorrow at the Battery. He has to work. When he is gone, I feel the old loneliness of solo paddling.

19

⟨flourish⟩

Last Night on River Time

8 P.M. From my tent I study the upper Manhattan skyline, orange Hudson River brick in an ozone sunset. The last two days of paddling have gone very quickly, and tonight I feel strange setting up a tent so close to the big city.

Through the spars and rigging of a sailboat, I watch the green-white shimmering lights of the nearby George Washington Bridge grow brighter in the gathering darkness. Tomorrow I will paddle eleven miles to reach the Battery, and I hope to arrive at noon during maximum ebb.

Part of me will be glad when the trip is finished, to have set a goal and accomplished something. But I'll miss the cowboy euphoria that I feel now at the edge of the water, listening to the hiss of my alcohol burner heating coffee, my canoe turned onto its belly close beside my tent on a strip of thick soggy grass just ten feet from a row of moored yachts at the foot of the Palisade cliffs.

Somewhere far above, a major highway runs along the escarpment, yet I hear only the halyards banging in a light wind. Even this close to so much traffic, I am alone with the river.

Directly across the river from my tent, a once-famous statue of Henry Hudson stands like a dwarf among the high buildings of the Bronx. Just north of the Spuyten Duyvil Bridge that links Manhattan to the Bronx over the Harlem River, the English explorer is engulfed by condos, and it took me a long time studying the opposite shore to spot him. But here he is, high on a pedestal, dressed in seventeenth-century garb, Henry Hudson himself gazing forever out to sea, down the shoreline of Manhattan and beyond. Perhaps he is thinking of home after his month of traveling up an unknown river.

The Vikings may have explored this river as early as the eleventh century. Verrazano saw the mouth of the river in 1524. Estevan Gómez noticed it in 1525. The French traded furs here in the 1500s. In fact, the Hudson River was known long before it was explored by Henry Hudson. On fifteenth-century European maps, it bears the mysterious name of *Norumbega;* no one is sure of the word's derivation.

Robert Juet, who chronicled Hudson's journey, writes in the log of the *Half Moon* that the last few days on the river were dangerous. On October 2, 1609, the *Half Moon* came to rest when the tide turned against it. One of the Indians "that swamme away from us at our going up the River" came out to the ship, but Hudson would not let him aboard. "Whereupon two Canoes full of men, with their Bowes and Arrows shot at us after our sterne."

Juet and his comrades fired "sixe Muskets, and killed two or three of them." Then a hundred Indians attacked from land. Juet fired a small cannon and killed two more. The Indians fled into the woods, then returned in another canoe with another ten men. Juet fired the cannon again and killed one Indian. More muskets were fired, and more Indians died. The *Half Moon* escaped downriver, anchored perhaps off Hoboken, and "There we saw no people to trouble us."

On October 4, the *Half Moon* set sail for England, but it had been a troublesome leave taking of the great river. The directors of the East India Company were disappointed with Hudson's journey. They had wanted a Northwest Passage to China, and Hudson had given them nothing. Not until 1623 did the directors of the company finally send a shipload of permanent settlers to Manhattan. They had heard that the French were making a lot of money off the fur trade, and the Dutch wanted a piece of the action.

The statue of Hudson fades into the condos at twilight as the lights on the George Washington Bridge grow brighter. The haze of the day seems to dissipate as the earth cools ever so slightly.

I make more coffee by candlelight, then dive for the tent. Light-

39. The George Washington Bridge on the last day.
Courtesy Pat Shafer.

ning bugs come out as I wait for the fatigue to overcome me. I lie
awake thinking of everything. Sleep will not come, so I pull out a
lantern, climb out of the tent, and place my dog-eared road map of
New York State on a picnic table. Tomorrow will be three weeks to
the day that I left for Lake Tear. I have marked each night I spent
along the river. Number 1 at the top of the torn map reminds me of
the long hike with Ernie and the night in the lean-to with no bears.
On my map, the Adirondack Park is a green patch above the big
cities. I miss that green section. Number 2 at Upper Works, 3 at Newcomb, 4 at Blue Ledge, 5 at the Glen and the Donohue house, then
that long sixth day from the Glen to Luzerne, and saying good-bye to
Ernie. I remember the last night in the Adirondacks at Luzerne, when
my father stuck a hundred dollar bill in my pocket and said, "Just in
case." Then that six-mile paddle alone upwind to Corinth leaving the

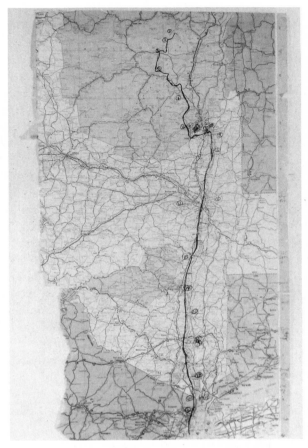

40. The author's road map marking his journey
and the nights he spent on the river.

Adirondack Park, encountering my first dam, followed by barrage after barrage, and winding around to Glens Falls past the Northway to the welcoming Bishops home and their dental lab. The ninth day at Lock 7, after a long ride through the Feeder. Then Lock 5, and a long haul from Schuylerville to Troy, a city of trains. Then the Albany wood boat show and urban terror in the night, followed by an enervating day of two ebb tides to Catskill. (I also notice all the towns I missed along the way, towns I had hoped to explore but will probably never see: New Baltimore, Coxsackie, Coeymans, Hudson, Athens, Tivoli, Glasco, Croton.) Next came the Saugerties lighthouse, the Rondout at Kingston, and a night paddle to Poughkeepsie with stories of pirates and caves, and in the morning one of the hardest, hottest paddles of the journey, coming home to a house that seemed like someone else's home. Then Captain Kidd's Highlands with the *Riverkeeper*. Followed by nuclear whitewater and then an old-time fisherman who said it is not a river for canoes. Finally with Scott in big water past the Tappan Zee to Dobbs Ferry and now Englewood.

Here at the very bottom of my map, the river does seem whole if I add the days and the fishermen together. Above North Creek, fly fishermen cast their flies into the swift water below rapids. Between the great power dams, loners fish in the big, dead, eerie pools. Wild bass fanatics race around Catskill, and serious commercial fishermen, when the shad stop running in the spring, turn to crabbing Jersey Blue Claws near the big city.

I don't know the hour. The gentle south wind is banging the halyards against metal—the sound of ships all over the world—and I worry I will tip over in the harbor in front of my family tomorrow. My mother and stepfather, Suzanna with Melissa, and Melissa's mother and father—all have promised they will come.

I cannot tell if my fear is a fear of embarrassment, should I tip over, or whether it is genuine fear of being swept out over the deepest, most invisible, and scariest Hudson of all, a Hudson no one knows, through the Narrow's and out over the deepest part of the old glacial river.

Before the last glacier covered the river as we know it today, the Hudson actually ran for another 150 miles, cutting a huge gash in the ocean floor. That deep gash is still there, but it has been filled in by thousands of feet of ocean. The ancient river used to run, as Carl Carmer says in *The Hudson*, "digging one of the deepest canyons the world has ever known . . . [reaching] a depth of 3,600 feet, a thousand feet deeper than the Royal Gorge of the Colorado."

Carmer speculates, "Had there been human life then, a traveler in a boat on the Hudson might have looked up to the blue sky between walls more than two miles high. But no man has yet seen, or probably ever will see, this stupendous natural phenomenon. After the river had created it, the salt sea returned and buried the canyon thousands of feet below the tossing waves."

To think my journey will end only where today's river ends, and another third lies buried under the Atlantic! That is what I am thinking when I finally fall asleep.

20

Maximum Ebb to the Sea

9 A.M. July 2, and I don't feel the city yet. I feel only the river, the accumulation of water off the mountains and down the tributaries. I feel the tides and the freedom, the gulls and the smell of salt. I feel the wide arrow of the river. But no city yet.

Cronin has appeared with Pat Shafer on the *Riverkeeper*. If I leave the marina now, I'll pass under the George Washington Bridge exactly at 9:30 when the CNN cameras are supposed to arrive. Then I can take my time crossing over to Manhattan, riding the tide past the Seventy-ninth Street Boat Basin and on down past the old Cunard Piers to Battery Park.

Cronin offers coffee from his thermos, and we float free of the marina. Still no sense of the city. No sound, only the sight of rush-hour traffic passing mutely over the great grey bridge. Before I pick up my paddle, I look over to Spuyten Duyvil to see Henry tucked inside the condos still trying to gaze south to the sea.

Goodbye HH.

I dig at the water. At the bridge within minutes, I scrutinize the upper and lower deck for television cameras. One year when Kunz made this trip, an ABC helicopter circled over him, and a TV camera-man tried to get into a canoe and nearly swamped it.

Directly under the bridge, I can hear the cars now and trucks like thunder but see no cameras, no cluster of fans and well-wishers. Maybe CNN will be at the Battery if they do not show here.

From New Jersey, a lone sea kayak paddles out to meet me. A young journalist from Hoboken comes alongside to ask why I'm making this trip. I tell him the usual answers. He tucks his notebook and camera into the shell of his boat and zips his roll flap. He works his double-bladed paddle hard to keep up with me. Shafer keeps waving him away, to get him out of the photographs, but I'm glad for the company. He comes right alongside, even runs into me once or twice. He's a nice guy enjoying his assignment. But he's no paddler.

Together we scoot across the Hudson just above the North River sewage treatment plant, a honeycombed white cement structure reeking of feces. From the day it opened in 1986, it had reached its capacity, its polluted water often spilling back into the river.

I hope I don't tip over here. Swimming is unthinkable. Storms that swell the river create sewage problems in many of the old cities along the Hudson, and Manhattan is the worst. As much as 90 percent of the coliform bacteria in New York harbor comes from overflowing sewage plants.

I move downstream beside thick West Side Highway traffic (a slight drone now) past Grant's Tomb, Riverside Church, and Columbia University.

The color of the water is grey-green as it whips up around the Seventy-ninth Street Boat Basin. I would like to stop to chat with the long-time residents of the basin, but I have to be at the Battery by noon.

The wharfs that shoot into the river look like the shells of burned barns, dilapidated warehouses, cement docks cracking with weeds. A helicopter rises off a landing pad a hundred yards off my port bow, but it's not a camera crew. These are executives heading to work. I stop waving.

A Circle Line tour boat passes. Only one tourist waves back at me. Then Cronin fires his foghorn to warn me about a small ferry that has darted out from between two piers without warning and will not vary its course crossing the river. I pry my paddle against the gunwale to bring the canoe out of the ferry's path just in time. Idiot.

The wind is up out of the northwest, thank God. The water deepens into oyster green under a pearl sky. I have only to steer now in this tide, which seems fiercely aware of its proximity to the Atlantic Ocean.

Cronin motors over to give me a walkie-talkie so he can communicate with me about where to land at the Battery. This still has not been resolved. Off he races to arrange a possible landing at Gangway 4 at the old fire station, home of the most powerful fireboat in the world.

Even now the town seems deserted. There is little sound, perhaps a faint hum. From out here on the river, all the crime I've read about in the city doesn't seem possible.

As I run along the big city, Kunz's words come back to me: "It's all beautiful—the whole river. But coming into Manhattan and seeing the skyline under the bridge, the greatest city in the world, we sensed that we'd actually arrived somewhere. It was a fitting end to our trip."

More remnants of former river activity appear. These abandoned Cunard Piers are the run-down docks of former commerce when the river was important in the daily lives of New Yorkers. From here the great ships *Lusitania* and *Mauritania* sailed. The survivors of the *Titanic* disaster found refuge on these wharfs. This was the very place where immigrants landed before going on to Ellis Island, and more than a million GIs in World War II shipped out from these now-broken docks.

Over the walkie-talkie comes the crackling voice of Cronin, "Hold off, Peter, we're having some problems. Take it slow."

11:30 A.M. Already somewhere past Greenwich Village. To bide my time, I have to pull off into a little watery alcove under Battery Park City, just in front of the green-tinted glass of the World Financial Center. The swell is so huge, it thrusts me up into the pilings, the underbelly of the city visible at low tide.

I'm trying to hang onto the pilings, which is probably stupid, but I desperately don't want to tip over and be swept out to sea in front of my family. Suddenly, from around the pilings, what should appear but another canoe! Two bare-chested men have just paddled half the river, from Albany. They look exhausted and lost. Where are they headed? I ask. "Well," they say, "we don't know if we should go up the East River or not." I advise against it. Fighting maximum ebb in that narrow channel is suicide. "You'll die if you try that."

41. The old fireboat at the Battery.
Courtesy Pat Shafer.

12:30 P.M. Cronin says over the walkie-talkie that he's changing my take-out plans. It will not be the firehouse Gangway 4 because the photographers cannot get a good shot from there. "They want the Statue of Liberty in the photo," he says. So he's trying to get permission for me to pull out on a small, private floating dock just the other side of the Circle Line. But for insurance reasons, the dockmaster won't let me do it.

"Just hold on, Peter. We're working on it."

I push off from the pilings because the swell threatens to cripple my boat against the cement. I brace in the deeper water and feel dizzy. Thank God for the brace. Off my bow I can see an ocean liner being pushed by five tugboats up the Hudson. Gulls swirl all over the sky. Everything has that green-grey color. The sun breaks the clouds apart and sends a sheen of aquamarine over the grey.

It's getting past lunchtime. I know Melissa and my baby must be just around the corner, but I cannot see them yet.

The canoe will not settle down.

1:25 P.M. After an hour of struggling to brace and keep afloat, I get the go-ahead from Cronin. Instantly, I swing the canoe into furious forward action. It's a handful of yards to Battery Park. I've been lollygagging only seconds away from my family. And here they are: Melissa and the baby, my mother and stepfather, Melissa's parents, and a few friends. They cheer, they clap, their voices are scant in all that wild seascape.

The seagulls swirl above me by the hundreds. Strolling tourists hardly know this sliver of a canoe has arrived from the mountains. Tourists from all over the world gaze out toward the Atlantic Ocean. Way offshore, the fireboat is spraying fountains of Hudson River water into the air as the tide rips furiously at the rock of the great city.

How easily I could be swept out to sea.

I paddle hard on my starboard to keep the canoe from straying. I shout at my stepfather, "I need some help, Pop."

I do not want to sound desperate.

He races over to the floating dock where the waves are smashing. The World War II veteran has the right stuff in him yet. He reaches down decisively. He grabs my hand. And I'm up. Then the canoe is up. And the dockmaster is screaming at us to get off the dock.

But the radio stations have put microphones in my face and one of the questions is "What do you want to eat more than anything else, now you're home?"

What is the right answer? "A deli sandwich?"

I look at the harbor, at the tugs and the gulls, at the fireboat that is gushing water, and the Statue of Liberty way out there. Nearly 400 years ago, returning from his three-week trip upriver, Henry Hudson was free of any fear he might have felt heading into the unknown.

It was here the *Half Moon* steered for home.

I have yet to carry my Odyssey to the car, but I will linger a minute or two and forget the screaming dockmaster. Tomorrow there will be no river for me, only a memory of adventure in my backyard.

As I speak into the microphones and hear the cameras click, I notice without really looking that someone is filming me from the

42. With Suzanna at Battery Park, July 2, 1990.

side—a movie camera! It must be CNN, I think. When the radio interviews are over, I glance at the cameraman. It is only my stepfather with his video machine. So much for fame and PR!

Meanwhile Melissa has jumped down onto the dock with Suzanna. With one arm around Melissa's shoulder, I tuck Suzanna in the other, a milk bottle in her mouth and her little sunbonnet blowing down over her eyes. She leans her head on my shoulder. The wind is brisk. This is home.